Chicken Soup for the Soul®

The Multitasking Mom's Survival Guide

Chicken Soup for the Soul: The Multitasking Mom's Survival Guide
101 Inspiring and Amusing Stories for Mothers Who Do It All
Jack Canfield, Mark Victor Hansen, Amy Newmark
Published by Chicken Soup for the Soul Publishing, LLC www.chickensoup.com

The publisher gratefully acknowledges the many publishers and individuals who granted Chicken Soup for the Soul permission to reprint the cited material.

Front cover photo courtesy of iStockPhoto.com/ktaylorg (© ktaylorg). Back cover photo courtesy of iStockPhoto.com/VikramRaghuvanshi (© Vikram Raghuvanshi). Interior photo courtesy of iStockPhoto.com/conejota (© conejota).

Cover and Interior Design & Layout by Brian Taylor, Pneuma Books, LLC

Distributed to the booktrade by Simon & Schuster. SAN: 200-2442

Publisher's Cataloging-in-Publication Data
(Prepared by The Donohue Group)

Chicken soup for the soul : the multitasking mom's survival guide : 101 inspiring and amusing stories for mothers who do it all / [compiled by] Jack Canfield, Mark Victor Hansen, [and] Amy Newmark.

p. ; cm.

ISBN: 978-1-61159-933-6

1. Mothers--Literary collections. 2. Mothers--Anecdotes. 3. Motherhood--Literary collections. 4. Motherhood--Anecdotes. 5. Human multitasking--Literary collections. 6. Human multitasking--Anecdotes. 7. Anecdotes. I. Canfield, Jack, 1944- II. Hansen, Mark Victor. III. Newmark, Amy. IV. Title: Multitasking mom's survival guide : 101 inspiring and amusing stories for mothers who do it all

PN6071.M7 C484 2014
810.8/02/0352/52 2013957153

PRINTED IN THE UNITED STATES OF AMERICA
on acid∞free paper

24 23 22 21 20 19 18 17 16 15 14 01 02 03 04 05 06 07 08 09 10 11

The Multitasking Mom's Survival Guide

101 Inspiring and Amusing Stories for Mothers Who Do It All

Jack Canfield
Mark Victor Hansen
Amy Newmark

Chicken Soup for the Soul Publishing, LLC
Cos Cob, CT

Chicken Soup for the Soul®

www.chickensoup.com

Contents

❸

~Sharing Good Advice~

❹

~Laughing After the Fact~

5

~Handling Housework Hassles~

6

~Learning from the Kids~

7

~Juggling a Career~

8

~Feeling Guilty~

9

~Slowing Down~

Introduction

You fall out of your mother's womb,
you crawl across open country under fire, and drop into your grave.
~Quentin Crisp

I love the above quotation because that's how motherhood can feel, especially when your children are young. The demands are relentless, you never catch up, and you're always tired. You are most certainly "under fire," as most of us try to pack an awful lot of living into our days—more than we should—but not as much as we wish we could handle!

This collection of stories is meant to entertain you and support you while it also painlessly imparts some valuable lessons about how you might want to run your life and your household. My husband and I have four kids, all grown now, but I wish I had been able to read stories like these when the kids were younger. They would have helped put things in perspective, and since the stories are short, they would have made for great reading interludes while waiting… in the pickup line, at sports, during tantrums, for late kids, etc.

In our chapter on "Making 'Me Time'" you'll hear from moms who have "been there, done that" and have already come to grips with the need to create some balance in their lives. In "R Is for Randi" we meet Randi Mazzella, who had an epiphany when her friend gave her a pendant with an "R" on it. Randi had focused so much on her kids' initials that it hadn't even occurred to her that she could wear her own initial. As Randi wrote, "I realized that to be a good mother, I also had to be my own person—not just someone who solely existed to take care of other people."

The "Feeding the Family" chapter will make you laugh, and for those of you who are not domestic goddesses in the kitchen, there is some comfort in these stories too, as mother after mother discloses her own food-disaster story. I have one of my own stories in there, which can be summed up by the following excerpt: "My daughter came home from school, excited about something new that she had learned in kindergarten. 'Did you know that in some families the mommy cooks?'" You'll also find some tips about how to bring the family together in the kitchen and around the dinner table.

Speaking of tips, we received so many wonderful stories filled with great advice that I wish I had heard when I was starting out as a mother. We selected a baker's dozen for our "Sharing Good Advice" chapter. You'll pick up some ideas for reducing sibling squabbling, for giving your kids some control over their lives, for managing privileges like watching TV, and for maintaining the romance with your significant other. Lori Lara sums up one of the most important themes in the book in her story "The Fantasy of Motherhood" when she says, "There's a special joy that comes from making peace with domestic chaos."

We all have certain stories that we love to tell over and over again at family gatherings. And most of them seem to involve disasters of some kind, which are quite funny in retrospect, but perhaps not so funny at the moment they occurred. If you need a laugh, turn to Chapter 4, "Laughing After the Fact." Patricia Lorenz's story, "The Longest Day Ever," is a perfect example of a story that we just had to include for you: On a very harried day, when Patricia needed help, she carefully explained to her two-year-old how to push the button to turn off the TV. He remembered "push" and "TV." After Patricia heard a loud crash and the sound of breaking glass, she went running. Her son proudly showed her how he had "pushed off" the TV... right off the stand.

And that leads us to housework, which never goes away. Between the housework and the repairs, my list never seems to get shorter. I loved Ann Kronwald's story, "A Busy Mom's Guide to Home Selling," in our chapter about "Handling Housework Hassles." Faced with a last-minute repeat visit from prospective homebuyers, Ann had to clean up the house in thirty minutes, no easy feat when you have four children under the age of five and you have been baking. In a panic, Ann stashed everything, including the dirty dishes, in her minivan in the garage, finally finding a good use for those tinted windows. It worked and they went to contract on the house the next day!

We moms are always teaching our kids, even as we are multitasking our way through our busy days. But they teach us too, and in the "Learning from the Kids" chapter, we read about the life lessons that our offspring share with us. Diane Stark has a great story called "Building Sand Castles that Last" about the day that her son insisted they keep building sand castles right next to the water, ensuring that each one would be destroyed almost immediately after its completion. Diane couldn't understand her son's joy, but then she realized that it was just like all the things she did for her family, like making dinner, and doing the laundry, and cleaning. They all had to be done again and again, and she had sometimes wondered if her friends with jobs were doing more important work than she was doing. Diane said, "I am building something important, something that will last forever. I'm building a family. And nothing matters more than that."

For those women who do have jobs, along with all the other work of motherhood, we have a whole chapter of stories called "Juggling a Career" that will make you feel like you're not the only one who has a crazy life. In "Why I'll Never Be Volunteer of the Month," author Amelia Rhodes talks about how her daughter seemed disappointed that her working mom was never named volunteer of the month at school. Amelia just didn't have the time to put in the hours required for the award. Then on a family vacation that occurred between Amelia's book release and a marathon she was running in (another passion that took her away from volunteering) her daughter said, "It's so cool to have a mom who writes books and runs marathons." Amelia concluded that "what matters most—following your passions, being there for your family, celebrating together—those all can be balanced in a way that everyone wins."

And that brings us to guilt, and why you shouldn't have it. In our "Feeling Guilty" chapter, attorney Sara Rickover has a story called

"Not So Guilty After All" about how her kids used to reprimand her for going over legal papers while she was watching their games. She really had no choice—she had to squeeze in her work whenever she could. Now that her children are adults, with their own careers, she is watching with amusement as they squeeze in conference calls and e-mails during family vacations. I recommend that those of you who are feeling guilty try to defer that guilt for a decade or two—I can almost guarantee that your kids will tell you how much they appreciate what you did for them once they are grown.

So now that you know that you are not alone in your multitasking madness, that you should take some time for yourself, and that you shouldn't feel guilty, you should read the last chapter of the book, "Slowing Down," and make a resolution for yourself and your family. Marya Morin wrote a wonderful story called "Special Hour" in which she explains how she decided to give her son his own undisturbed hour with her several days a week after she realized that she was letting too many other obligations interfere with their time together. She says that she is "grateful that I discovered the importance of making time for what was most precious in my life—before being a busy mom made me too busy to be a mom."

Since we love quotations at Chicken Soup for the Soul, I'll conclude with one by Anton Chekhov that beautifully describes what it's like to be a multitasking mom: "Any idiot can face a crisis—it's day-to-day living that wears you out." I'm glad that you are taking a little "me time" to relax and read this collection of inspirational, entertaining, and educational stories. I hope that you will enjoy reading this multitasking mom's survival guide as much as we enjoyed making it for you!

~Amy Newmark

to do list:
Pay bills
- Get Laundry
- Call Mom
- Pick up kids from birthday at 6 p.m.
- Buy groceries

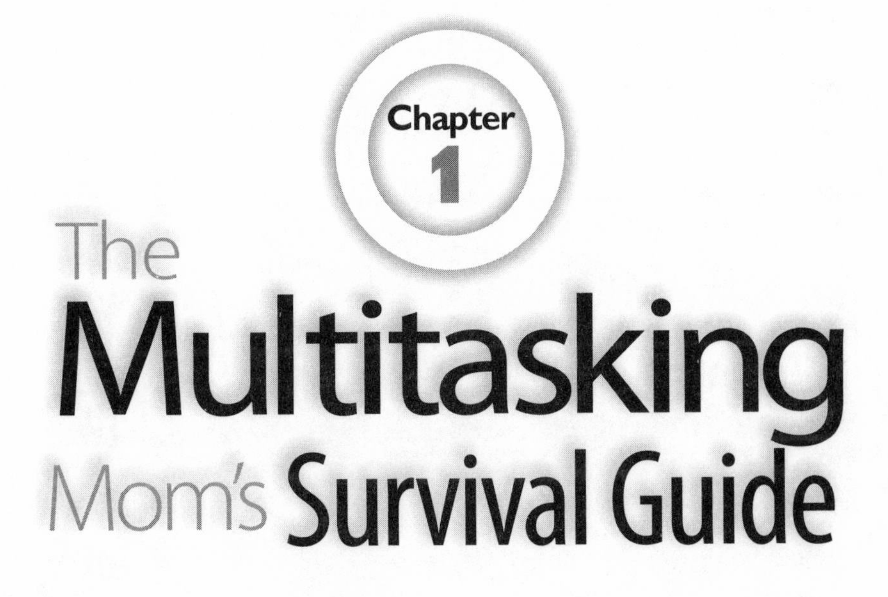

Making "Me Time"

I took some me time.
I think that's a really important thing to do for yourself.

~Ashlee Simpson

R Is for Randi

All discomfort comes from suppressing your true identity.
~Bryant H. McGill

Several years ago for my birthday, a friend gave me a necklace that had a small charm with the initial "R" on it. It was a simple gold necklace and a lovely gift.

The necklace was very similar to another one I had with three initial charms—A, J, and J—the initials of my three children. I remember I looked at the necklace for a while. It seemed odd to me to wear a necklace with the initial "R" even though it is the initial of my own name.

I realized after a while that the reason the necklace seemed odd to me was because I was slowly starting to lose my own identity. I had kind of forgotten who "R" was.

In recent months, I had introduced myself to several people by saying, "Hi, I am J's mother (or A's mom)" rather than starting with my own first name. One of the other mothers actually asked me, "And do you have a name?"

My sister-in-law called a few days before and asked, "What's going on with you?" I proceeded to talk for five minutes about my son J loving his basketball team, my daughter A's SAT prep and my daughter J's recent track meet.

When I finished, my sister-in-law asked, "So, is there anything going on with *you*?"

At first, I didn't understand why she was asking me that. Hadn't

I just told her what was going on with me? But then I realized that nothing I said had actually been about myself. It was all about my kids.

I love being a mom. When other kids dreamed of being pilots or doctors, my ideal career was always to be a mother. In first grade, we had to draw pictures of our ideal careers, and I drew a picture of my mom. I divided the paper into eight sections and drew her in her eight different roles: cook, chauffer, player, cleaner, teacher, shopper, advisor and nurse. My mom made being a mother look so great; I could not wait to be one myself.

After graduating college and a false start in accounting, I began a very successful career in retail. I travelled around the world—Singapore, Malaysia, Japan, Germany, Italy. I had to get extra pages in my passport because I didn't have room for all the stamps. I lived in New York City with my husband and was out almost every night at the movies, dinner and clubs.

Even though I had a dream job, I still had the same dream from first grade: to be a mother. Although I discussed going back to work after my maternity leave with my boss, my husband and I ultimately decided that it would be best for me to stay home with our daughter for at least a year.

The first week as an official SAHM was odd. Prior to my maternity leave, my husband and I had commuted together, and we both worked ten-hour days. Now I was home alone with my newborn, and she was not much of a conversationalist. Even though we had lived in our home in the suburbs for over a year, I had never really "lived" there. I just slept there and changed my clothes.

Those first few months, finding time to take a shower was a challenge some days. I had been a world traveler—one of United Airlines' top flyers—and now I was huffing and puffing trying to lock in my daughter's car seat for a trip to the market.

But I adjusted, and that year at home turned into more than a decade. I made other mommy friends, and I had more kids. I loved being a mom and doing all the jobs I had drawn in my picture. I cooked, I drove, I played, I cleaned, I taught, I shopped, I advised and I nursed. The kids were my world. Or rather, it was my kids' world, and I just lived in it and made sure it didn't fall apart.

The necklace, the introductions, the conversation with my sister-in-law all made me realize that I needed to start thinking about who I am in addition to being a mother.

When I was a little girl, my mom bought me a nameplate necklace. Years later, for my sweet sixteen, I got not one but two different initial rings. It did not seem weird or egotistical to wear these items of jewelry; it was my name, my initial, and I wore them without reservation. When I became a wife, I took my husband's last name, but still maintained my own identity. Somehow, I had lost that identity a little as a stay-at-home mom.

I put on the "R" necklace and then set out to figure out who "R" was in addition to being A, J and J's mom. I realized that to be a good mother, I also had to be my own person—not just someone who solely existed to take care of other people. Not having my own identity was making me a little boring, frustrated and embarrassed.

I joined a spin studio and started doing more volunteer work. I made a monthly date to go to the movies. I took a writing class online. I started submitting my work to local publications. At first, I got a lot of rejections. But then a few pieces of my work got published. I am now a regular contributor to several magazines and write a bi-monthly blog. I don't make a lot of money, but I feel more fulfilled as a person. I am learning and growing, and that makes me happier—and a better mother.

Now when I introduce myself, I say, "Hi, my name is Randi," and it feels good to be me.

~Randi S. Mazzella

Time for Music

Music produces a kind of pleasure which human nature cannot do without.
~Confucius

"Can I take piano lessons like Nicole?" Tami, my blue-eyed seven-year-old begged, tugging at my shirtsleeve as I stirred spaghetti sauce for dinner.

Nicole, our next-door neighbor and Tami's best friend, was eight. In my mind, it was the perfect age to start piano, probably because that's how old I'd been. "Maybe next year," I told Tami, adding a bit more basil to the sauce.

"I want to take lessons now." Tami tugged at my sleeve again.

I winced at the hope in her voice. If we were able to budget for piano lessons, I would have to drive her there, and that was on top of second-grade worksheets, soccer, Brownie Scouts, laundry, shopping, cooking, and the care of Tami's little brothers, ages two and four. Next year, my youngest would be in preschool, the middle child in kindergarten. There would be a little more time. For now, the strains of the Beethoven sonata wafting from our stereo would have to be enough piano music for Tami.

"Please, Mommy? Pleeeze?"

I turned from the stove and looked at my wispy-haired daughter. My heart melted the way a mother's heart does when faced with that pleading look of her child.

"I'll talk to Nicole's mother. Find out who the teacher is and what it costs. I'll need to talk to Dad."

"Thank you!" Tami hugged me around the waist and skipped off, probably to tell Nicole.

Had I said yes?

I looked at the old upright that had sat in our living room unused for the three years since we'd seen an ad and I'd begged my husband to buy it. I loved piano music. I usually had a piano CD on at home, and scrimped for tickets to the symphony, especially enjoying the guest pianists. I had taken lessons as a child. I hadn't been a child prodigy, certainly, but I'd performed for a room of beaming parents several times in recitals. I longed to play again.

When we bought the piano, I produced the right hand to "Happy Birthday" and "We Wish You a Merry Christmas" on the appropriate occasions. But when I attempted the left hand to "Silent Night," Tami, then four, looked sadly at me and patted my shoulder. "You made a lot of mistakes, Mommy," she said. "That's okay."

Obviously, a sonata was not going to magically pour from my fingers. I needed to take lessons again and practice daily if I was going to create anything resembling music.

As the years passed, my husband had the grace to say the piano made a nice piece of furniture and left me to nag myself. I would play again, I swore, when the children were older and I had more time. In my current hectic life, there was not a remote possibility of devoting a half-hour a day to practicing. Tami would be our pianist.

After dinner, with the family settled in front of a Disney movie, I called Nicole's mother. She liked the teacher very much, and the rates were reasonable. My husband agreed that Tami could begin lessons. So I called the teacher and a piano tuner.

Two weeks later, on a sunny Thursday afternoon, I took Tami to her first lesson.

My heart quickened as I watched the teacher lead my daughter to a mahogany upright that resembled the one at our house and sit beside her on the bench. Tears sprang to my eyes. Was I sad to see my little girl growing up?

I should slip out the door, but I stood transfixed.

The piano teacher looked back at me and rose from the bench. "You want to play too, don't you? I can give you a family rate."

Did my face show my longing to feel those ivories under my fingers? The teacher didn't sound like a salesman; she sounded like a compassionate friend.

"I don't have time," I stammered. "Maybe when the children are older."

"Of course." She nodded, and I left.

"Family rates," I murmured as I drove home. But no, it was out of the question.

Over the next week, I made sure Tami practiced every day. She willingly sat down at the piano the first few days. Then, one afternoon, she resisted. "I'd rather go to Nicole's."

"Do you know how lucky you are?" I scolded. "I'd love to be practicing."

"Then you do it," Tami said.

I recoiled. Not because my daughter had talked back to me, which she seldom did, but because I heard my own words. I would love to be practicing.

My older son was engrossed in his Legos, and the younger one was taking a nap. I could snag a few minutes at the piano. "You go to Nicole's for a while," I said. "Then you need to practice."

Tami was out the door before I finished my sentence. I opened her *John Thompson's Modern Course for the Piano—First Grade* and put my fingers on the keys.

I could feel my smile growing as I teased out the simple pieces with one hand, then both hands. Could I take lessons and find a half-hour a day to practice? I didn't have time for all the things I did now. But each day I juggled the minutes, and somehow when bedtime came, the have-tos were done.

Could I make playing the piano a have-to?

I worked my way through ten songs before Joel woke up. At some point, Ben came to stand beside me and watch as my fingers sought out the keys they hadn't touched in years.

That night, I arranged for my own lessons every other week

during the time Ben was at preschool and Joel at a friend's. For a half-hour every day, often in five- or ten-minute segments, I settled down with *John Thompson's Modern Course for the Piano—Second Grade* and *Bach for Early Grades*. Sometimes one or both boys plunked keys along with me for a few minutes until one or the other of us grew tired of the din. Sometimes Tami and I practiced the same piece, with me on the keys an octave lower, a sort of duet. Some blissful times I practiced alone.

"I'm glad you're playing again," my husband commented one night when I went to the piano after the dinner dishes were done. "How did you find time?"

"I made it a have-to," I explained with a smile, and turned to Bach's "Minuet in G Major." For the early grades, it was fine, but if I kept at it I'd be treating the family to sonatas.

~Samantha Ducloux Waltz

Ode to a Quiet Bathroom

Not merely an absence of noise, Real Silence begins when a reasonable being withdraws from the noise in order to find peace and order in his inner sanctuary.
~Peter Minard

This year I'll turn forty. I'm just waiting for my husband to ask me what I want for my birthday. I've got my answer all prepared. It's probably not what he expects though. In the years before kids, he'd have gotten off easy with jewelry or clothes, dinner out and a gift certificate to a day spa. But after ten years and three kids, my idea of the perfect birthday gift has evolved. What I want this year, what I really want, is four hours alone and uninterrupted in my own bathroom. Just peace and quiet and porcelain. I suppose that makes me a cheap date but, after ten years of doing whatever I've got to do in the bathroom with an audience, four hours of bathroom solitude sounds better than anything he could buy me.

My birthday fantasy looks like this—me loitering in the tub with my eyes closed. Around me are no action figures, no stick-on alphabet letters, no naked Barbies. (Talk about depressing. The last thing I need, when I'm bent over shaving my legs, is a naked Barbie smirking up at me.) I want no little urchins there to offer commentary on my breasts or belly or buttocks or anything else. I don't want to hear that I'm getting fat but "Don't worry, Mommy, you look good that way."

I want to shave my legs without delivering a safety lecture about my razor. I don't want to share my shaving cream with anyone no matter how much fun it is. I want to fog up the mirror without having to peek around the curtain and answer, "What letter is this, Mommy?" I want the curtain to stay shut—not be fanned open every few seconds leaving me to explain once again the mechanics of a shower curtain keeping the water OFF the floor.

I want the water as hot as I can stand it and not to hear that anyone is taking up all the room. I want all the room. I don't once want to hear, "Oops! Guess I forgot to tinkle before I got in the tub." I want to stretch out my legs without it being seen as an invitation for a pony ride. I want to step from the tub without hearing, "Boy, the water goes way down when you get out, Mommy!" and to towel off without having to teach an anatomy lesson entitled, "Why Mommy looks different than Daddy."

And while I'm at it, I want to do what I need to on the toilet without spectators. Not to have to remember who tore off the toilet paper for me the last time so I'm sure everyone gets their turn. I want to pick up a magazine, read an article from start to finish, and actually comprehend what I'm reading. I want to close the door and not have little notes slid underneath with my name on them or tiny fingers wiggling up at me.

Then I want to paint my nails—only mine—no one else's. Not to have the "But, sweetie, nail polish is for girls and mommies." I want to give myself a pedicure, a facial, and touch up my roots without once stopping to yell, "I'm in the bathroom. No, I can't come to you. You come to me."

I don't really care where my husband takes the kids. I just want four unbroken hours to luxuriate in my own bathroom alone! Maybe I'll remind him while he's sitting in the McDonald's play yard staring at his watch that he's turning fifty this year and I'm toying with the idea of declaring the remote control off limits to anyone but Daddy for one long, glorious afternoon. Consider the possibilities.

~Mimi Greenwood Knight

When Mom Gets Sick

Written on her tombstone: "I told you I was sick."
~Erma Bombeck

There's something about being sick and being a parent that doesn't mesh. The very instant we give birth, it seems that all mothers are slapped on the back with a bright red bumper sticker: CAREGIVER: NO SICK DAYS ALLOWED.

Mothers understand what I'm talking about. It's the unspoken, unwritten, but very real rule about how long a mother is allowed to be sick. I think the rule says something like two or three hours every fifth, even-numbered year in a month that ends in E.

Don't get me wrong. I'm not a bellyaching sort of person who conjures up imagined headaches or three-day flu bouts the way some people do just to get a break from the routine. I just think mothers deserve a little more consideration than most families seem willing to give them when they are sick. And that's why I'm spouting off.

I remember the last time I had the flu as if it were the day before yesterday. The year was 1987. I left work early that day, head pounding, body shivering, glands aching, nose sniveling, mouth dry, chest full.

The drive home in the snow was no basket of cherries either. As I tried to keep the car on the road, I wondered why I couldn't get sick in July and lie on the cool sheets in my underwear, sipping cold drinks until the fever passed.

At home, that cold, gray December day, I undressed, pulled on my bleakest-looking, washed-out jogging suit with the elastic waist and ankles, popped two extra-strength cold tablets, slid between the flannel sheets and pulled three blankets, a bedspread and a heating pad over my body.

It was 2:20 p.m. I could sleep for an hour before my oldest daughter arrived home from high school. I'd already made arrangements for a neighbor to take her to her piano lesson at 4:00 p.m.

At 3:40, my two junior high teens would be waltzing in the door, stomachs growling, ready to eat Milwaukee. One of them would walk to the babysitter's to pick up the five-year-old. If I got out of bed right then and wrote them a note telling them I was sick and to please be quiet and let me sleep, I might even make it a two-hour nap.

So I wrote the note. Back in bed, I dreamt of the day when the children would all be grown, and I wouldn't have to write them any more notes of any kind. Just letters telling them I'd be jetting out to Denver, Phoenix or New York or wherever they all lived by then. I'd tell them to get the guest room ready and that I'd take them out to dinner in a fancy restaurant. After a long, luxurious candlelit meal, we'd walk to one of those elegant round restaurants that rotates ever so slowly on top of a skyscraper and order an oversize fruit drink with a name that sounds like a Hawaiian volcano, and we'd talk about our exciting, fulfilling lives. Then later, I'd fall asleep in the guest room of their new condominium....

Aaaaa-choooo!! The phone rang. "Hi, Mom. I hate to tell you this but you know I have my drum lesson after school, and I forgot my drum sticks and music. Could you bring em down right away?"

The front door opened. "Mom! Where are you? I brought Lisa home with me so we could practice our new cheers in the family room."

I deserved my bed, my heating pad, some quiet time. I had earned it. No matter what they said or how much they pleaded I was just going to lie there and be sick.

By 9:00 a.m. of day two (after somehow getting them all off to school amid one exaggerated crisis after another), I practically overdosed on flu and cold medicine, trying desperately to get my household back in order. By evening of day two, the whole darn family was mad at me for being sick. I had to beg the oldest to come and sit in my room and talk to me that night. I was lonely, but did they care?

That night, I paged through my Bible. There it was, proof that mothers weren't supposed to get sick. Right there in Matthew 8:14-15: "When Jesus came into Peter's house, he saw Peter's mother-in-law lying in bed with a fever. He touched her hand and the fever left her, and she got up and began to wait on him."

By ten o'clock that night I actually wondered where Jesus was when I needed him.

By morning of day three, I figured that I would feel just as bad whether I was lying on the living room sofa or in my bed, and the sofa at least provided a central place from which to direct family life and/or at least help solve one family crisis after another.

By day four, I couldn't take it anymore and was off to work, still sneezing and aching but having learned my lesson—that it's impossible for a mother, especially a single parent mother, to escape under the covers for four days without the entire household threatening mutiny.

Getting sick is simply not in the mother's handbook of life. Since then I've only thrown up once. I resumed my phone conversation two minutes later and went to work twenty minutes after that. I figured by the time my youngest graduated from college... then, and only then, could I get away with being sick. In the meantime, if I felt a shiver coming on, it was simply time to pull on the long underwear and forge ahead with gusto.

~Patricia Lorenz

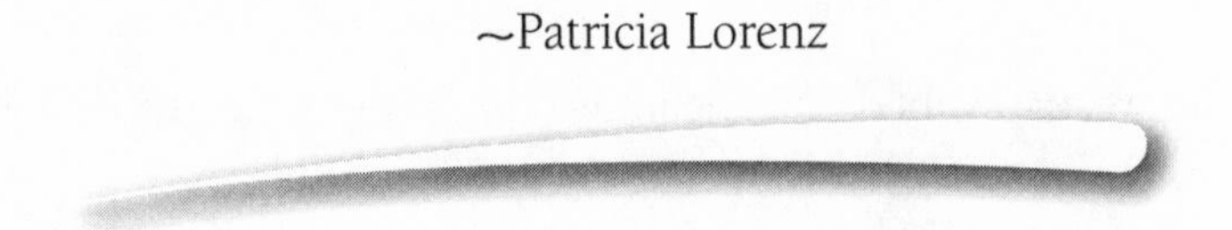

How I Became a Ballerina at Thirty

I think it is wonderful for everyone to take ballet classes, at any age. It gives you a discipline, it gives you a place to go. It gives you some control in your life.
~Suzanne Farrell

In my tomboy youth growing up in Texas, the only dancing I did was line dancing in gym class—brush kick, grapevine, and boot-scootin' boogie across the basketball courts. And hours of *Dance Dance Revolution*, if that counts as dancing. In college, I bobbed and swayed through formal dances and participated in some choreographed Bollywood numbers for the fun of it. Freshman year, I met my soulmate. About seven years later, we did a cheesy wedding dance to Shania Twain's "You're Still the One."

As I spent more time on the dance floor, two things became apparent: I love to dance and I am a terrible dancer. And I'm not the kind of terrible dancer who has an infectious sense of confidence, who can pull out zany disco moves in a cleared-out circle and people start clapping. I'm awkward, clumsy, and have all the rhythm of a quarter clanking in the dryer.

In 2009, my husband was offered a professorship at McGill, so we moved to Canada that fall. After three years of settling into a new life in Montreal, welcoming two beautiful daughters into my life, and turning thirty, I took my insistent three-year-old to enroll in ballet at a local studio.

Maybe it was the dramatic black-and-white photographs of elegant ballerinas mid-leap on the studio wall and the fantasy that I could look like that one day—perfect, weightless, ethereal. Maybe it was some deep inner, partially formed desire for self-expression suddenly lifted out of the existential miasma of being an expatriate and a mother and a woman no longer in her twenties. But I signed myself up too, and there was no looking back, at least for the next twelve-week paid session.

My daughter and I went shopping for leotards together. The woman at the store brought me two black ones to try on—XL and XXL. (Usually, I'm a small or a medium.) I suddenly felt like quitting before I even started, but my daughter was watching me, so I tried on the leotards and bought the larger size with three-quarter sleeves to hide my arms.

The first class, I desperately tried to copy the person next to me at the barre while deciphering what the instructor said in French about *les orteils* (toes) and *les épaules* (shoulders). My frustration prodded me. Instead of feeling discouraged, I became determined to improve outside of class. Something in *mon coeur* (my heart) shifted, and I was filled with a desire to take dance seriously.

I went home and downloaded *Ballet Beautiful* workouts from Mary Helen Bowers, who got Natalie Portman in shape for her Oscar-winning role in *Black Swan*. I tried to eat fewer cookies and did Mary Helen's bridge series and inner/outer thigh toning exercises until I could actually make it through the whole sixty-minute workout without wimping out in the middle.

By the end of three months, I hadn't dropped a leotard size, but there was a perceptible change in my physique. It had less to do with muscle tone and more to do with how I carried myself—how I stood up from a chair, how I walked to the park, how I twirled in the grass with my girls.

Even though I enjoyed ballet, it was private, something I did for myself because I felt elegant and "ballet beautiful." So when my daughter enthusiastically declared to another mom at the playground that I was a ballerina, I smiled politely to hide my embarrassment and quickly dispelled any misconception: "No, no, I'm just in a beginner ballet class." Not that my Rubenesque form could be mistaken for one of those black-and-white prima ballerinas on the studio wall.

Later, as I was recounting the incident to my husband, I began to wonder why I had such a hard time describing myself in terms of what I like doing. My daughter likes to dance, paint, and play with a plastic light saber. In her mind, she is a dancer, an artist, and a Jedi Knight. The moment at the playground was a reminder that, as a grown-up, I spend time doing things, but I don't allow myself to be those things. I fear criticism, ridicule, and dismissal. I seek perfection. Why is it that I have to be good at something in order to be that thing?

Yes, I have to coax my body onto wobbly tiptoes—being a long way from *en pointe*—but there has always been an untapped dimension to my spirit that I didn't fully explore in my insecure boot-scootin' boogie days. I've always had dance inside me. It may find its expression in weird and awkward ways, but it's still dance.

My class rehearsed the past three months for a performance to Respighi's "The Cuckoo." On the day of the show, my hair tightly pinned into a bun, I put on a purple costume with matching tutu, rose pink tights and slippers. Heart nervously fluttering in my chest, waiting for the music's opening flutes on stage, I realized that I may not be a professional ballerina—I may not even be a good ballerina—but I am a ballerina.

Then the stage lights rose, and the curtains opened. Suspended in the magic of the performance, arms outstretched like wings, for a moment I saw myself in black and white.

~Mitali Ruths

Time for a Shower

Mirth is God's medicine. Everybody ought to bathe in it.
~Henry Ward Beecher

With a newborn and two toddlers, I was a mess. No one had bathed in three days. I couldn't seem to get the house clean. There were dishes in the sink and toys everywhere. To top it all off, we were having guests that evening.

Thankfully, naptime was coming. That blessed time when all three little girls would lay their heads down and become perfect sleeping creatures with angelic faces. If I could get them all to sleep, I might be rewarded with enough solitary time to get the dishes done and take a shower. Oh, the luxury of a shower without interruption.

I managed to feed the children a fairly healthy lunch and corralled them all up the stairs into their bedrooms. After being rocked in the rocking chair, my newborn, Anna, fell right to sleep.

One down, two to go.

I then cuddled my two-year-old, Kait. I sang her a lullaby, all the while dreaming about my shower and a clean house. Kait fell asleep with little protest.

Then came my three-year-old, Emilia. She wanted to talk instead of sleep. I kept hushing her, reminding her she needed her sleep so she wouldn't be tired when our guests arrived. She finally stilled. I snuck out of her room and back downstairs. I waited at the foot of the stairs, listening to see if little feet would follow me.

Silence.

Not sure how long my good luck would last, I practically ran to the bathroom and started the water. Steam filled the tiny room. I pulled the curtain aside to step in when the quiet knock sounded on the door.

I was so close! The door opened, and there was Emilia with her curly blond hair, big blue eyes and precious little grin.

"You takin' a shower, Mamma?" She swung the door back and forth in its frame, letting all the warm air out of the bathroom.

"I was trying to," I sighed.

"Can I get in the shower?"

I considered her question, but she really needed to take a nap or she would become a whiny monster later. "I'm sorry, lovey, but you need to rest right now. I'll get you washed up after your nap."

"I don't want to nap." Her face instantly changed as her lower lip stuck out. She crossed her arms and stomped her foot, and then let out a loud, disheartened cry.

My mind raced. *If she wakes her sisters, I won't get this shower. I won't get time to clean house. I'm so very tired from being up with her baby sister.* My shoulders started to clench.

"Emilia, watch your voice. You're being too loud for naptime." I rubbed her back, trying to ensure the quiet that would still allow me to shower.

"Why do you always need to be alone?" She wiped her tears. Her nose started to run.

If only she understood how little time I actually had alone. "I need time to bathe myself, time to think about how to get the house in order, and to make sure you and your sisters get cleaned up before our guests get here." Just saying out loud all I had to do before the guests arrived, my chest tightened with an overwhelming stress. I helped her wipe her nose as I guided her back upstairs to her room.

Downstairs, I sprinted back toward the shower determined to feel like a clean human being again. I stepped quickly into the shower and lathered my hair to a sudsy mess. The water turned from warm to cold then to steaming hot. Someone had flushed the toilet upstairs. I rinsed my hair and jumped out of the shower.

From upstairs, I heard Emilia and Kait. *Oh great, now she woke up her sister.*

Emilia's little voice sounded clear as day. "You want a shower, Kait?"

We don't have a shower in the upstairs bathroom so when I heard a large amount of water splash on the floor, I raced up the stairs two at a time. I found Emilia standing on the bathroom stool next to the toilet, dipping the hand towel into the toilet bowl and holding it over Kait's head for another shower. I was too late to stop the toilet shower. I watched as Kait was drenched from head to toe in toilet water, mouth open, grinning like a fool. There was already a large puddle around her feet, covering the floor and snaking into the hallway from previous showering.

"Emilia! What are you doing?" I stared at both girls, who clapped and played in the water.

"You were worried about baths." Emilia patted my leg with a damp hand, and in total confidence stated, "Now Kait is clean."

I could have blown a fuse or broken down in exhausted tears. Both seemed practical, but instead, a laugh bubbled up from somewhere inside of my tired body. My shoulders relaxed, and my chest loosened. The stress I had felt just seconds before dissipated. "Okay, girls, let's go get you a real shower."

My children were cleaned as well as the bathroom floor. My house was still a mess when my guests came to visit, but at least my kids were bathed—and not by toilet water this time. Over the years, there have been plenty of stressful times like that day, but I've learned to let laughter wash the stress away.

~Sarah Shipley

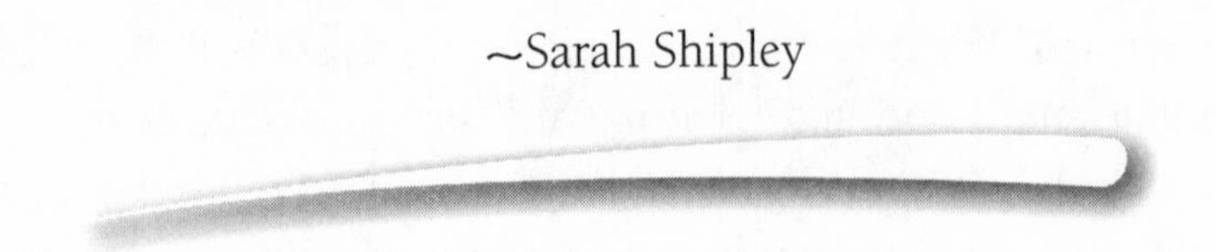

The Art of Porching

We benefit from doing nothing, from going out to play, from giving from the heart and spending time in nature.
~Jo Ann Davis

When I was a small child, I noticed how much time my grandmother would spend on the front porch of our North Bay, Ontario home late in the afternoons. I used to wonder what she thought about as she sat in her lawn chair, gazing at the highway that ran through our town. Naturally, I assumed she was counting cars. In fact, one day I joined her on our porch and came right out and asked her: "Granny, are you counting the cars?" She gave me a little smile before answering, "Yes, I am."

I've often thought about my grandmother during moments of reprieve from the frantic cadence of my life's various activities. "How the heck did she do it back then?" I muse while driving to work, driving home from work, sifting through loads of laundry to find the missing pink sock, buying groceries, making appearances at school functions, and ferrying children to karate and gymnastics classes. When I compare the shape of our lives, I am embarrassed to admit that on most days I feel more than a little overwhelmed. I'm raising two children; she raised six. I have a home filled with all the modern conveniences; she had a wood stove and no hot water. I have a vehicle at my disposal; she did not. And when I complain about having to empty the washing machine for the third time in the same day, I think about her doing laundry for eight people with a washboard and a bar of soap.

When I put it on paper, it's plain to see that in the game of hardships, there is no contest: Lucy: 0, Granny: 1,000,000. So why does it feel like my life is so damn difficult all the time?

Though it is true that women today in the developed world enjoy freedom of choice far more than at any other time in history, I feel that many of these choices have also enslaved us to a life of overextension, exhaustion and, in some cases, much unhappiness. Just because we live in a time when we can do everything, it doesn't necessarily mean we should.

As I have learned during those times when I have backed away from some of my out-of-home responsibilities, there is a lot to be said for living life in its simpler form. And while I don't mean to insinuate that women should be abandoning their careers by the masses, or tossing their chili-pepper-red front-loading washing machines by the wayside, I do encourage any and all women who, like me, are many things to many people, to take inventory of all the places in which you expend your precious energy, and how (not to mention how often) you make the time to replenish your limited reserves.

I recently finished reading *Gift from the Sea* by Anne Morrow Lindbergh, a highly acclaimed author of the twentieth century (not to mention the first female glider pilot in the U.S.) whose accomplishments often bloomed in the shadows of her husband's notoriety. In one particularly resonant chapter of her book, she speaks of the insidious breakdown of the female spirit due to overwork. Keep in mind, this book was written back in the fifties. Since then, we've evolved five-plus decades worth of other ways in which to overextend ourselves. She paints an interesting portrait of the exhausted spirit by cautioning readers against attempting to water a field with the reserves of one pitcher.

I, Lucy Lemay Cellucci, being of sound(ish) mind and body, mother of two, wife of one, teacher, writer, trapeze artist (only on my downtime), citizen, and barista, plead guilty to first-degree, premeditated pitcher-depletion. I hereby accept my sentence—ninety days of porching.

On my porch there are no plot arcs to craft. There are no lessons to plan. There are no customers to be served. There are no walls to be painted. There are no children needing my immediate attention. (They're actually just on the other side of the door, draining what little sanity is left in their father. And, yes, I admit, I'm not above taking pleasure in that fact.) There are no sticker-reward charts to update. There is no laundry to be folded, no meals to be prepared, no tidying to be done.

There is just me, sitting on my Adirondack chair, cup of tea in hand, surrounded by the flowers and shrubs in my garden. There is the sound of birds chirping nearby and the warm glow of the sleepy pre-dusk sun peeking out between the branches of the trees as it slowly begins its descent behind the houses.

For one hour each evening, I sit on my porch, taking refuge on a concrete life raft. Beneath its shelter I am offered amnesty from the irreverent pace at which I have lived my life during the last five years. Here I am connected to that part of me that actually has the ability to sit quietly and be still. Here I am not compelled to fill the silence with jokes, wisecracks, and other inessential chatter. Here I am simply living in the present moment, experiencing the joy of sitting on a porch with a cup of chamomile tea on a lovely summer evening.

How grateful I am for this opportunity to temporarily detour out of the race of life and replenish my poor, long-emptied pitcher. I'm more thankful yet that this much-needed respite has happened during the summer months. Somehow I don't think my evenings spent on the porch would have been so comforting during the middle of January. There's only so much relaxation one can soak in from behind a snowsuit and balaclava, after all.

Occasionally, my son pokes his head out the door to observe my uncharacteristic inactivity.

"Mommy, are you looking at the sewers?" he asked me one night.

I looked up at him and smiled before I replied, "Yes, I am."

~Lucy Lemay Cellucci

Time-Out for Mommy

Coloring outside the lines is a fine art.
~Kim Nance

It all started out quite innocently. My two older girls were home sick from school, and my youngest was toddling around, still refusing to be potty-trained. I had run out of ideas for keeping everyone happy, so I decided to set my daughters up in the playroom to watch a movie. (Exhaustion makes you believe that you can trust a six-year-old, a four-year-old, and a two-year-old to just sit and watch a movie while Mommy takes a break.)

Feeling like my girls were sufficiently mesmerized by the television screen, I slipped out of the room for what I rationalized would be a quick minute. Now, I want to tell you I headed to do noble mommy things—like scrubbing toilets or making my own baby food or folding my thousandth load of laundry—but I didn't. Nope. I checked my e-mail.

Keeping an ear open for any tears or sudden crashes, I happily clicked away on my laptop. And with nothing but the sound of cartoon characters coming from the other room, I decided it would be okay to read one short blog post—which may have led to another one and then possibly another one after that.

When sweet giggles drifted out of the playroom, I smiled and thought to myself, "Oh, how nice. Listen to the love. They are having fun." Perhaps if I had not been so caught up in reading my favorite blogs, my mommy alarm would have gone off—the alarm that notices there is too much quiet and that everyone is getting along too well. The alarm that sends you to see what everyone is really up to.

But instead of hearing that inner alarm, I soon heard my oldest daughter's tiny voice cheerfully declaring, "Mommy, Lauren is coloring us!" Sure enough, there she stood—her face and sweatshirt scrawled with pink marker, the joy in her voice revealing she had been a willing canvas for my two-year-old.

I bolted to the other room to assess what else bore the mark of my little Picasso. There I found my middle child colored on, toys colored on, and even a sippy cup colored on. I went from distracted mama to angry and disbelieving mama in a matter of seconds. Prying the marker from my toddler's hand, I swooped her up and marched her to her crib.

With my marker bandit safely behind bars and my older daughters in their rooms for a time-out, I stomped back toward the kitchen. Angry thoughts swirled in my mind. "Couldn't someone have gotten me before she colored everything but the TV? Come on now! I'm not promoting tattling, but there are things I need to know about. They know we only color on paper and the dry-erase board!"

As I internally huffed and puffed about my now pink ladies, a humbling question bubbled up inside of me. "So, who is going to put YOU in time-out?"

And then I realized that I shared the blame. Should my older girls have known better than to let my littlest color on them and everything in sight? Yes. But should I have also known better than to leave them unattended for so long? (Sigh.) For sure.

With a corrected heart, I thanked God no one ended up hurt during my time of distraction. Sure, a sweatshirt that once could be worn in public would have to become a sleep shirt, but other than that, everyone was fine. Pink, but fine.

In the end, we all learned a few life lessons that would keep us from having quite as many time-outs. My girls learned that sisters are not for coloring on. And me? Well, I learned there are times I am just going to have to ignore the siren call of the Internet—at least until all my adventurous girls are sound asleep.

~Kimberly D. Henderson

The Knock

How long a minute is depends on which side of the bathroom door you're on.
~Zall's Second Law

As a homeschooling mom of two active boys, I'm on duty 24/7. And even with my showers down to six minutes, I'm always nervous when I close the bathroom door. Who knows what's going to happen in those six minutes, right?

Exactly.

On one particularly humbling occasion, I started my shower time with the usual threats and warnings. It somehow makes me feel a little better about being out of earshot.

"Hey, boys!" I shouted from my bedroom. "I'll be in the shower for a few minutes. Get along. Don't fight. Don't use the stove. No weapons in the house. Don't throw a rope over the banister and try to shimmy down like Batman. And don't knock on the door and start tattling on each other or ask if you can have cookies."

My showers always start with the appropriate warnings and reminders. But I can never seem to remember everything to warn them about. And since I never know what creative version of a crisis or urgent argument will erupt, I'm usually stressed the moment I turn on the water.

"Did you hear me? I'll be out in a few minutes, okay?" I said a little louder.

"Okay, Mom," they said in unison.

Yeah, right. Who am I kidding?

One minute later, I hadn't even lathered my hair when I heard knock, knock, knock.

Oh, seriously! I just got in! What the heck could have happened so quickly?

"Leave. Me. Aloooone," I said in my stern mommy voice.

Lather.

Knock, knock, knock.

"STOP! KNOCKING! ON! THE! DOOR!" I yelled with clear enunciation.

Knock, knock, knock.

"That's it! Someone better be BLEEDING!" I shouted as I rinsed my hair and decided I didn't have time to shave my legs.

I heard running footsteps and raised voices at my door.

I squeegeed the shower doors in a full mommy-fit. My mind raced. You'd think I could get just six minutes to myself. But, noooo. They were probably arguing over that darn video game again. This was ridiculous. No more electronics. They needed to learn how to respect my time!

As I reached for the towel, I saw something out of the corner of my eye. It was a very large bird clinging to the side of the house just outside the bathroom window. To my surprise, it started pecking on the exterior wall.

Knock. Knock. Knock.

Oh, my gosh. It was the bird knocking!

As I quickly got dressed, I heard urgent footsteps coming up the stairs. I opened my bedroom door and saw my boys with worried expressions.

"Mom! Are you okay? You said you were bleeding! We're sorry to knock on the door, but we were so worried about you!"

They were worried about me and had no idea how mad I was at them. I had misunderstood the entire situation.

"I'm okay, guys," I said as I hugged them. I didn't have the heart to explain.

Oh, the humbling experience of mommyhood.

~Lori Lara

A Little Piece of Quiet

True silence is the rest of the mind; it is to the spirit what sleep is to the body, nourishment and refreshment.
~William Penn

Today it is quiet in the house. The rain taps a busy staccato outside while inside there are only the hums of the appliances to break the heavy silence.

I am not sure I like all this quiet, even though I am usually the one who is asking for it: "Could you turn it down?" "Please, shut your door!" "Who's making all the noise out there?"

Quiet. This usually only happens for an hour or two. It's something I have only when my children go off to visit friends, or when my husband is out doing errands. To have the house to myself for a whole day is both delightful and perplexing. I find myself torn between doing something sensible, like scrubbing out cabinets, or doing something wicked, like looking for stashes of sweets.

I should use the time to get caught up on the housework, maybe plan a month's worth of meals, or even re-wallpaper the kitchen. I should do something constructive, something for the family. And yet, I find myself drawn to doing "me" things, like taking a nap, and it's not even the afternoon yet. I would like to read a book from cover to cover. Then there are those dresses hanging in my closet, the ones that have been waiting patiently for those seven pounds to drop off.

Trying them on requires privacy. Or maybe I will do something radical to my hair, beyond just touching up the streaks of gray coming in.

I don't do any of those "me" things. Instead I organize the kitchen drawers.

My mother tells me of the time when she enrolled me in preschool. "I'm going to use these few quiet hours and finally paint that dresser," she had sighed to another mother. The other mother exclaimed, "Are you crazy? I'm going home to take a long soak in a bubble bath." It hadn't occurred to my mother that she could have done the same. She still ended up painting the dresser.

When I find myself surrounded by the family, I get things done. Laundry gets folded, toilets are scrubbed, the garden is weeded, bills are paid, and ironing is conquered. All this is done amid solving sibling conflicts, fielding questions, and finding stuff. Now that it is quiet, I don't feel as productive. Do I only function best with noise surrounding me?

When the youngest finally entered first grade, I realized that amazing possibilities lay ahead. I could paint the bathroom. Lounge in my pajamas. Take up the harmonica. Abandon common sense and binge on cheesecake. I did none of those things. I filled the hours with a part-time job. I confess—I couldn't face all that quiet at home.

I wonder if my attempts to fill up these momentary gifts of empty hours with meaningful busyness are because I am not used to being by myself anymore. After all, for more than fourteen years I have had at least one child to account for and my husband to keep track of. It's going to take me awhile to reprogram myself to make decisions in solitude, while accomplishing something without the pressure of others demanding my attention. I need to get used to having peace in my quiet.

And so, in my quiet house, I am reminded of the maxim, "Be careful what you wish for—you just might get it."

Today I have the quiet I so often longed for, and yes it is pleasant. On the other hand, I realize that laughter, voices and the noise of my family fill up the empty corners of the house, making it a home. They are the sounds of love, the sounds that complete my peace.

I realize it's just a *piece* of quiet I long for, more than *peace* and quiet.

~C. Muse

Substitute Mom

Teamwork divides the task and multiplies the success.
~Author Unknown

I missed teaching, but my husband and I had agreed when I became pregnant with our first child that I should be a stay-at-home mom. It was an adjustment, alone in the apartment with a new infant, away from the chatter of my students and teaching colleagues. There were very few young families, mostly elderly retirees, in our apartment complex and I often found myself feeling lonely, wishing for the camaraderie of my teaching days.

I was thrilled to learn of another new mother in a different wing of the apartment building, with a son a few months younger than my daughter. We were introduced and were soon walking our babies in their carriages together, or arranging to put them down to nap in the same crib so we could bake cookies together or just enjoy a cup of coffee and conversation while they slept.

As we compared notes, we discovered that we both missed our working days and although we were both often asked if we could come in to substitute for an absent employee at our old places of work, we had to say no because we couldn't leave our babies. Doris had been a lab technician in a local doctor's clinic; I had taught in our local middle school and high school.

Over time, we came up with a plan. Since our kids loved being together, and were comfortable with either one of us, we decided that whoever received a call to fill in at their old place of employment for a day or two should accept the offer and immediately alert the other that she would be babysitting. That way, if Doris got the first call, I'd know not to accept an assignment the same day and I would take care of her son, Keith. Conversely, if I had a call from the school district, she would agree to take my Alice.

By the time our second children, my son Eric and her daughter Karen, came along, we were both moving into our first homes and away from the apartment complex. Even though the houses we bought were in different towns, they were close enough to continue the arrangement. Although my children always protested when left with an adult babysitter, they were delighted to be left with my friend Doris. They didn't feel I was leaving them. They felt they were going on a play date with their friends Keith and Karen.

Although we had put some miles between us by moving from the apartment complex to different towns, there was no way Doris and I were going to give up our arrangement. Far more valuable to us than the extra money from our substituting stints was the joy of seeing our old friends at work again and keeping our skills fresh. It was glorious to be able to spend an occasional day back in the adult world, where people were your own size and expressed ideas in full sentences.

Years went by and as our kids started school in different towns, our arrangement became too complicated to continue. But by then, the children had neighborhood friends. If Doris or I received a call to substitute, we could send our kids off to school with the knowledge that they would go home with a particular friend. Neighbors' children filled my house as often as mine filled theirs. It was a great arrangement for us stay-at-home moms, a chance to have it all: the extra income and occasional change of routine, spending a day back at work while being a full-time homemaker.

~Marcia Rudoff

to do list:
- Pay bills
- Get Laundry
- Call Mom
- Pick up kids from birthday at 6 p.m.
- Buy groceries

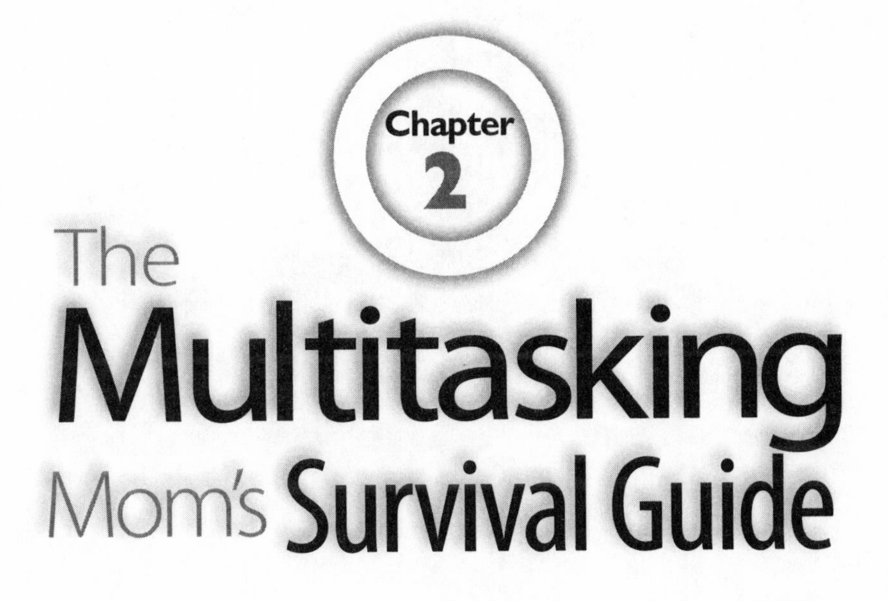

Feeding the Family

The people who give you their food give you their heart.

~Cesar Chavez

Confessions of a Lunch Maker

I come from a family where gravy is considered a beverage.
~Erma Bombeck

According to my mother, my generation has it easy. She's referring to bread machines, microwave ovens, smartphones, Internet banking... the list is endless. But I can stop her cold with two words: school lunches.

When I was a kid, she made me a peanut butter and strawberry jam sandwich. On white bread. And tossed it in a brown paper bag with an apple. That was it. Simple, simple times.

My daughter uses brown paper bags to make hand puppets. Lunch bags come with insulation, pockets, zippers, water bottles, mini ice packs and a matching thermos. Peanut butter is banned in most schools, and white bread is looked upon as a nutritional wasteland. That leaves the apple. And that's precisely what my children do: leave the apple. But I keep sending the apple. No mother worth her minivan sends her child to school without fresh fruit for the teacher to see. (Tip: An apple can go back and forth for a couple of weeks before it bruises, rots and needs replacement. A banana, on the other hand, has no longevity.)

Of course, every September I hope it will be different. I approach a fresh year of lunchmaking with a fist-full of "kid-proven" recipes torn from newspapers and magazines. I vow to buy breads with flax seeds and ancient grains, certain that if I use a cookie cutter to shape them like a star or a horse, the kids won't notice the lack of fluffy white dough. But within days, the sandwiches begin returning.

It's important to me that all the food groups are represented, but I confess, as the school year progresses, each group is open to interpretation. For example, by Christmas I consider chocolate-covered raisins a fruit. By April, so are those rubbery "fruit" chews. By spring, I'm so worn out I consider cheddar popcorn both a vegetable and a dairy product.

I have one disguised vegetable trick that has yet to fail me, but it takes great commitment. The kids know it as "chocolate bread." It's actually a low-fat zucchini loaf made with applesauce. Cocoa and a half-cup of mini chocolate chips are its cover. The most important step is grating the zucchini so fine that it isn't visible to the naked eye when baked. I grate late at night when my children are sleeping.

I shared this recipe with a friend. Her children loved it, but the late-night grating wore her down. She became careless and grated while they were still up. I think it was a cry for help. She was caught, and her kids never touched "chocolate bread" again. She tried to act disappointed, but I think she was secretly glad to have her life back.

I soldier on. So, Mom, have a little sympathy. I may bank in my bathrobe, but at night as you sleep, I'm bleary-eyed in the kitchen, silently grating zucchini.

~Kim Reynolds

Blue Waffles

If we're not willing to settle for junk living,
we certainly shouldn't settle for junk food.
~Sally Edwards

We're a busy family, but what family isn't? My husband and I both work full-time outside of the home. Our two daughters are involved in softball, golf, basketball, theater, orchestra and church activities in addition to their schooling. They both volunteer with animals and missions and enjoy fun hobbies like swimming, running and reading.

But we've always strived to have dinner together. Unfortunately, that dinner was often called something like "Number Three Value Meal" and was eaten from a paper bag in front of the television as we all collapsed from our busy days. As much as I wanted to cook dinner for my family, I knew that I wouldn't have time, or I'd spend a great deal of energy making something that would not be pleasing to everyone.

"I've got an idea," I announced one Saturday as I sat down to make out our weekly grocery list. "What if each of you—even Daddy—took one day to fix dinner? Anything you want. You tell me what day you want and what you want to fix, and I'll make sure that we have all the groceries you need."

My ever-supportive husband jumped right in and said he'd take Friday nights. This week, he'd fix sausage casserole, his favorite meal.

Our daughters were a bit more reluctant. My older daughter voiced her concerns first. "You are sure we can fix anything we want?"

I nodded my head.

"Anything at all?" her sister clarified.

"Anything at all."

"Even blue waffles?" my older daughter asked.

Blue waffles? I wasn't sure that I had even heard of blue waffles. "I guess," I said tentatively.

"I'm in," my older daughter agreed. "And this week, I want to make blue waffles, fried chicken and scrambled eggs."

I nodded and wrote down her menu.

The night before she was to cook, my husband asked me, "What are blue waffles?" Honestly, I had no idea what blue waffles were, but I was willing to let my daughter make them in order for us to gain more quality family time and to give myself a break from the kitchen.

When her day to cook dinner arrived, my older daughter asked me if I had a recipe for blue waffles. I confessed that I didn't even know what blue waffles were.

"They are just waffles that are blue," she answered. I handed her the waffle recipe and the blue food coloring.

Since that meal, our daughters have turned out some mighty delicious pans of enchiladas, a great Italian quiche, homemade pizza and an awesome grilled steak salad. I did nix the pepperoni and oatmeal casserole—we're not that adventuresome!

More importantly, we have a great time gathering as a family in the kitchen to assist the cook of the night, and we have come to appreciate being together at mealtime.

I'm no longer stressed about providing a good meal every night, our daughters are contributing to our household, and they're learning some delicious culinary skills.

We all sit down together at the table to talk to each other about our days, and we've all learned to appreciate the effort it takes to put together a meal. We've also learned to appreciate blue waffles—they've become a staple in our meal rotation.

~Heather Davis

The Wrong Bag

Every survival kit should include a sense of humor.
~Author Unknown

I stumbled to the kitchen. It was way too early to be up after a long night writing. I filled the coffeepot with water and tilted the coffee bag over the filter. Nothing! I opened the bag wider and looked inside. Empty!

"Mom!" Lee called from the other room. "Mom?" I rummaged in the cabinets. There was another bag of coffee somewhere.

"Mom?" He walked into the kitchen. "Didn't you hear me calling you?"

"Yeah," I answered. "Whatever it is, just hang on a second. I'm trying to find some coffee." I checked the pantry. No coffee there either.

"This is important," Lee demanded. I paused and looked at him. "You have to make my lunch today. I'm going on a field trip to the courthouse." Oh, no! Was that today?

"Okay, I'll take care of it." I gave up the search for coffee and started looking for things to put in a bag lunch. We were out of lunchmeat so he got a PB&J sandwich minus the jelly because we were out of that too. There hadn't been time to go to the grocery store yet this week.

Ring! Ring! I snatched up the phone with one hand while searching for the Hostess cupcake hidden behind the canned veggies with the other. "Hello."

"I'm not going to be able to help decorate for Karen's bachelorette party tonight," my friend Amie said. "I have a job interview but I have all the decorations. Can you come by and get them before you take the kids to school?" Just great! As if I didn't already have enough to do. But I agreed. What else could I do?

I hung up and looked with longing at the cupcake in my hand. I'd hidden it away for a day like this, when things were crazy and I needed the comfort of chocolate. Sighing, I put it next to the sandwich I'd made for Lee. I didn't have any chips or anything to put in his lunch, so the least I could do was give him dessert.

Cody came running in. "Mom, I can't find my T-ball uniform."

"It's in the dryer." I looked over at my middle son, Rob, calmly eating his cereal. He was always so calm while the rest of us ran around like chickens with our heads cut off. I grabbed a Walmart bag from under the sink and handed it to him. "Would you grab Cody's uniform for me?"

I grabbed another Walmart bag and started packing Lee's lunch, glancing at the clock. We were running late and Cody and Lee hadn't eaten yet. I popped two waffles in the toaster; they could eat on the way. I rushed everyone out to the car and started to back up.

"Wait," Lee yelled. "I forgot my homework." I watched the minutes tick by while we waited for him to find it. He got back in and I pulled out of the driveway heading to Amie's.

"Don't forget Chelsea," Rob said from the back. Shoot! I forgot I was supposed to give the girl down the street a ride. I pulled back in and went the other way. We were really running late now. At least Amie was waiting outside with the decorations when we got to her house.

I was lost in thought, trying to figure out how I was going to do everything that needed to be done. Drop Chelsea and the older boys off at school, spend the day volunteering in Cody's classroom, pay bills at lunch, pick the boys up after school, take Cody to his T-ball game, drop the kids off at my mom's house, and decorate for Karen's party before it started at 7:00.

"Mom," Lee interrupted my thoughts. "You missed the school."

I turned around in the nearest driveway. "Sorry, guys. My mind isn't working very well today. I haven't had my coffee."

"You know coffee is a drug don't you?" Chelsea asked. "My class went on our field trip to the courthouse yesterday and the policeman told us all about drugs."

I pulled in the parking lot. "That may be," I answered, handing Lee his lunch. "But I could sure use some."

Thankfully, the staff lounge at Cody's school had coffee made. I sipped a cup and felt my mind begin to work again.

The morning passed without incident. At lunch, I ran out to drop off some bills and order a burger from McDonald's. While waiting in the drive-thru, I noticed the bag of decorations sitting on the floor. Curious to see what naughty items Amie had picked out for the bachelorette party, I opened it. The first thing I saw was the cupcake. Oh no! I had given Lee the wrong Walmart bag. I glanced at my watch. If I hurried, I might be able to make it to school before they started eating.

I pulled out of line and rushed to the courthouse. As I parked, I could see Lee's teacher getting the class settled on the courthouse lawn. I grabbed Lee's lunch and ran across the street. Where was he? There! I spotted him talking to a police officer and hurried over.

"My mom does drugs," Lee was saying. "But she ran out this morning and her mind isn't working right." He held his bag up. "That's why I got this instead of my lunch."

He turned the bag upside down and dumped assorted party supplies, many shaped like… man parts… on the ground at the officer's feet. I was standing there mortified, wondering if I could just slip away, when Lee saw me.

"There's my mom right there." I hurried to scoop the stuff off the ground under the watchful eyes of Lee's teacher and the policeman. I could feel my face burning as I mumbled something about a friend's bachelorette party and not having any coffee. I glanced around to see both the teacher and the police officer trying unsuccessfully not to laugh.

Later on I was able to appreciate the humor of the situation but not right then. I was too embarrassed. But I did learn a valuable lesson that day. Always double check the bags to make sure the right things go with the right people. And keep a spare bag of coffee in the pantry.

~Kimber Krochmal

Into the Fray

You can learn many things from children.
How much patience you have, for instance.
~Franklin P. Jones

Years ago, when I was a newlywed, my older sister asked if I would babysit her five children for a week. At the time I was still tanned from a honeymoon and eager to embark upon married life. I was also unemployed. Thus, when my sister made her outlandish request, I had no reasonable excuse.

Dorie followed by adding that she and her husband Gerard hadn't been away in three years. She also mentioned she was pregnant with number six.

"They deserve a break," my husband concluded. Easy for him to say; he wouldn't be the one moving in for a week.

My sister was fifteen years older than me, and our lives were vastly different. My husband and I lived alone in a quiet suburban condominium. My sister's life, on the other hand, was a dizzying whirl of kids, dogs and carpools. I never left her house without feeling frazzled, wondering how she managed it all and still maintained her sense of humor. It helped that she was no perfectionist.

"The first one up is the best dressed," she said.

At twenty-three years old, I was ill prepared to care for five children under thirteen. For one thing, I couldn't cook. Yet despite my deficiencies, I was conscientious. I didn't want my nieces and nephews to get scurvy on my watch, so I gave in and bought a cookbook. I was determined they'd have a hot meal every night.

While perusing the book, I learned a clever tip: Make sandwiches for the week and freeze them. In the morning, remove from freezer. By lunchtime, the sandwich will have thawed.

I'm sure the tipster didn't have five kids in mind when making that suggestion. Nonetheless, following my arrival, I cleared the kitchen table of hockey masks and video games and set up an assembly line. Before long, the freezer held twenty-five sandwiches piled in neat stacks: peanut butter and jelly, bologna and cheese, tuna salad, and liverwurst and Swiss. Organization was the key, I decided.

Nonetheless, I wasn't prepared for the first early morning alarm and the resulting chaos as the kids fought over the bathroom. Following that, they raced into the kitchen. Here they emptied boxes of cereal into bowls and dragged gallons of milk from the fridge, sloshing it over the table. All the while they bickered, elbowing and nudging each other.

Before racing out to the bus, they grabbed the sandwiches from the freezer. The peanut butter and jelly vanished immediately. Needless to say, on subsequent mornings, they rejected the other selections. I discovered that liverwurst is "gross" and tuna fish and bologna freeze poorly.

When the house was blessedly quiet, I wearily phoned my husband for support as the dog lapped up the milk and soggy cereal on the floor.

With the kids in school, I looked through my cookbook. I knew it was important for children to have vegetables, so I selected an easy casserole of spinach, eggs and creamed corn.

I was dozing on the sofa when I heard the sound of air brakes followed by an ungodly roar. The front door burst open, and all five kids raced in accompanied by an assortment of friends. They tossed jackets, hats and books on the floor while rushing to the kitchen. Once again the refrigerator and cupboards were flung open, and everything I'd carefully put away was dragged out. Rivers of milk flowed amidst the constant elbowing, pushing and bickering. This was the afternoon "snack time" my sister had mentioned.

Soon the stereo was blasting while my nieces and their junior high friends sang and danced in the living room. Down the hall, the boys fought over piles of sports equipment, punching each other until I broke it up.

When dinnertime finally arrived, I called the kids to the table. For a moment, seeing them sitting together, I had a feeling of satisfaction. But only for a moment.

"What's that?" Terry said, when I placed the casserole on the table. Unbeknownst to me, kids and casseroles are not compatible, especially those made with spinach.

"This tastes better than it looks," I promised, though I had no idea. Because they were hungry, they dug in, and before long discovered the—unwashed—spinach.

"Yuck," Butchie spat. "That's dirt."

"Don't spit on me," his brother Shawn said, elbowing him sharply.

"I didn't spit on you." Butchie elbowed back.

With that, Shawn picked up his runny square of spinach casserole and threw it at his brother. Some of it hit his sister, who threw hers back at him. A food fight ensued until I stopped it by yelling the loudest. With the walls splattered with spinach and corn kernels, I piled everyone in the car and drove to a local pizza parlor. At least it was a hot meal, I rationalized.

My week at Dorie's has become an oft-told family legend. Yet it was during that endless week that I learned about compromise, something my sister already did well. I found out that kids won't die from eating pizza for breakfast, and matching socks—or shoes—aren't mandatory for learning. And though the house shook on its foundation when all the kids were at home, at least they were accounted for.

The lessons came in handy when I later threw caution to the wind and had two children of my own. My sister never offered to babysit.

~Sharon Love Cook

Everything But Cooking

I was thirty-two when I started cooking; up until then, I just ate.
~Julia Child

"Mom, I can't believe you submitted this," exclaimed my twenty-four-year-old daughter, laughing, as we looked at her nursery school recipe book, which sported her smiling three-year-old face on the cover. I thought back to that day, long ago, when she came home from nursery school with a note saying that each mother had to provide two recipes for a cookbook the school was making. I had reluctantly submitted two: one was for chocolate chip cookies and was copied right off the back of a Crisco can. The other was for an hors d'oeuvre I called "salmon roll-ups," said recipe consisting of the following instructions: 1) sprinkle smoked salmon with lemon juice, cracked pepper, and dill weed; 2) cut into long strips; 3) roll up strips and insert toothpick.

I spent the first four decades of my life completely unable to cook anything. My first cooking disaster occurred when I was twelve and I obtained my grandmother's coveted fudge recipe. I carefully followed the instructions, right down to including her secret ingredient—one tablespoon of coffee. The fudge came out black, shiny, and hard. It looked and felt like a polished piece of lava. Even our Golden Retriever, who would eat anything, refused to go near it. It was only two decades later, when I became a coffee drinker, that I realized my grandmother meant that I should include a tablespoon of actual brewed coffee, not the instant coffee flakes that I had carefully stirred into the mixture.

The next cooking disaster that stands out occurred years later, when I attempted to make pancakes for my young children. The pancakes came out so hard that the kids used them as Frisbees. They were inedible, but perfectly round and aerodynamic. After playing with them all day, the kids left them in our back yard, which was fully populated with deer, coyote, raccoons, rabbits, birds, and other hungry creatures, but the pancake Frisbees were still there the next morning. It was only after another night outside—and the sprinklers running for six hours—that the pancakes apparently softened up enough to be eaten by the animals, since they had finally disappeared by the third morning. The kids still talk about my baked Frisbees. So I guess children can have favorite family recipes even if they are not for something edible!

Another time, I decided to make iced tea for my book group. It may be hard to believe, but I actually had to look up the recipe for iced tea. I diligently placed the tea bags in a saucepan full of water, with the paper tags hanging over the edge as instructed, and turned on the gas. It was good I had the water, since every one of those paper tags immediately burst into flames.

I was married to the second son of four sons, and his mother had decided that he would be the son who learned to cook. He was great at it, so I did not know how to cook anything. He even made our coffee every morning.

It wasn't an issue in our marriage. I was a Wall Street analyst and ran a hedge fund, and I was contributing to the family in many other ways. I worked full-time from home, handled all our investments, took care of our tax returns, and even managed to be class mother every year for one or the other child. I drove on field trips, read stories out loud every night, bought all the gifts. I was also responsible for all the kitchen cleanup after every meal. I just couldn't cook the meal.

My aversion to cooking was only a problem when it came to dealing with the other mothers—I had to discretely avoid baking or cooking assignments for school functions. I was the mother who always volunteered to bring the paper goods, spending umpteen dollars on paper plates, cups, napkins, etc. just to avoid bringing in a theoretically edible item. My downfall came with birthday cupcakes—moms really do have to make those for their kids' birthdays. One time, I tried to make cupcakes, from a mix no less, and instead of rising in the oven, they came out shaped like cups. My kids thought it was great—I had to fill in the craters with lots of extra frosting before I could even add the frosting domes on top. The poor teacher must have wondered why her students were bouncing off the ceiling that day.

A couple of years after the cookbook crisis, my daughter came home from school, excited about something new that she had learned in kindergarten. "Did you know that in some families the mommy cooks?" she asked, as surprised as if she had just discovered that women could be NFL linebackers or Catholic priests.

She was even more surprised a few years later, after a divorce, when I did indeed learn to cook. It turns out my problem all along had been a dislike of recipes. Once I realized I could "cook by feel" and just throw whatever made sense into a pot, I began cooking up a storm. And now my new husband helps with the dishes, because he can't even boil water!

~Amy Newmark

I Blame My Mother

The most remarkable thing about my mother is that for thirty years she served the family nothing but leftovers. The original meal has never been found.
~Calvin Trillin

It is no secret that I have never been nor ever will be a Martha Stewart type. I am the "anti-Martha Stewart" if anything! That said, I have managed to raise three relatively healthy children into adulthood, and my husband has never lost weight due to my dysfunction in the kitchen. I don't have a huge repertoire of recipes so I go for the tried and true, the meals tested over time and family-approved, because if I digress from those formulas there are always serious repercussions.

I blame my mother. She failed to instill household skills of any kind in her one and only daughter—me. She didn't much like to cook or clean, and she was a meat, potatoes, and gravy cook. I suggested cooking spaghetti one night, and she almost had a coronary. After her first grandchild was born, my mother attempted to become the stereotypical perfect grandmother. On my daughter's third birthday, she decided to bake her favored grandchild a birthday cake. Being close to Easter, my mother thought she could combine bunnies and birthday cake. The result was a two-tiered vanilla concoction that my father thought looked like a "motor scooter." My mother never baked again.

My mother once shooed a Fuller Brush vacuum cleaner salesman away from our door by turning the garden hose on him and yelling as she did: "I don't use the vacuum cleaner I've got. Why in the world would I want another one?"

Knowing I have a DNA disadvantage, there have still been times when I have been forced to overcome my inbred homemaking impediments and venture out to uncharted territory. I was hosting a large family-and-friends gathering, and it was imperative that the meal be edible, the house be impeccable and the evening be delightful. I had planned a simple, foolproof meal, one that I had successfully time- and family-tested in the past. I brushed off the cobwebs on my vacuum and attacked every dust bunny in the house until the infestation was gone! I set a table with a plethora of cutlery that would impress royalty. All was perfect until I realized I had neglected to plan a dessert. I knew baking was out of the question. I could buy something at the local grocery store, but my guests were about to arrive so there was no time for me to duck out and find something to plop onto a fancy plate and claim credit for later.

In a panic, I raided my cupboards and found some pudding cups, fruit cocktail, and marshmallow fluff. First, I scooped some pudding into bowls, then the fruit, and then the marshmallow fluff. I added more pudding, more fruit and a little more marshmallow fluff on top. It looked fabulous! With no time to spare, I popped the little bowls into the fridge and welcomed my first guest.

All was going splendidly. I may not know how to cook or bake, but I do know how to play a good host. When it came time for dessert, there were many "ooohs and aaahhs" at the presentation—until each guest tried to dip a spoon into their bowl. My mistake was in not realizing that marshmallow fluff hardens to concrete when refrigerated. One guest managed to pickaxe his spoon into the goo and wave it around like a bowl flag before the rest of the guests dissolved into frenzied laughter.

Mortified at the dessert disaster around me, all I could say was, "I blame my mother."

~Lynn Dove

Lunch Date

The only person you should ever compete with is yourself.
You can't hope for a fairer match.
~Todd Ruthman

Head held high, I strode through the front door of my son's new school and down the corridor to the lunchroom. His challenge had been new classmates. Mine would be the new School Parents Team. It was tough changing schools halfway through the school year, but after a week he was doing fine. It was my turn, and this Family Lunch Day was my debut as a school mom.

I paused outside the lunchroom doorway and surveyed the buffet table from afar. I noticed the bowls of salad first—a great idea for a school lunch, I thought. There were real plates and salad forks that one of the parents had brought from home. Lettuce, red and green peppers, tomatoes, spinach leaves, gorgeous really. Farther along was a large dish of something grainy and beige, wisps of steam rising from its surface. Was it brown rice? That was odd.

On one side of the table a line of slow cookers shared a power strip, their contents bubbling gently. Little colored cards beside each dish identified the contents in clear capital letters, suitable for elementary students: SOYBEANS AND CELERY, ROOT VEGETABLE STEW, and LENTILS WITH ZUCCHINI. A bright yellow happy face decorated each card. Right at the end of the table, mostly hidden behind pitchers of filtered water, were several small paper plates. On each was a personal-size pizza from a nearby take-out, cut into neat quarters for easy eating and sharing. Pepperoni. Ham and Pineapple. Double Cheese. But there were no cards identifying the pizzas and no happy faces, none at all.

The school notice was still in my handbag. I discreetly pulled it out. "The School Parents Team announces Family Lunch Day this Friday!" it said. "Bring food to the school kitchen by 10:30." I had done that. "Lunch at noon," it continued. No other information; not a word about soybeans.

As soon as the noon chimes sounded, children hustled into the lunchroom and surrounded the table. Curiosity and enthusiasm vibrated in the air. I squared my shoulders and walked in, too. A stay-at-home dad handed out the china plates and silverware.

Mothers manned the serving stations, ladles in hand, prepared to dish out what the children chose.

"Try some of these yummy turnips and beets, Melinda."

"Bean stew, children?"

"Roberto, have some spicy tofu. Here, try a spoonful. Roberto! Take some tofu!"

Like homing pigeons, the children brushed past the garbanzo casseroles and made for the pizza. I spotted my son and headed that way, too. He saw me coming. With a happy smile on his face and pride in his voice, he announced, "My mom brought the pizza!" A few of the children emitted a ragged cheer. One offered a high-five with her left hand, while brandishing a triangle of Meat Lover's Special with her right.

"Adam's mom brought the pizza!"

"Yeah, it was Adam's mom!"

All of the parents turned to stare as I stood there surrounded by children in the rapidly chilling room. I slipped out the back door at the first opportunity. It was going to be a long year on the School Parents Team.

~Eleanor Thomas

Snack Attack

Red meat is not bad for you. Now blue-green meat, that's bad for you!
~Tommy Smothers

Have you ever had one of those days where you have a plan, you are working so hard, you are checking things off the task list and things are flowing just fine, and then suddenly it all slides right through your fingers like sand?

I was at my computer, mid-morning on a weekday, mind on task, tapping away at the keyboard when the phone rang. The familiar voice of my husband spit out the words, "Are you trying to kill me or what?"

Take one step back. That morning, I had gotten up nice and early to make healthy lunches for the three of us and even packed a snack of bread, peanut butter, jam and a tea bag for my husband. We had discussed that he'd save a few dollars a day at the cafeteria if he brought his own lunch. All good intentions. I even gave him a tiny container of sugar for his tea, which I pinched from our camping supplies.

Back to attempted murder... I had no idea what I could've done. It turns out the bread I had sent was moldy, and not just the white fuzzy beginnings of mold, but the green-blue variety. This also meant his lunch sandwich could be moldy, which also meant my son's sandwich at school would be suspect. So he chucked the bread and just made himself a nice cup of tea. Then he took one sip of his tea with two teaspoons of—wait for it—SALT and gagged, spewing tea all over the table. I must have grabbed the camping salt! Not only was his morning less pleasant than usual due to my irresponsible family care, but I broke into an unstoppable fit of laughter on the phone when he told me all of this, which didn't help. Then, realizing the time, I quickly snapped out of it and said, "Gotta go!" I slapped together a quick bologna wrap for my son and slipped over to his school to make the sandwich switch before the lunch bell.

The result of all this nonsense was a family conversation the next day in which we decided that lunches would be made the night before so as not to be rushed and that we would also take turns. It's been a wonderful change for Mom... and no rotten episodes since.

Sometimes I think I'm really putting "for better or for worse" to the test!

~Brandy Lynn Maslowski

The Show Must Go On

I learned that there's a certain character that can be built from embarrassing yourself endlessly. If you can sit happy with embarrassment, there's not much else that can really get to ya.
~Christian Bale

We had a dinner guest a few Sundays ago. Our parish secretary, a lovely, refined, mild-mannered lady in her seventies, came to join us for a roasted chicken.

All day we had prepared the house for our company. The linens were ironed, the floors were steamed, and the food was bubbling joyfully on the stove. The children were napping, with cute outfits laid out to wear upon waking. Mia, my three-year-old, had helped wash the windows and set the table. She was quite excited we were having a special guest.

Ms. Night has been working at my church ever since I was in middle school. We never spoke much as she's a quiet soul, but I was always curious about her. I knew she lived alone and dressed very conservatively, always in skirts with a kerchief around her neck, never in pants. Now employed by the parish myself, I came in contact with Ms. Night quite regularly and felt it would be appropriate to have her over.

And so it was that Ms. Night arrived exactly at five, in kerchief and skirt, bearing a fruit tray. We welcomed her, and Mia flittered about, chattering about one thing or another. After giving her a tour of the house, we sat down to carve the grand roasted chicken. So far, everything was going excellently. While we are never so reserved or proper about our meals, Mia and her two-year-old brother, Jack, were picking up the cues perfectly, and the meal began with light conversation and a salad.

I had a Bridget Jones moment of "Sitting at table with guest, am poised, graceful host serving succulent chicken. Talking about how we can aid the crisis in Japan. Am proper, intelligent host. Husband is sounding calm and serious. Children are also waiting calmly for dinner. Mood is Stepford-ish, but good. Certainly guest will be impressed with our family."

Suddenly, like a dying helicopter landing in the middle of a blissfully still meadow, Mia began to pass gas. At the table. At an incredibly audible level and rate of expulsion.

The conversation came to a halt. Mia was seated directly across from the guest of honor. The guest of honor stared at Mia.

I was seated directly across from my husband, Tom, which was not good considering that our eyes locked, and we started twitching simultaneously while trying to remain serious.

The concert continued, and I began to worry about two things: losing my "inner poise" and wondering how long this was going to last. As if sensing my nervousness, Mia decided to break the ice by announcing to our stunned ears, "I am farting!" She then grinned, glanced from adult to adult, and continued even louder, "I love farting!"

I glanced at my husband to see how he was handling the situation. His head was downcast, hidden in a napkin, pretending he was mourning the loss of our dignity or something.

"Perfect," I thought. "All Tom has to do is look at me and we'll both lose it. How am I going to get out of this one? What do I say?"

To make the situation just a little more awkward, our guest was ignoring my daughter's shouts and continued to calmly munch her arugula and baby spinach.

Then baby Jack began to chime in. Mia turned to her brother and decided to narrate the event to us as well.

"Jack likes pooping! Wow, that's a big one!"

Both kids burst out laughing.

Tom and I looked at each other, trying not to laugh. Then, at Jack's next round, we both lost it.

Never in a million years would I have imagined that scenario.

Our kids have never, ever done this at the dinner table. Especially together on cue. Which is impressive, but horrible, timing to showcase their newfound talent.

"I'm so sorry!" I moaned between fits of laughter, practically hanging off my chair under the table from sheer hysterics. "I don't know what to say. This has never happened to us..."

Luckily, Ms. Night has plenty of nieces and nephews and was able to carry on with us the rest of the evening as if nothing had happened. But I'm pretty willing to bet that was the only time she ever witnessed such an event.

When we headed up for the night after our company had left, we burst out laughing again. I shook my head.

"Time to review manners with them, I guess."

Tom shook his head, laughing.

"Time to invest in Beano."

~Annemarie Thimons

Cooking for Special Needs

Let food be thy medicine...
~Hippocrates

My mother used to cook a traditional dinner each night. We had broiled meat, potatoes or rice, a vegetable, and a salad. Dessert was always fruit—sometimes fresh, often canned. There was one rule: we had to eat what was offered whether we liked it or not. My sister was frequently in trouble because she didn't like the canned asparagus Mom regularly served.

I thought about those dinners when I had my own family. I tried to make dinnertime a pleasant experience, encouraging our young children to try new foods but not punishing them if they didn't like the new tastes. All went well until the kids grew older.

And then dinner became a challenge.

My teenage son had been eating voraciously and yet he seemed to be losing weight. I took him to the doctor, and he was diagnosed with diabetes. I had to re-appraise what I was serving. I became aware of the impact of fats and carbohydrates on blood sugar and tried to balance his meals to help him stay healthy.

Then one day my daughter looked at the dishes on the table and said, "Mom, I can't eat that." She was having some health problems and started experimenting with an allergy-testing diet. It seemed to me that she was hardly eating anything—a typical mommy response—but she needed to identify those foods that caused a reaction.

But my dinner woes didn't stop there; my husband discovered he needed a lactose-free menu. And although I had been vegetarian for many years, I was now vegan, which caused more issues.

I found myself needing to cook one dinner for four special needs diets. In general, I liked to cook, but it wasn't fun anymore. How could I keep everyone happy—and healthy—and maintain my sanity, too? I could just imagine the turmoil this would have caused for my mother. But now I was a mother, too, and I had to do what was necessary for my family.

I developed a multi-meal plan. It was based on a Mediterranean model with several dishes offered from which we all could choose. A meat or fish platter, a few plain, steamed vegetables, a non-embellished carbohydrate, the makings of a salad sliced and served on different dishes, seeds and nuts put out separately as condiments, and a variety of fruits allowed us all to choose what we each needed. Sauces were served on the side to be added or not, as desired.

We all seemed to thrive on the new regimen. Yes, it was a little more work for me, but the results were worth it. My son was able to keep his diabetes under better control, and my daughter found out which foods she would do well to avoid. The grown-ups, too, could have a meal with appropriate foods to eat.

We went back to enjoying dinner together. And we discovered that we actually liked the new plan. It gave us all a degree of culinary freedom and, because of the differences in our dietary needs, offered us a sense of discovery in dining.

~Ferida Wolff

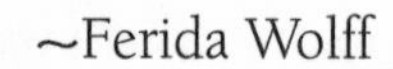

The Circus Show of Motherhood

Spaghetti can be eaten most successfully if you inhale it like a vacuum cleaner.
~Sophia Loren

"There! Dinner is served. Everyone be quiet, eat, and be satisfied." I placed the spaghetti in front of everyone and sank into my chair with a big sigh. It was Thursday, and like every Thursday, I was exhausted, overwhelmed, and just irritated with everyone and everything. These long workweeks with two little kids at home drained me like nothing else.

"Mom?" asked my older daughter, looking at me with her little button nose scrunched up in mock horror.

"What?" I practically screamed. Couldn't they just eat without demanding something?

"Why is the spaghetti, like, mushy?" she asked.

No, not again, I thought in desperation. I glanced at my husband, and he just gave a slight nod in agreement with my daughter. Why couldn't I even cook something as simple as spaghetti? Then I remembered why. Because while I was trying to get dinner cooked and on the table, the baby kept crying at my feet; my older daughter wanted milk, then her necklace tied around her neck, then she was fighting with her sister; the dog was bugging me to go out and then be let back in; and I was trying to finish up the dishes I hadn't finished from the night before and squeeze in a load of laundry so it wouldn't be a ridiculous pile by the weekend. Once again, I was distracted by so many other things besides the task at hand, which was supposed to be cooking us all an easy spaghetti dinner.

I picked up a forkful of my own spaghetti. I tried to hide the horror on my face as I realized how overcooked the noodles were. There was no way we could eat them.

I hung my head in defeat once again. Sometimes, I just wanted to cry. Throughout my journey in motherhood, I have concluded that my multitasking abilities are an absolute failure at times. This spaghetti dinner was just another example. How did everyone else on Facebook make it look so easy? Sometimes I feel most mothers are graceful trapeze artists, while I am the goofy clown juggling too many balls in the air at my three-ring circus show of motherhood.

I have succeeded not once, not twice, but three times in flooding not only my kitchen but my basement while washing dishes because I got distracted doing something else. Laundry has become my worst enemy. It wins the battle every week. I can wash clothes and fold them, but I just can't get them put away. I am the most unfocused chef ever. This was not my first failed meal. A few spaghetti meals back, I undercooked the noodles to the point that they crunched when we ate them.

And I don't even know how to balance the "wife" with the "mother" anymore. Romance is a distant memory. My only goal in this multitasking circus of motherhood is to survive, because not burning down my house or losing a kid would be an accomplishment.

"It's okay, honey," my husband said as he patted me on the back. "I'll see if we have a frozen pizza or something."

I nodded. I knew we would laugh at this later, but for now it was just another frustrating moment of failure.

"Mommy?" I looked down at my older daughter as I got up to carry the awful spaghetti to the sink.

She wrapped her arms around me and looked up at me with her big brown eyes. I couldn't help but smile. Then she said the words that make every mother's day better: "I love you, Mommy, and I still think you're the greatest mommy ever!"

~Angela Williams Glenn

She Needs Groceries

Preconceived notions are the locks on the door to wisdom.
~Merry Browne

I remember those days clearly. There I'd be, shopping in Target with all of my disposable income, buying something frivolous, like a CD, and then BAM!—my peace would be shattered by a shopping cart full of wailing toddlers. Or one wailing toddler—but we all know that one is enough.

"Ugh," I'd mutter to myself, "that woman should take that child home. He is clearly overtired, and he's disturbing the rest of us."

Or I'd be at the grocery store, selecting Lean Cuisines and light yogurt—the kind of food that twenty-something women like to eat. A haggard-looking mom in sweats would rush by, chasing a kid carrying not one, but three candy bars, and yelling, "I hate you! I hate you!" After watching him nearly knock down old women and displays of soup, I'd frown at the macaroni and cheese and chicken nuggets in her abandoned basket, and then smugly picture the lentils and kale I would prepare for my well-disciplined eventual children, who would never, ever run away from me.

Fast-forward three years. I'm at the store, trying to buy groceries with my one-and-a-half-year-old daughter. I'm trying to figure out the cheapest items I can buy that she won't simply throw off her highchair tray. Too bad I can't focus enough to actually do that, because my newly walking child refuses to ride in the shopping cart. I could try to make her, but I fear for her safety when she stands in the pitiful excuse for a seat belt and tries to writhe her way out of the cart. Instead, she gleefully tries to bolt away, and I consider abandoning the entire grocery trip.

When I am finally done buying food for my family, I try again to strap her into the cart so I can push it to the car, but her outraged response tells me it's too close to naptime to bother. She wants to walk—of course she wants to walk—but I can't let her dart into the rainy parking lot. I tuck her under my arm, where she writhes and screams, and I subdue my rage and try to push my groaning shopping cart with one hand through the downpour. This is when he appears.

He's probably twenty-five. He's smartly dressed. He's alone with his small bag of groceries, and I'm willing to bet a million dollars that he's single.

He smirks, walking past me to his car, and my rage boils up into my head. I can hear his thoughts: "Ha! That's why I'm not having kids till I'm forty. When I do, boy, mine sure aren't going to be little jerks like that lady's. Kids need discipline, you know."

I almost run after him, screeching, "Does it look like I don't need help? Whatever happened to chivalry?" I remind myself that I already look crazy and unhinged... because I am the mother of a screaming, writhing, uncooperative one-and-a-half-year-old. He, on the other hand, is an arrogant jerk.

And this is when I realize how wrong I was. I can't apologize to those parents I judged; I can't go back and offer to hold their bags while they wrangle their children. I can't go back and tell my younger self, "Look, she shouldn't take that child home because he does this every stinkin' time they go to the grocery store. And because SHE NEEDS GROCERIES!"

Fast forward another three years. Now I have a son, too. He's one and a half. He really likes those little carts for kids at Trader Joe's. I don't. I hate them. Every time I set my son on the ground, he grabs the little cart and runs as fast as he can, usually straight toward the Two Buck Chuck wine display.

So I strap him into the cart, and he screams with rage. My

daughter, now four, laughs when he tries to stand up in the cart. Everyone is staring at us, especially when he manages to flip himself over the cart seat so that he is dangling upside down in the basket of the cart, still strapped in with the little buckle. He bellows and screams, and his face turns red. Everyone looks at me like they can't imagine what is wrong with me. My cheeks flaming, and my eyes threatening to tear up, I lift him up and over so that he is back in the seat. And then the same thing happens again, in the same aisle, within two minutes.

A lady snaps at me, "That's not SAFE"—as if I had been encouraging him to stand in the cart. What could I possibly say? "I'm sorry, but I didn't want him to break forty-eight bottles of wine, so I strapped him in upside down like this."

Suddenly, I can understand that man in line, the one with the kid, when I worked as a teenage cashier. He showed up with his merchandise—and a child dangling upside down in the crook of his left arm. It was as if the man was not aware that the child was there at all, despite his screams. I didn't understand it then.

Now I understand. Now I have three children, and I really, really can't take them anywhere. But I have to. Because I need groceries.

~Laura Garwood Meehan

to do list:
- Pay bills
- Get laundry
- call Mom
- Pick up kids
from birthday
at 6 p.m.
- Buy groceries

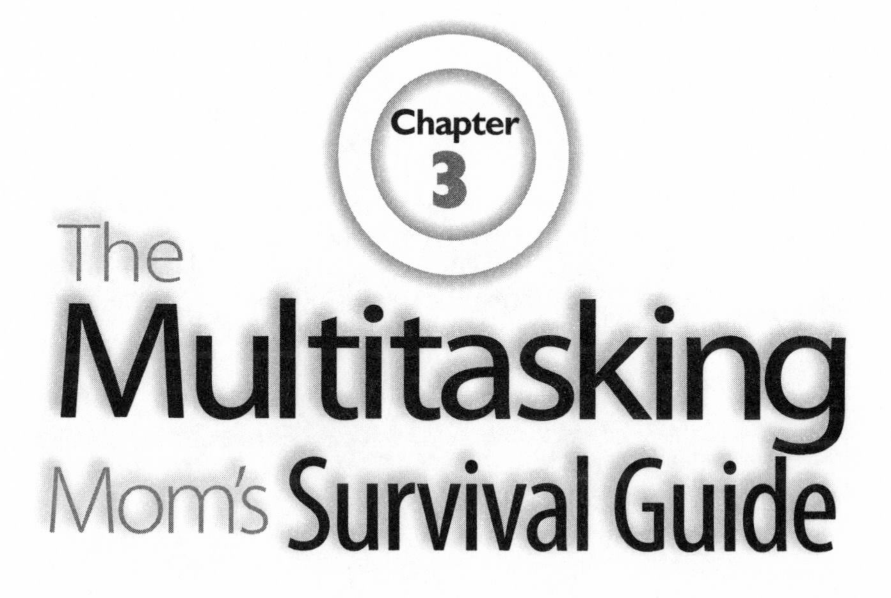

Sharing Good Advice

It is easier to be wise for others than for ourselves.

~François Duc de La Rochefoucauld

The Fantasy of Motherhood

Reality is the leading cause of stress amongst those in touch with it.
~Jane Wagner

I had big mommy dreams before I had kids. I pictured myself chasing ladybugs and butterflies through open fields with my children as they giggled with curiosity and delight. I could practically hear the *Chariots of Fire* soundtrack in the background.

I imagined our little family sitting at the dinner table for long periods of time with my husband and I calmly explaining our hard-earned wisdom to our eager little ones as we ate nutritionally balanced meals. And I envisioned our family doing chores together on Saturday mornings and going on field trips to interesting places.

My husband and I were married for almost eight years before our first son was born, so I had a lot of time for these fantasies to become well rooted and unchallenged.

And then we had kids.

When our first son was born I turned into a complete lunatic because of lack of sleep. I can say with all my heart that I understand why sleep deprivation is used as torture tactic. Feed, burp, change the diaper, cajole to sleep, pray for sleep, beg for sleep, do anything for sleep, wake up after a catnap with spit-up all over you, and then do it all again. Whoever said time flies never had a newborn baby. Every day felt like *Groundhog Day*. I was buried in monotony, and I felt guilty that I wasn't barefoot and happy about it. Did I love my baby? Of course I did. I just wanted his mother to show up so I could take a nap.

We did, in fact, chase ladybugs and butterflies in an open field. Once. But the kids were more interested in arguing and throwing weeds at each other, so I ended up growling at them while I begrudgingly gathered ladybugs in the stupid habitat container. The jar sat on the dining room table for a week, serving as a reminder of how not fun it was. Needless to say, I didn't hear *Chariots of Fire*.

Dinnertime, my prized fantasy, ended up being the most awful time of day when our boys were young. Our kitchen table turned into a perpetual battleground complete with lines drawn and complaints and preferences rifling at me so fast I needed a catcher's mitt. We had antsy, energetic boys who'd rather jump up and down making weird sound effects than sit and listen to any words of wisdom. It was crazy mayhem wrought with tears and loud noises, and eventually I stopped serving myself because I couldn't swallow my food through all the stress. Dinner was over in a flash, and even though I was glad when it ended, I felt resentful that my two hours of cooking organic, homemade meals were dismissed with horrified expressions and pinched noses as if I dished out sewer contents. The only wisdom we shared at the dinner table revolved around the fact that if they didn't eat their vegetables they couldn't have dessert. Period.

Chores were a joke. No one cared about a clean house. I felt more like a drill sergeant than a loving mother. The kids just wanted to play with Legos and leave them out wherever they fancied. Have you ever stepped on a Lego brick right in the arch of your foot? Two words: primal scream.

Can you hear my dreams shattering like glass on the floor? I could seriously write the best selling, most effective parenting book of all time: Do the complete opposite of what I did and you're guaranteed to be a successful parent.

On top of wanting to be perfect so I wouldn't mess up my kids, I had some other major issues to sort through. I had undiagnosed PTSD and suffered from major depression, which only compounded the ordinary struggles and adjustments. I loved our kids so much it hurt, but I was treading water in the deep end of the pool long before they were born.

Motherhood was a shock beyond shocks to my psyche and it took years of butting my head up against my dreams before I realized I needed to let go of the fantasy, so I could make my reality work. Life improved dramatically when I realized I was trying to fit my children into the mommy dream box instead of meeting them where they were. I had to start from ground zero and work my way through all of my unresolved trauma while trying to be a good mom. I walked step by painful little step until life opened up and things started to click. Those early years were tough.

Out of pure survival, I chucked my ridiculous expectations of our children and myself. Forget running in fields and sharing insight; my goal was to keep our children one step above feral, so I could work my way through the depression.

Thanks to the grace of God, I found a great therapist who lovingly witnessed my breakdown while teaching me the tools to process my layered, complicated grief and PTSD. Slowly but surely I was able to manage quasi-sanity and chicken nuggets, and I made a promise to myself I wouldn't quit until I was well. And it worked.

There's a special joy that comes from making peace with domestic chaos. After years of dedicating myself to that adjustment, I can tell you with all sincerity that when I tuck my children into bed at night and I lay my tired mommy self next to them, my world is complete. As they open their hearts and reveal their secret wishes, dreams, and fears, I'm leveled by their compassion, untainted truth, and willingness to forgive. They're far wiser than I ever imagined, and I'm humbled to know that I'm the one learning most of the lessons in this sacred relationship.

Yes, no one ever told me how hard motherhood was. But they also didn't tell me how my life would really begin the moment my children were born.

Chasing an active, tantrum-slinging toddler around the park well past his naptime while hauling a crying baby on your back is no fun. And if anyone says otherwise, it's a lie. Whether a mom has depression, PTSD, or a solid background, any mom worth her weight will admit she wasn't born a good mom; she had to work at developing past her natural abilities. She'll also swear that every moment of frustration and fatigue pales in comparison to the holy bond she has with her children.

Long gone are the days of expecting things to be perfect. Instead of a sparkling, clean house, our visitors are promised nothing beyond flushed toilets; and I'm okay with that. Friends might not be able to eat off the floor, but they'll be greeted with happy hearts and a genuine desire to connect.

And, yes, after almost twelve years of being a mom, I will agree that time flies… but only in retrospect.

~Lori Lara

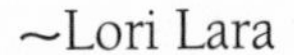

Learning to Communicate

A friend is a person with whom I may be sincere.
Before him I may think aloud.
~Ralph Waldo Emerson

Fred and Shari introduced themselves the day Phil and I moved into a house two doors down from them. While Fred helped my husband unload the moving truck, Shari chatted with me about the neighborhood. Over the next few years, as the men hiked and camped with the local Boy Scout troop, they developed a strong friendship.

During that same period, I gave birth to three little ones. I didn't necessarily plan to have three children under the age of three—perhaps God thought it would keep life interesting. If so, He was right. And with each precious arrival, Shari was first on the scene with a delicious casserole, a thoughtful gift, and a helping hand.

Shari and I swapped recipes and traded the proverbial cups of sugar. My mother had died before I married so I called Shari instead when one of the children came down with an earache or a stomach virus. The mother of five, she always knew what to do.

Our friendship was polite and comfortable. That is, until a situation pushed us to a deeper level of intimacy and bound us together as kindred spirits.

It was a sweltering Saturday in late July. The children were four, five, and six. The previous evening, Phil had tossed his sleeping bag into the back of Fred's pickup. The men took off to the mountains for a weekend of camping with the Scouts. Not long after they left, our air conditioner decided it would take a vacation too.

I had been in and out of the house all morning, trying to catch up on endless loads of laundry. The laundry room was outside the kitchen door, to the rear of the carport. Sweat rolled down my back as I transferred loads from the washer to the dryer or from the dryer to the laundry basket. I usually folded the clothes as I pulled them from the dryer, but the suffocating heat made that impossible. Of course, the living room wasn't much cooler without an air conditioner.

The oppressive heat made the children cranky. They whined, picked fights, and ran to the kitchen door every few minutes to tattle or complain. I waited anxiously for the buzzer to tell me the last load of towels was ready to come out of the dryer. I wanted to fold them, make lunch for the children, and then soak in a cool tub of water.

The buzzer sounded, and I went out to the laundry room. Just as I opened the dryer door, I heard glass shatter. High-pitched little voices began to assign blame.

I flew into a red-faced tirade. "Stop fighting! What have y'all broken? I've had enough of this! If your daddy ever gets home from this stupid camping trip, I'm going to—"

That's when I saw Shari. She walked down our steep driveway with her head thrown back in laughter.

"Stupid camping trip? Oh, Arlene, you've been holding out on me. All this time I thought you were the perfect little wife and mother. Always supportive of Phil. Always patient with your children. I'm so relieved to know that you are just as human as the rest of us."

I was too mortified to speak. I turned my back to Shari, covered my face with both hands, and bawled.

Shari nudged me toward the back door. "Go on inside. I'll be in there in a minute."

When she pulled a hand towel from the dryer to fold, I tried to object. She pointed to the kitchen door with mock sternness. Inside,

I collapsed on the sofa. I didn't even bother to wipe away my tears of frustration and embarrassment.

Shari came in and poured two glasses of sweet tea. She sat next to me and offered me one. "What's the problem, honey?"

I tried to pretend everything was fine, but my neighbor wasn't putting up with any nonsense. So, for the first time in years, I let it all out. "I'm exhausted, I'm overwhelmed, and I'm mad at Phil for being gone so much."

Shari tucked a short, blond curl behind her ear. "Now we're getting somewhere. I know what you're going through. I feel the same way about Fred sometimes. And you know what's really lousy? We can't complain. Complaining about the Scouts is like saying we hate motherhood, apple pie, and the flag!"

My friend laughed at her own joke. "Scouting isn't the problem. That program has done a world of good for my boys. Our husbands are just too involved in a good thing." She placed a hand over mine. "I'm going to be plain with you about three things. First, I'd bet money you haven't told any of this to Phil. He can't read your mind, Arlene. You have to tell him if you need help."

She squeezed my hand. "The second thing. No one around here expects perfection from you except you."

My children—Joseph, Rachel, and Rebecca—were spying on us from the hallway. Shari motioned for them to join us. She pulled the girls into her lap and put an arm around my son's waist.

"Here's the last thing. Motherhood is a hard, thankless, never-ending job. I should know since I have a houseful of kids. But I'm convinced it's the most important job in the world. And you're a good mother, sugar. You just need a day off every now and then."

Shari eased the girls to the floor, stood, and made a grand gesture with her arms. "Well, good news! Today is your day! I'm taking the children home with me. After I feed them lunch, we're going to bake cookies all afternoon, aren't we?"

My children danced around the room in answer to the question.

"Before I bring them home, I'll make a casserole big enough

for your supper tonight and for tomorrow night when Phil comes home."

Tears spilled over as I shook my head. "Shari, I can't let you—"

She put a sassy hand on her hip. "I don't recall asking your permission. Besides, you need to save your strength. The laundry the men bring home will reek of campfire smoke."

My friend tossed her signature goodbye over her shoulder, "Kissy-kissy!" She ushered my children out the front door. I half-laughed and half-cried as they skipped up the road.

Twenty-five years have passed since that hot day in July. Phil and I had many a talk as we slowly, sometimes painfully, learned to communicate our needs. His job eventually took us to another town. Shari passed away. Fred followed her a few years later.

Even though my kindred spirit no longer lives two doors down, I've never forgotten her important advice. Don't expect people to read my mind. Don't expect perfection of myself. Don't expect motherhood or anything else of great value to come easily.

Shari taught me one other thing, but not through any of the words she spoke. Her actions painted me a picture of a true friend.

~Arlene Ledbetter

Silly Mommy to the Rescue

Do, every day, something no one else would be silly enough to do.
~Christopher Morley

Weekday mornings at my house were like one of those action movies in which the hero has only a short amount of time to defuse a bomb. Each day, I had about fifty minutes to get my kids out the door to start our day. But instead of a bomb exploding, it was usually my temper.

"Jack, we have thirty minutes before we have to leave. Can you please get dressed?" I'd ask my eight-year-old son, who was too busy watching the local morning news to acknowledge me. And so the countdown would begin. "Mary, we've got twenty-five minutes," I'd tell my five-year-old. "Can you stop dancing around the table and finish your breakfast so we can get going?" She would sit, only to pop up again about twenty seconds later, usually trailing toast crumbs onto the floor as she did.

And this is where my blood pressure would start creeping upward. I just wanted to get the kids out and on their way to school on time, and usually it was because I needed to get back home for a phone call for work, or to finish a project on deadline, or make it to a meeting.

Beseeching, pleading, begging—it would only go so far as I prodded (okay, nagged) them. Ten minutes to put your clothes on!

Five minutes to brush your teeth! Do you have your homework folders? We have to leave NOW! All it would take would be one small trigger—say, Jack not wanting to wear the shirt we had picked out the night before or Mary crying about a lost baby doll—and I would snap. You know that point in the movie where the hero tries to defuse the bomb by snipping a wire, but he cuts the wrong one and the ticking timer on the bomb starts moving faster? Well, my mistake was choosing to let my frustration get the better of me. And boy, did the tension escalate fast after that.

"Mommy, I don't know where my shoes are," Mary would cry as I tried to find her a new pair. "You can be very mean sometimes," Jack said after I got mad when they were still lagging behind. Invariably, it made for a very grumpy walk to school and a bad start to the day.

Then one morning, Mary was watching *Mickey Mouse Clubhouse* while picking at her food. I was putting their lunches together and could tell by a glance at the kitchen clock we were going to fall behind. "Mary, please eat," I said. And then, probably a little loopy from not enough sleep, I switched over to the voice of Clarabelle Cow. "Or else I'm going to eat your breakfast with Minnie and Daisy."

Jack and Mary looked at me. And started to laugh. "Say something else as Clarabelle," Jack said.

"Okay," I drawled, "go up and get dressed for school. And don't pull a Donald Duck and forget your pants."

And instead of fighting me on it or ignoring me, Jack laughed and went up to his room to get ready. Mary started to eat again and said, "You're silly, Mommy."

It turned out Silly Mommy was better than the average action movie hero—she was a super hero. That morning, for a few moments, I didn't stress about schedules, or what I'd be working on that day, or reminding myself about the coming PTA meeting or errands that needed to get done. I didn't push the kids, or nag them, and we still made it to school on time. And we had fun.

Since then, I regularly call on Silly Mommy. I've added more crazy voices to my repertoire, done a few wacky dances. In the mornings, Jack and I have raced around the house to see who could make it upstairs first, and I've jiggled and spun Mary around while we pretended she was on the Star Tours ride at Disneyland.

And Silly Mommy's useful not just on crazy weekday mornings. I've learned that taking the time to laugh and have fun with my kids actually helps me get my to-do list done—it should be at the top of that list every day.

~Anastacia Grenda

The End of Sibling Squabbling

Siblings are the people we practice on, the people who teach us about fairness and cooperation and kindness and caring—quite often the hard way.
~Pamela Dugdale

It seemed like there were shouting matches every evening. My children were always fighting over their chores and their privileges. They never agreed on who had last washed the dishes, or who had last picked the TV program. I was tired of constantly keeping score and refereeing.

One day, I mulled over what my life was like a decade earlier—before marriage and little ones. In my reverie I stumbled on it—the simple, obvious solution. I recalled my high school days when the terms "O" day and "E" day meant something. My class schedule alternated between "O" days (odd days) and "E" days (even days). On O days I might attend Phys. Ed. And on E days I'd go to another elective class, such as First Aid or Art.

So I explained our new system to my second- and fourth-graders. "Jolee, you were born first," I said. "Is one an odd number or an even one?"

"It's odd, Mom."

"And Al, you arrived second. Is two odd or even?"

"Two's an even number, Mom."

"Okay, so Jolee, from now on, every odd day is automatically your own special day. That means you get to pick what to watch, or where to sit, or which board game to play. Al, the same applies to you on even days."

He thought about it a minute, then said, "But there are more odd days than even ones in some months. Jolee will get 'her day' two times in a row when a month ends in 31, and the next one begins with a one."

"True," I said, "but that also means she'll be taking the smelly, disgusting trash out, scrubbing the dishes, and doing other less-enjoyable things two days in a row, and you won't. It's part of life's give-and-take."

For the first few days after that, whenever one kid shouted, "Mom!" I'd just call out, "Whose day is it?" That settled it. Soon, the bickering ceased.

Ah, the sheer joy of peace and quiet!

~Florence C. Blake

Privilege Coupons

Successful enterprises are usually led by a proven chief executive who is a competent benevolent dictator.
~Richard Pratt

It's frustrating to be a child. Adults are always telling them what to do, and kids crave some control over their lives. As the 19th century writer Josh Billings said, "To bring up a child in the way he should go, travel that way yourself once in a while." In other words, imagine what it feels like to have no say over your life, even for little decisions as to whether you get to stay up an hour past your usual bedtime. After years of skirmishes with my kids over the little things, I realized there had to be a better way for us to coexist with me in charge but with the kids feeling like it was not a total dictatorship. So I decided to make it a benevolent dictatorship.

I had always found that my kids behaved better if I gave them some control over the things that didn't even matter to me, such as how they styled their hair or what clothes they wore. My daughter could wear her brother's pants to school with her pink shirts, and my son could wear a red cape to nursery school for an entire semester if that made him happy. My theory was that if I let them make decisions about the unimportant things they wouldn't feel the need to rebel about the things that mattered, such as doing their best in school or avoiding self-destructive behavior.

One Christmas, when they were preteens, I surprised the kids with homemade coupon books. I took their most requested privileges, made coupons for them, and stapled them into a little booklet that included:

1 coupon for "Shopping spree at the mall"
2 coupons for "A day with Mom doing anything you want"
2 coupons for "Have a party for whatever reason you want"
4 coupons for "Pick a game to play with Mom"
4 coupons for "Double your allowance this week"
4 coupons for "Triple your allowance this week"
4 coupons for "Get candy while shopping with Mom"
5 coupons for "Order pizza whenever you want"
12 coupons for "One can of soda whenever you want"
12 coupons for "Stay up one hour past bedtime"
12 coupons for "Watch one hour of TV on a school night"
12 coupons for "Watch one hour of TV on a camp night"

In the early years, I included coupons like "Have Mom read a book to you" and in the later years I included things like "Get a ride for you and your friends to the movies."

The kids loved their booklets. They presented me with a coupon whenever they wanted to exercise one of their privileges. They had power, we had peace, and we could spend more time enjoying each other instead of negotiating. They learned how to budget their TV time; they chose when it was really important to stay up late; and they learned to view candy and soda as occasional treats over which they had control. After all, they had to make those coupons last an entire year until the next Christmas.

I continued to give them their privilege coupons through their middle school years. I think it was one more contribution to making them the responsible adults they are today. They still talk about those coupons and how much they liked them, and I won't be surprised if my grandchildren end up getting coupons from their parents too!

~Amy Newmark

Busy

If you are too busy to laugh, you are too busy.
~Proverb

All my life, I thought it was good to be busy. Idle hands are the devil's work. I was a busy kid, a busy teen, a busy student. I graduated on a Saturday from college and began my master's on Monday. After that summer of courses ended, I taught school while continuing my studies with night classes. The next summer break, I completed my advanced degree and launched my career. I taught high school, pursued an administrative certificate, joined clubs, and dated my boyfriend. I married, moved, acquired a new job and kept doing what I'd been doing, including taking groups of students to France on spring break. Then, at thirty, I had my first child and quit work. Life as I knew it came to a grinding halt.

I doted on that baby, and the one who came twenty-one months after him, and the one who came two years later, and the last one who came twenty-one months after the third. I stayed busy. All the while, I kept adding duties: sundry volunteer jobs, clubs, subbing, pets.

My father-in-law often advised that folks need to take it slow when raising kids. When I'd tout the educational benefits of some toy, he'd say, "Let the kids bang on pots and pans." When I'd sign up for some exercise class that would take me out of the house, he'd say, "Vacuum more." I'd furrow my forehead at the suggestion, and he'd add, "Grow a garden!"

"Next year, maybe," I'd say, not really planning on doing it.

"I like sweeping myself, and it's great exercise," he'd comment and pick up a broom and sweep out my garage. I thought he didn't want me to spend money on babysitters or classes. He encouraged more domestic work. I dismissed his advice and did as I pleased, which is what most thirty-something mommies would do. And then our folks got sick. My mom passed first. Then my father-in-law became gravely ill.

I remember the last time we saw him, wheelchair-bound, pale and aged. He called each of the boys to him. He gave a marble weight to one son, a brass eagle weight to another, and a signed baseball to the third boy. He hugged my little girl and rubbed her head. He delighted in watching them run around the lawn. In his last hours of his last days, he liked nothing more than to sit on the stoop and gaze at the kids romping around his front lawn. He'd been a busy man with a demanding career. He was a joiner. He had engaged in multiple civic duties and sundry clubs and Sunday school, but in the end, he sat serenely viewing his grandchildren doing nothing, just existing.

As I noted his fading eyes pore over them, I pondered the joy he gathered studying their movements and taking in their energy as they frolicked and rolled around on the grass. Something occurred to me. Maybe it's not good to be busy all the time. Maybe being a good mother doesn't mean you have to sign your kids up for every activity that comes down the pike. Maybe you yourself don't have to participate in every social function. It's good to plant a garden and watch the flowers grow without having to till it constantly.

One of the last things I said to my father-in-law that day, the last time I saw him alive, was this: "I'm going to become calmer. I'm going to become less busy."

He smiled weakly as he tilted his head up at me and said, "That's a good idea, Erika." And then he returned his gaze to the kids tussling under the magnolia tree. He smiled.

~Erika Hoffman

A Priceless Privilege

The deepest principle in human nature is the craving to be appreciated.
~William James

"If I had one million dollars, and I paid someone half that amount to do the grocery shopping, how much would I be paying?" I asked my six-year-old son, Andrew, whom I'm convinced is a math genius.

"Mom!" he said with exasperation. He knows when I make up word problems like this, they are not completely hypothetical. He answered anyway.

"Five hundred thousand dollars."

The truth is that I dread grocery shopping like I'd dread a migraine. If I suddenly became independently wealthy, I'd still clean the house, cook all the food, and care for Andrew and his sister, three-year-old Gracie, because I find joy and fulfillment in those tasks. But grocery shopping? I'd hire a personal shopper in a heartbeat. There are so many things I'd rather do than shop, like weed the yard, scrub the toilets, or clean the oven. I'd willingly have a mammogram, Pap smear, and root canal all on the same day to avoid shopping.

Okay, I'm exaggerating. I hate cleaning the oven, too.

One reason I detest grocery shopping is the time it takes on a Saturday when I would rather be playing with my kids. Another is that it is the most underappreciated task I do for my family. The only time they notice my effort is when I forget something. Or so I thought.

On my latest shopping trip, I pushed my cart through the aisles and tried to push away my bad attitude. Because we had recently moved, I wasn't familiar with the store's layout, which only made the task more frustrating. And I was having a most forgetful day, even with a list. I wheeled from the side that had the toothpaste to the side that had the pork roast, and then remembered I needed shampoo. After getting the shampoo, I realized I needed a meat thermometer. After that I rolled back to the food department. Then I remembered I promised to get Gracie some hair accessories. I rolled back over to the health and hygiene aisle, and picked out ponytail holders, barrettes, and a neon pink and orange brush and comb set. It was a little loud for me, but perfect for Gracie.

At home, after I put all the groceries away, Gracie came into the kitchen.

"What did you get for me, Mommy?"

I showed her the hair accessories, and her face lit up like sunshine.

She opened all the packages immediately, brushed and combed her long ringlets, and begged for me to fix her hair. After I pulled her hair up into a bouncy ponytail, she wanted to wear the new barrettes—all of them, all at once. I dutifully obliged, snapping them into her hair above the ponytail holder.

"You look beautiful!" I said.

"I'll go get ready for the park!" she announced, flashing me a brilliant smile.

Gracie quickly dressed in her turquoise shirt, purple leggings, hot pink tutu, and ladybug shoes. I kissed her on top of her head, on the one spot there wasn't a barrette. Even a Scrooge-like shopper like me had to admit Gracie's excitement over the barrettes felt pretty good.

As Gracie and her purple and pink barrettes zoomed, jumped, and danced all over the park, I reevaluated my view of shopping. Why did I hate it so much? My husband, the safety expert and *Consumer Reports* reader, buys toys and products that require research, which helps me immensely since I'm always pressed for time. But that means he brings home Legos, Barbie dolls, and awesome gizmos like the family camera, flat-screen TV, and a cool new telescope. I bring home scintillating items like bread and toilet paper, which are very important, but not exactly backflip worthy.

Gracie's barrettes reminded me that sometimes my weekly purchases do matter to my family—the occasional box of Froot Loops, Spider-Man and Hello Kitty Band-Aids, Colombian coffee for my husband, Batman pencils for my son's schoolwork. Every week, I bring them these humble offerings and, hopefully, a little brightness. Maybe shopping wasn't such a burdensome chore after all.

Later that night, after the kids were bathed and in bed asleep, I crept into their rooms. I wanted to see their angelic faces one more time before going to bed myself. As I tucked Gracie's pink and plum butterfly blanket under her chin, I noticed she was holding something. I pulled the blanket away. Her plump fingers clutched her new hairbrush to her chest. She held it close so it would be there first thing in the morning when she awoke.

From then on, shopping for my family would be a priceless privilege.

~Janeen Lewis

The Secret Life of a Busy Mom

A man travels the world over in search of what he needs and returns home to find it.
~George Moore

There are days—and if you're a mother you know the kind of days I'm talking about—when I feel like ditching my SUV at the airport and hopping a plane to Bora Bora. No one would know me there or, better yet, need anything from me, so I could spend my days whiling away the hours at the beach, turning my ghostly shade of pale skin to a golden bronze.

Or, on other days, I imagine myself appropriating a red convertible and riding across the country, *Thelma and Louise*-style, yahooing all the way. I would be a red-hot mama, visiting truck stops and seedy hotels, and staying wherever it strikes my fancy. On the road again, with the music cranked up, I wouldn't have a care in the world.

On other days, I imagine quite a different life for myself. On those days, I'm a single career gal, à la Mary Richards in *Mary Tyler Moore*. I'm striding confidently by a pond of ducks, a gaggle of schoolchildren, alone in the streets and tossing my knit hat up into the air.

In my dreams, I am remarkably free of the overwhelming responsibility of the care and upkeep of a home and family. I don't have to worry about the laundry getting done, the kitchen cleaned, the living room made livable, the carpet vacuumed, the toilets scrubbed, the field trip form filled out, the birthday planned, the bedtime story read, the prayers said, the toilet paper roll replaced.

"What's for dinner?" is a question I would never hear unless I asked myself. All I would have to think about is Me! Me! Me!

Yes, there are days I imagine my life without a family and children. While eating lunch at a sleek Art Deco restaurant on Miami Beach, I look at the waitress/aspiring actress and imagine how much fun her life must be. It must be a whirlwind of parties, dates and the possibility of an amazing future.

And then reality strikes, and I remember what my life was like before I married and had kids. My life, pre-children, was rather lonely, even when it included parties, dates and the possibility of an amazing future. There was something missing, and what I wanted, more than anything, was someone to love, who would love me back.

Yes, I have to remind myself that on days when the house never seems to get clean, the kids are constantly fighting and I wonder where I disappeared amid my roles of wife and mother, an impromptu hug around the waist, a sweet kiss goodnight and hearing "I love you, Mom" brings it all back into focus.

It is then that I realize I am exactly where I want to be.

~Gina Lee Guilford

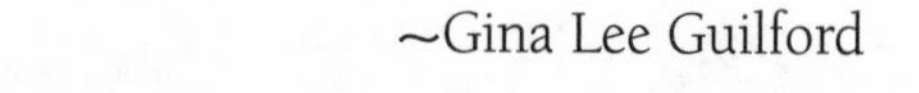

While Time Flew By

Time is what we want most, but... what we use worst.
~William Penn

I remember the stay-at-home days when my two toddlers, just two years apart, filled every minute of my day. A short walk to the mailbox during their afternoon nap was like a trip to the park. Just having a few minutes to take a deep breath and feel the sunshine on my face was heaven. I loved my little boy and girl with all my heart, but I wondered if I would survive motherhood.

Don't get me wrong. Although I was exhausted most of the time, the rewards were great. Not everybody had the privilege to stay at home with their children and see their first steps and hear their first words. I wouldn't have missed it for the world. I really should be writing all this down, I thought. But there simply wasn't time.

Sometimes, I selfishly longed to go back to work. It would have been so much easier on me, and on our budget. But looking back at my own childhood, I never remembered coming home to an empty house. Mom was always there, waiting to welcome us. I wanted that for my kids, too.

I continually asked for God's help. Ironically, Sunday church service was one of my biggest challenges. It had seemed easy for my mom. But I had no idea how much work this commitment was going to involve. It might have been a day of rest for some, but for me it was a day of stress.

It didn't take me long to learn one thing—all the planning had to take place on Saturday night. Clothes had to be ironed, shoes had to be polished, socks had to match, baths all around.

The next morning, getting everybody fed and dressed—in the right order—took more talent than I thought possible. To me, I had the cutest kids in the world, and I wanted them to look their best. That meant my son wore a shirt and tie; my daughter, a frilly dress. Keep in mind, this was the 1970s. We had yet to integrate dressing "casual" into worship services. The first time I wore a "pantsuit" to church, my grandmother nearly fainted. "I never thought I'd see the day," she said. In her way of thinking, I was treading on dangerous ground.

By the time we got to Sunday school, I was so tired and drained that I was sure it showed. Wiping faces and combing hair, I hurried the kids to class and made a quick stop at the restroom to run a comb through my hair and try to smooth the wrinkles out of my dress.

By the time I got settled into the adult class, I was out of breath, and not in any shape for concentrating on God's word. My mind couldn't slow down after running at full speed for so long. Then, out of nowhere, the cute things the kids had said all week replayed in my head. I have to write them down, I thought. But there was never any time.

Before I knew it, both my kids were in school. Now, I thought, I'll have time to write things down. But school activities and homework presented new challenges. When the kids caught the bus in the morning, I had so many things to do at home. And before I turned around, they were back again.

Then, all of a sudden, they were grown up. The years of bottles and diapers were over. The years of learning to crawl, walk, and talk—gone for good. The years of school functions, ballgames, and homework—long past. The years of being best buddies with their mom—a distant memory. Instead, I was watching them start their own lives—leaving home, getting married and having babies. The most precious days of my life were gone in the blink of an eye. I wish I had written it all down.

~Linda C. Defew

Man of the House

You have to leave the city of your comfort and go into the wilderness of your intuition. What you'll discover will be wonderful. What you'll discover is yourself.
~Alan Alda

"You're the man of the house until Dad comes home!" A neighbor is addressing my three-year-old son. I nod politely, pulling the child away. The man's expression becomes more serious as he speaks to me: "If you need anything…" I remind myself that he means to be helpful, but his words sound more like an order than an offer.

The year is 2000. My husband is overseas for several weeks. How many? Five? Two? I hope no one asks where he is. I've forgotten that, too. He's a pilot. Travelling is his job. I was a military officer too, but now I raise our two kids. That's my job. We're happily married, but our lives are very different. We don't spend our time together discussing the details of our workdays. He needs to know that the kids and I are safe. I need to know when he'll be home—just the day, and whether it'll be morning, afternoon, or middle of the night. The exact time isn't important. He's rarely on time, anyway.

My husband's schedule is unpredictable. I ensure that my children's lives are very predictable. They eat meals at the same time every day. Nap time, bath time, and bedtime are strictly observed, as are nightly rituals. We read a story, say a prayer, and I tell them our plan for tomorrow. I kiss them and say "I love you" before turning off the light. Children crave routine. Surprises are unsettling. Calm kids make for a happy mom.

My children adore their father, but they rarely ask when he'll be home. His comings and goings have no impact on their lives. He calls daily when he's travelling. When he's not, he calls from the office. I won't delay dinner for him, even when he says he's on the way. Why? Because one thing I've learned about my husband is that "I'll be home in ten minutes" is often followed thirty minutes later with another "I'll be home in ten minutes." It's not his fault—not always. He's needed at the squadron, and he often gets stopped on his way to the car by someone wanting a solution to a problem that just can't wait. I've delayed dinner for him before. I ended up frustrated. The kids, responding to my tension, acted up. Evening ruined. Now, I cover his plate in plastic wrap and put it in the fridge.

"Take care of Mom for your dad, now." It's 2003. My husband is at war somewhere around Iraq. I've brought the kids to church, and now I'm making polite conversation at coffee hour. I appreciate the concern of others, but I'm growing weary of the men who speak to my six-year-old son as if he's just joined a secret fraternity. I've noticed that those who'd urged him to "take care" of his mother three years ago don't tell his three-year-old sister the same thing now.

I'm not much for small talk, but I need to socialize with adults. So, I force myself out of the house. At home, mundane chores keep me from excessively worrying about my husband. I try to eat right and make time for exercise, but I won't dwell on my shortcomings. Taking care of myself is important to caring for my kids. So, even when I feel like crud, I do it for them.

The war hasn't led me to uproot the kids—even temporarily—and I'm proud of my ability to run a tight ship at home. The kids are old enough to understand the importance of simple rules and consequences. They follow them, generally, because I enforce them. No one respects wishy-washy parenting.

In addition to managing the finances and day-to-day operation of the household, I've kept the TV and computer operating, performed maintenance on a few appliances, and repaired at least one broken toy. I'm feeling pretty good about myself, until the morning I notice that the back door has been tampered with. I notify the police and ask the property manager to put a dead bolt on the door. I don't want to trouble my husband with unnecessary drama, so I don't tell him about it when he calls from somewhere in the Middle East. Several days later, when one of his coworkers asks me how things are going, I mention the incident and the fact that my property manager still hasn't tended to the lock. He says he'll talk to the property manager. Within twenty-four hours, the new lock is installed—thanks to his call. I'm grateful for his help, but my confidence wanes.

I miss my husband. Time for a meltdown. I make sure the kids are safely engaged in an activity before closing myself in a room to cry. I won't come out until I'm completely composed. The kids must continue to believe Mom has her act together. If they feel insecure, I'm in trouble. Some days I deserve an Oscar.

It's 2007, and I'm homeschooling both kids. My husband is away from home about fifty percent of the time, and when he's not travelling, he works long hours at the office. He says he's not in danger, though; life is good. I'm active at church and in our homeschool support group. The kids are at least one grade ahead in their schoolwork and score well on tests.

During one of my husband's deployments a friend offers to babysit my kids for me so that I can "take a break." This isn't the first time I've received such an offer but, as always, I gratefully decline. I don't need a break from my kids. They're what keeps me going.

My son gets another "man of the house" comment, and I wonder about the impact it might have on my daughter, now old enough to understand. Both kids are bright, well mannered and respectful. My husband and I are proud parents. I can tell that my son has a healthy respect for women. I like to believe that's partly because he has a strong mother, and partly because his father doesn't express disrespect toward females. Our daughter is mature for her age and aware enough to notice subtle differences in the way she and her brother are treated. I'm concerned about the deficiency of strong female role models in the media.

It's 2013. The kids are teenagers. They don't need me at home all day, so I've rejoined the workforce. Meanwhile, my husband is nearing the end of his military career and rarely travels. He's involved with both kids' sports teams and other activities. He even makes dinner—usually late, but still appreciated.

Our kids are strong and independent. They'll be ready to make their way in the world when the time comes. My husband and I are making the most of the few years we have left with kids at home. Our marriage is in transition; our roles are changing. We're aging, and we know we'll soon need each other more than ever. The "division of powers" strategy that worked for most of our marriage is evolving. We're mutually supportive—a team. There's no "man of the house" here. There never was.

~Debbie Koharik

The Moveable Vacation

There are no seven wonders of the world in the eyes of a child.
There are seven million.
~Walt Streightiff

One year my children came home from school asking where we were going on our summer vacation. It seemed that all the other kids were discussing where they were spending the summer. I couldn't afford to take them anywhere but I didn't want to tell them that so I just said, "It's a surprise!" They were delighted. That bought me a little more time.

I went over my budget several times to see if I could take them anywhere. I called several amusement parks in the state to see if there was a half-price day during the summer but no such luck. I tried everything, with no success, so I called some of the other moms to see what they were doing. Most were in the same position that I was. We decided to come up with something fun for our kids to do. We had a meeting, all five of us, and came up with what is now called a "playcation."

One mother was a gardener, so on Mondays the kids would all go to her house. They would play games using plants and vegetables, such as a relay race where they had to pass a green bean held between their teeth. They also planted vegetables and watched them grow over the summer. They even had a salad in August after picking their veggies.

The wife of our assistant pastor had Bible contests on Tuesdays.

She got red, blue and green sample rugs from a carpet store. All the kids would stand out on the lawn while she asked a question. Then she would give them three answers. If you thought the first answer was right, you would stand on the red carpet. The blue carpet was for the second answer and the green for the third. Once all the kids were standing on a color, she read the true answer. The ones on the right color rug got a penny, which they all turned in at the end to buy their goodie bags.

At our house on Wednesdays, I made an outdoor obstacle course complete with my spare tires. The kids also walked a balance beam on a two-by-four from my garage and raced through large cardboard boxes taped together that I had gotten from an appliance store. We also had a contest to see who could hula hoop the longest.

On Thursdays they had arts and crafts across the street. Fridays were hosted by a wonderful single dad with a metal detector who took everyone out treasure hunting.

The summer was a big success. Okay, it wasn't Disney World, but the kids didn't miss anything. My son actually said to me, "Mom, I think we had the best vacation ever, not like all the other kids who only got a vacation for a couple of weeks." My daughter added, "We got to spend it with our friends, not just with our parents, and it lasted the whole summer long. I can't wait to tell everybody about my summer vacation." This did my heart good but I was still thinking about putting aside a little each month so that I could take them on a real vacation the next summer. That is, until my son asked, "Can we do this again next year?"

~Diana Perry

Too Bad You Lost Your Jacket

"I must do something" always solves more problems than "Something must be done."
~Author Unknown

When my children were little we went to Disney World every fall. My friends thought I was crazy, but the kids loved it and I think I enjoyed it even more than they did. Except for one thing. Souvenirs. The kids would drive me nuts asking for souvenirs, to the point that in the stores I would try to block my daughter's view of the stuffed animals and my son's view of the superhero items.

Then I discovered Disney Dollars! The next time we went to Disney World, I gave each child fifty Disney Dollars to spend on souvenirs. They started evaluating every possible purchase as if they worked for Consumer Reports, and we returned home with half their Disney Dollars unspent.

That gave me an idea a few years later when I was at my wit's end over my son's remarkable ability to lose his clothes. Our school had a dress code and it could get expensive. I'll never forget when my twelve-year-old son Mike went off to the first day of school in a brand new navy blue blazer and came home wearing a bedraggled old one that barely fit him. The $100 blazer that I had bought just a little too big for him, so that it would last the entire school year, was gone. He said his friend Gideon needed a larger jacket so they swapped.

That was the last straw in a series of clothing disappearances. I decided it was time to change the dynamic in our household. I sat the kids down and laid out their annual clothing budget. Their father and I would give them half their budget in the fall and half in the spring. My daughter opted for a debit card that I refilled every six months; my son opted for a savings account.

It was heavenly. I drove them to the stores, we shopped together, and we each paid for our own purchases. If my son lost something, it was not my problem, and he learned a lesson about caring for his possessions. There were no arguments over clothing, no pleading for more, and no frustration on either side. We actually had fun shopping.

The advice columnist Abigail Van Buren summed it up perfectly when she said, "If you want children to keep their feet on the ground, put some responsibility on their shoulders." I gave my children the responsibility for what they wore on their shoulders, literally! My son became much more careful, although he did lose his blazer one more time, the night before an important ninth-grade event. With my new attitude, I just thought it was funny when he had to wear a pastel plaid jacket from the lost and found.

~Amy Newmark

Multitasking a Marriage Too

It's what you learn after you know it all that counts.
~Attributed to President Harry S Truman

I am a planner. With each stage in my life I thought I had it all planned out. I married my high school sweetheart, and after five years, during which time I earned my college degree, we felt we were ready for the next phase of our lives… parenting. We discussed the perfect time to have a baby and said things like "this baby is joining our lives, we are not joining his." How wrong we were!

We thought we had the perfect plan, my pregnancy was easy and I worked all the way up to my due date. There wasn't a doubt in my mind that I would have no problem delivering our baby and going right back to work, as we were going to stay a two-income family. Plus, I loved my job and I was positive I was the queen of multitasking and could do it all. I thought I had it all under control.

The delivery day arrived and my six-week maternity leave started and all I could think about was who could I possibly trust to love and take care of my baby as much as I did. I was fortunate enough to have my mom and grandmother to fill in on days when my husband was at work. With his job as a firefighter he was home every other day to be Mr. Mom.

My husband works twenty-four-hour shifts, so he would arrive home in the morning and I would hand him our baby at the door and head out for my one-hour commute. During his "Mr. Mom" days he handled everything: the feedings, napping, and household chores. When I would arrive home anywhere between six and seven at night he then would pass the baby to me at the door and head to the gym for some alone time. I understood his need to "get away" and he understood my need to bathe and bond with the baby. When he would return home we were both so exhausted from our day that we would have a quick bite to eat and fall asleep on the couch.

This routine went on for the first year of our son's life. We did not ask for help on the weekends or evenings as we felt my family was chipping in enough during the week. We didn't know of any babysitters. From the outside it all seemed perfect, but in reality we were living very separate lives centered on the baby.

What happened to the baby joining the life we already had? Now our lives consisted of taking care of the baby but we had forgotten that we were also a couple, not just parents. Without either of us realizing it we had become roommates, not companions. I am sure it was a gradual change but before we knew it everything had changed. We were too young to live as roommates and deserved more, but neither of us knew how to fix it… so, he moved out!

I worked so hard trying to prove I was a superwoman I forgot about the man I vowed to love and spend the rest of my life with. Now we were even more stressed, with double household bills and even more passing of the baby back and forth.

Asking for help may have been one of the hardest things we had to do, but we wanted our family intact. We started seeing a marriage counselor. We learned that being multitasking parents didn't mean we could stop being multitasking spouses. Date nights were important, babysitters were a necessity, and putting each other first was a must. With open minds, help from others, and a lot of love we were able to put it all back together for the better.

That was sixteen years ago, and while the road has not always been easy we learned to appreciate each other and value the stolen moments we have alone. We are best friends, lovers… and parents. When people compliment us on the success of our twenty-one-year marriage, I am the first to tell them that creating a wonderful family and life is easy if you always remember to take time to nurture each other.

Our son is now seventeen and has his own social life and will be going off to college in a little over a year. We still are very involved in his activities but once again we are rediscovering each other, spending Friday nights home alone, going on random date nights, and loving every minute of it. When I watch our son hold his own girlfriend's hand I know it is because he witnesses firsthand the love his parents have learned to share.

~D'ette Corona

to do list:
- Pay bills
- Get laundry
- call Mom
- Pick up kids
from birthday
at 6 p.m.
- Buy groceries

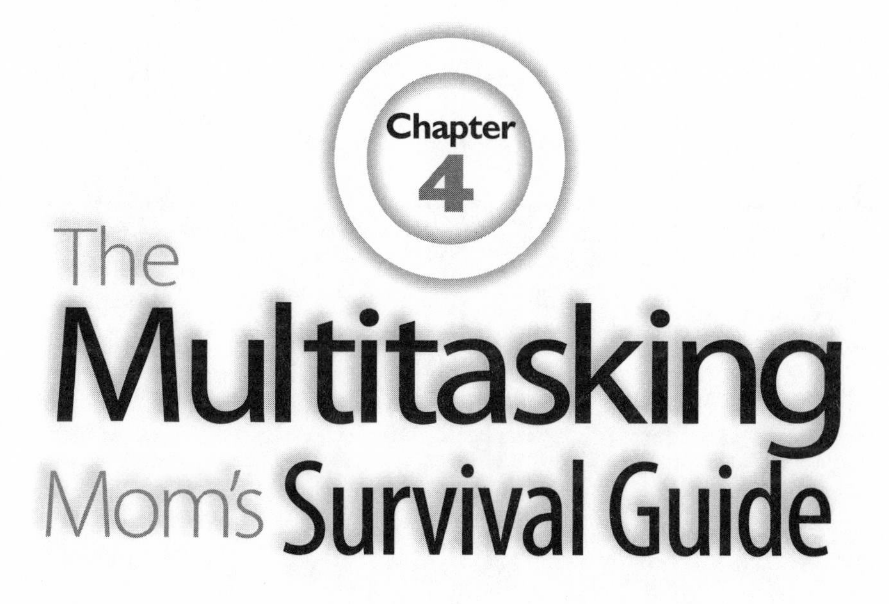

Laughing After the Fact

How embarrassing it is to be human.

~Kurt Vonnegut

The Meltdown

Temper tantrums, however fun they may be to throw,
rarely solve whatever problem is causing them.
~Lemony Snicket

My daughter has never been what you would consider an easygoing child. In fact, she has a bit of a temper. Okay, if the truth be told, she has a temper like a raging forest fire. Some kids just seem to be born with a temperament that is intense, sensitive, emotional, and dramatic. She is definitely one of them.

I knew we were in trouble when she was three weeks old. I put her down for her nap and she still wanted to be held. She looked up at me, frowned, and absolutely screamed, "MAMA!" I know babies aren't supposed to be able to talk at this age, but I know what I heard.

She entered the full-blown "terrible two's" just before her first birthday and never left them. We tried everything at one time or another—time-outs, taking away favorite toys, ignoring her, talking. The only thing that seemed to work (sometimes) was prevention—making sure that she never reached that cranky place where she was too hungry or tired or rushed. With two working parents, of course, this plan was doomed to failure.

We were driving home from daycare one day, both exhausted, and it was dinnertime—a set-up for problems. When I refused to stop for junk food, she went into "meltdown mode"... a full-blown tantrum, complete with hitting, screaming, kicking, and biting. I couldn't possibly drive safely, so I pulled over for a roadside time-out.

She continued to scream and flail around. After ten minutes of this, I turned off the engine and got out, standing beside the car with my back to her, hoping the lack of attention would calm her down. Instead, she upped the ante, screaming louder and banging on the windows. People were starting to slow down and stare.

Suddenly, she opened the car door and dashed away, screaming at the top of her lungs how much she hated me. I stood by helplessly. I was too tired to chase her, and even if I tried, I didn't think I could catch up to her. I struggled to hold back the tears.

Her timing was astonishing. At that exact moment, a policeman drove by, slowed, turned around, and then stopped. He got out of the police car, tipping his hat back as he scanned the situation, and scowled at me.

"Is that your child, ma'am?"

"Yes." I was growing more embarrassed by the moment. By the way she was screaming, he must have thought I was kidnapping her. Or abusing her. To make matters worse, I am a social worker, and part of my job at the time involved child abuse investigations.

"Well, what is going on?"

"Oh, nothing, officer. She's having a tantrum, and I'm trying to get her back into the car."

Halfway across the field, my daughter stopped dead in her tracks, watching us. I don't know what went through her little four-year-old brain. Maybe she even thought that I had called him. Meanwhile, the policeman apparently decided that I was the mother, after all, and that I was not abusing her. His tone softened.

"I'm a father. Is there anything I can do to help?"

"You could try talking with her."

He walked briskly across the field. She just stood and stared at him. I can only imagine what he said, but after what felt like an eternity, they both walked slowly back to the car. I managed to mumble a thank-you, and she climbed into the back seat. We drove home in utter silence.

At home, my husband asked how our day had been. My daughter looked sheepish, obviously horrified at the thought of her father knowing about her brush with law enforcement. She shot a look my way, her eyes pleading.

"Oh, nothing unusual."

I winked at her. I could always tell him later.

~Beth Andrews

Frenzied

Cats can work out mathematically the exact place to sit that will cause most inconvenience.
~Pam Brown

I had four kids in six years. My last child was born on the eldest child's sixth birthday. At the same time, I had a cat that reproduced twice. Because of the kids' relentless whining and begging, we kept the kittens. When they grew up, I had them spayed before they followed in their mama's wanton footsteps. Our family also included an oversized Golden Retriever that never hurt the cats but enjoyed chasing them. He'd bounce around them, unnerving them until they swatted his nose with their outstretched claws. Often, our cats scrambled atop the cars to escape him.

Because my multitasking efforts paled in comparison to my friends, my boys were habitually late to Little League. Frequently, I had to plead with one coach to get him to play my oldest son, who would rather pick dandelions than catch a fly ball. One afternoon, with cleats in hand and two boys semi-dressed in their baseball uniforms, plus a four-year-old fellow clinging to my dress, I scurried out the door.

"Come on. Pile in, kids," I ordered the troops. Then I raced back to fetch my baby girl, tote her to our van, and strap her in her car seat as she sucked on the multicolored plastic keys that had just fallen on the garage floor. "Lace up each other's shoes," I instructed my players.

I commandeered our truck-sized recreational vehicle out of the dark carport into the blazing sun.

"Can we play Nintendo?" my seven-year-old asked.

"No!"

"Can we watch TV?" my six-year-old asked.

"Those devices are for long trips, boys! We're just going to the baseball park ten minutes away. Remember? Got your mitts? Gloves? Caps?"

I heard them fidgeting with the knobs to the entertainment console as I was racing down the hill and over the bumps.

"Wheee!" they yelled in unison as they popped up out of their seats.

All of a sudden, I heard a mad honking behind me. I glanced in the rearview mirror. A neighbor was banging his steering wheel in agitation. He was throwing up his hands and gesticulating wildly out the window. I figured he thought I was a reckless driver so I slowed down. Yet, he was still banging the horn with the heel of his hand.

"What does crazy Mr. Reed want?" I asked aloud.

The kids all swiveled around to look. Now Mr. Reed was trying to pass me on the narrow two-lane street, while he was yelling at me and signaling for me to stop.

I couldn't. My oldest's Little League coach had threatened to replace him if we were late one more time. I kept going. The dang fool behind me accelerated past me. With mouth agape, I looked to the side as if to say: "Have you lost your mind?" His pointer finger made circles as he gestured for me to roll down my window. When he paralleled my van, I finally put down the window. I worried that the guy was slated for a head-on collision.

"Stop your car!" he yelled.

"What?" I mouthed.

"STOP your car!" he screamed and pointed upward.

And then I saw them. Two sets of clinging paws protruded over the roof onto my windshield. I pulled over. Mr. Reed halted in front of me. I stopped short. I was lucky nothing tumbled off. I jumped out, hustled to the back of the van and climbed the ladder to the roof. My uniformed sons trailed behind me.

Sunshine, our cat, and her grown offspring stood wide-eyed with tails in the air. The three looked shaken as if they knew they'd lost a few of their nine lives. I grabbed the cats and handed them down to my two older boys, who carried the mewing cats inside the van.

"Thank you, Mr. Reed," I said breathlessly.

"That was quite the rollercoaster ride your cats got," he said. "What's your hurry?"

I glanced back at the van with smiling kids and curious cats peering out the windows. All were happy and safe.

"Nothing. Nothing that's really important." I turned the van around and headed home with my cargo. Baseball could wait.

~Erika Hoffman

The Holiday Card

Mistakes are the usual bridge between inexperience and wisdom.
~Phyllis Theroux

It was two weeks before the holidays, and I still hadn't sent out my holiday cards. Each year, my family gets dozens of holiday cards from friends and family, and I wanted to send one out as well that year. We get all types of cards, like pictures of an entire family, pictures of the children, vacation pictures or even professionally produced pictures. Sometimes we receive cards with no pictures at all, just wishing us happy holidays in bright, bold letters.

After giving it some thought, I decided to go with the family picture taken by a professional photographer. After dropping off my two boys at grammar school, I called the local photographer and made the appointment. The photographer told me since there wasn't much time before the holidays, he would come first thing Sunday morning and told me to have the whole family in white shirts. It sounded perfect.

Now, not only now did I have my usual five million things to do—carpooling, volunteering, buying last-minute presents, grocery shopping, cooking and making sure my family was happy—but I also had to find matching whites tops for my entire family. After visiting a bunch of stores, I decided on white polo shirts for all of us. I couldn't have asked for a smoother morning. I was able to continue doing all my other errands with a smile, knowing that my family was going to look great for the holiday photograph session.

I'm not sure where the rest of the hours went, but when I went to tuck in my younger son on Saturday night, I noticed his hair was a complete mess. OMG! He needed a haircut. With all my running around, I hadn't noticed how badly he needed one. I didn't know what to do. It was 8:00 at night, and every salon or barber was closed. The photographer was coming the next morning. I then became resourceful... or so I thought!

I got out the scissors I used to cut fabric and told my son to come into the bathroom where I set up a little salon. My younger son is very easygoing and cooperative. I wet his hair, combed it and started snipping away. When I was done, we looked at each other and both knew that the haircut was a disaster! I started to panic. What had I been thinking? I had never cut hair in my life. Why did I think it would be so simple? Now my adorable little boy was paying the price.

Now, I had no other choice but to tell my husband. When he saw my son, he went completely bonkers. He said, "The pictures are tomorrow morning, and our son has the worst haircut I have ever seen on a little boy!" I was now sweating, and words would not come out of my mouth. I had no excuse. All I could do was apologize. My husband told me to go downstairs and have a cup of tea while he took care of the situation.

I am a woman of many talents, but obviously cutting hair is not one of them. As I sipped my tea, punishing thoughts ran through my head. I was always trying to juggle everything, fix everything, and have all the answers. Sometimes, I needed to take a step back. If something didn't get done or fixed, it was not going to be the end of the world. If I had taken a breath, I would have seen earlier that my little one needed a haircut. As tears filled my eyes, my son came downstairs with his older brother.

I couldn't believe my eyes... I saw the two cutest boys with buzz cuts! And minutes later, my husband joined in with a buzz, too!

My beautiful family holiday cards went out on time—just with a little less hair!

~Jacqueline Davidson Kopito

Six Hours Until Takeoff

Rivers know this: there is no hurry. We shall get there someday.
~A.A. Milne

With six hours until takeoff for a long international family trip, I had fifty things left to do. On the Sunday morning of departure, I took a deep breath, glared fiercely at my long list of last-minute to-dos, and dressed for church. I drank in the aroma of extra-strong coffee brewing on the clean countertops, energized by the race before me that would lead to a long, quiet flight.

Church stood in the way. One of us had a meeting; one had to teach Sunday school; one had to play an instrument; and one had to be the timekeeper for our carefully choreographed dance. "We can do this," I cheered to the family on the night before. "It will all be worth it!"

My adrenaline surged at the challenge before us. With my husband gone early, I roused our sleeping son and dashed for the car keys to drop off our teenage daughter. With one last swallow of coffee, even the minefield of suitcases and carry-ons could not hold me back as I leapt around the floor like a chorus girl. I smiled in defiant memory of the relatives who said our plans were unreasonable, far-fetched, and too stressful. Only a masterful multitasking mom of travel like me could manage such a journey. I relished the chance to train my children in the ways of a job-juggling mom on a mission.

Imagining how a racecar driver feels, I buckled my seat belt for the short ride to church. We had given the garage door opener to the house sitter the night before, so after we pulled out of the garage and up our steep driveway a little way, I asked my daughter to jump out and manually press the button. I put the car into park and paused, idling impatiently, as if I was at a starting line. When my daughter jumped back into the passenger's seat, I shifted gears and pressed the gas to accelerate.

Scraping, cracking, screeching sounds assaulted our ears. The car had slipped back down the hill when I took my foot off the brake, right into the garage door. The double garage door was hanging from the rails in a twisted mangle of wood and steel. A cable snapped like the final clash of a cymbal at the end of a symphony.

"Oh. My. Gosh! Oh. My. Gosh!" I announced, gripping the steering wheel in unplanned panic, trying to remind myself to breathe.

"Mom? Mom? It's okay, Mom. It's okay," my traveler-in-training daughter cautiously offered.

"No! No! It's not okay. THIS. IS. NOT. OKAY. Find Dad. Call Dad!" I screeched back to her.

The full scope of the calamity washed over me. Six hours until takeoff, and my well-planned list didn't matter.

As our daughter ran inside to make the call to extricate my husband from a meeting full of quiet church people, my slumbering teenage boy appeared, forced awake by my raucous deed. Taking in the scene through his sleepy eyes, no explanation was needed.

"Oh, Mom. I'm so sorry. It's going to be okay, Mom," he ventured.

"No! Some things are okay. THIS is not okay," I retorted.

Within minutes, my husband arrived to see the dangling door for himself. I knew he was counting the six hours until takeoff, though he said little and waited for the play-by-play description of how I managed to assault the house.

With tears wiped away and suitcases loaded, a friend took our insurance information, our key, and our thanks. In exchange, he gave us a giant blue tarp to cover the gaping hole left by my well-meaning rush. Like my teenage travelers in training, he assured me it would all be okay. And so we left it all behind: the unfinished to-do list, the good intentions, the tears, the mangled mess of a door.

Somewhere over the ocean, the long to-do list loosened its grip on me. My shoulders relaxed, I closed my eyes, and I stopped reminding myself to breathe. By the time we were told to raise our tray tables and buckle our seat belts, I began to chuckle about what the neighbors would say and I crossed worry off my list. I opened my heart for this once-in-a-lifetime chance to make memories with the people who assured me it would all be okay when I was sure it would not.

Instead of training our two young travelers in the ways of a juggling mom on a mission, my young vacationers showed me that victory comes in letting go of lesser things and moving forward with the best things. And when pulling out of the garage, moving forward is always the best thing.

Three weeks later, we returned with full hearts and a load of memories to replace those of my garage door destruction. I threw away the long-forgotten list of things that didn't matter, and we were grateful to find a new door covering the hole we had left behind and to discover that it was, indeed, all okay.

~Julie Sanders

Can't See the Forest for the Keys

The existence of forgetting has never been proved: We only know that some things don't come to mind when we want them.
~Friedrich Nietzsche

The Lost Keys Curse came upon me at the same time as motherhood. When it struck, I was basking in the glow of my eighth month of pregnancy, sorting through names for my soon-to-be-born son. It was one of those mornings when the weight of the watermelon-sized bump in my middle had me feeling a bit sluggish. I'd gotten up late for work and was rushing around—as much as you can with an eight-pound baby boy practicing karate in your womb. I was ready to leave, purse in hand, when the urge pounced upon me—as it had about ten times in the past hour—to pee. I dropped my keys on the table in the hallway, made a quick bathroom stop, headed out with my purse and pulled the door closed behind me on my way out. No sooner had the door clicked than I realized what I had done. Peering through the sidelight, I could see them in plain sight. My keys were sitting on the table.

I did not panic because I, the brilliant and organized woman who had thought through all possible pregnancy-brain scenarios, had a spare key. I probably got the idea from one of those Paranoid New Mom books and I had hidden a key around back. I trudged through the shrubs in my one-size-larger-than-I-usually-wear-but-my-feet-are-so-swollen shoes and felt the underside of the deck. It took a pregnant woman's version of downward-facing dog to grab it, but I eventually nabbed it and went back in the house. My bladder situation being what it was, I figured I'd better make one more trip before heading off for my twenty-minute commute. So I used the bathroom, headed to the garage, locked the door behind me and… left the spare key on the table next to my other keys!

When I admitted to the dispatcher that I was almost in my ninth month, she sent a very amused locksmith to the house right away. He didn't know it yet, but he and I were going to become very good friends.

Certain that pregnancy had permanently altered my short-term memory, I gave spare keys to everyone I thought might be able to rescue me if I managed to double lock myself out again. Even so, I learned how to appropriately tip the AAA guy who jimmied the car door open for me from time to time.

Fortunately, the Lost Keys Curse lost its mojo over time. The space between incidents gradually lengthened until it seemed that the curse might be broken. Each day, I was beginning to feel more like that brilliant and organized young woman who hid a key under the deck so many years ago.

Though the foggy New Mom Brain was a thing of the past, I began to face a new challenge in Motherhood Stage Two: The Attack of the Killer Schedule. One kid at soccer, another needing a ride to a friend's house, volleyball at 6:00, the roast in the Crock-Pot, my dad's doctor's appointment, rounding up volunteers for the class owl pellet dissection, and squeezing in a haircut. Over time, I've learned to handle it with the skill of a circus fire-torch juggler—unless I'm distracted.

And kids' illnesses can be pretty distracting. One fateful day, I had one child waiting to be picked up from kindergarten, one at home recovering from the flu, and I was on the way home from the pediatrician with child number three and a second flu diagnosis. Would I make it to kindergarten pickup on time? Is it okay to leave a still-sick middle-schooler at home alone watching TV? How were we going to make up all the missed homework? I stopped at the corner store to pick up some chicken soup for my newly diagnosed daughter. As I headed back to the car, I felt in my purse for the keys but they were not there. How could this be? I used the keys to get to the store, didn't I? I searched my purse, the car, every aisle and checkout lane in the store. My feverish little one was in the back seat slumped against the window. I couldn't call my dad for a rescue—I certainly didn't want him getting the flu. Could I wait an hour for the AAA guy? Would we have to walk home?

It was all just too much in that moment, and I started to cry. My poor, sick daughter tried to comfort me. "Just relax, Mom, and take a deep breath," she said. "If you slow down and say a prayer, maybe you will find them."

Good advice for lost keys—and much, much more.

After a few moments of meditation, I decided that they had to be in the car. I had undoubtedly dropped them in my purse on the way into the store. Another thorough search turned up nothing. So I shook my purse and heard the faintest jingle. As I scrounged around in there, I noticed that my sunglasses case had taken on an odd shape. I opened it, and there they were. Smiling at me, it seemed. I suppose I had the case open in my purse, and when I dropped the keys in, that's where they landed. When I had slung my purse over my shoulder, the motion must have closed the case back up.

Suddenly, I wasn't so worried about the flu. My daughter would get better in a few days. Missing after-school activities were not a big deal. And homework would wait until everyone was feeling better. The Lost Keys Curse was not some mystical curse of motherhood. It was my own doing, and I vowed to undo it. Clearing my schedule—and my mental to-do list—would give me the space to pay more attention to life's little things. And to where I put my keys.

~BJ Marshall

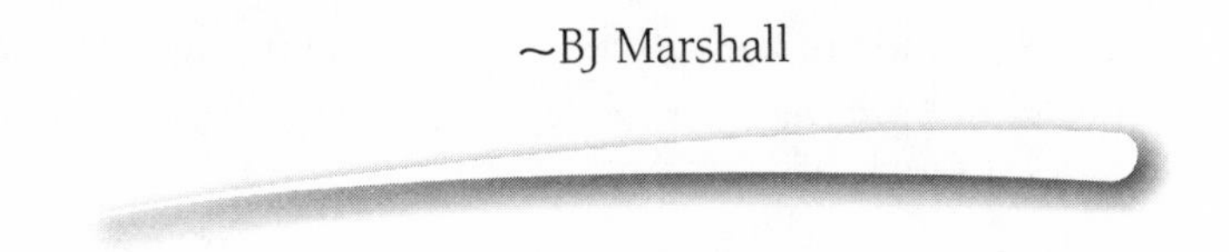

Where's Roger?

No day is so bad it can't be fixed with a nap.
~Carrie Snow

When Roger was in kindergarten, I was a single mom, and we lived in an apartment complex that had a playground. One afternoon after I had picked him up from school, I told him he could go to the park after we got our errands done. We got home that day, and he wanted to go to the park immediately. I told him I needed to change the baby and get a few other things done first. I juggled the baby carrier and groceries along with Roger up the stairs. Just as we entered our third-floor apartment, the phone rang. I thought Roger went into his room, and I went about everything I had to do.

As I answered the phone, I put the groceries away, changed the baby, checked the mail, separated the laundry, and started dinner. I noticed that Roger was really quiet; he was not under my feet as he usually was. I called him, but there was no answer. That wasn't really surprising, though, because he doesn't always answer when called. I looked in his room. No Roger. Well, the apartment was not that big; he had to be somewhere, and I had seen him come in. I looked in my room. Nope. I called out, "Roger, I'm not playing! Where are you?" No answer. I was starting to panic. I looked in the bathroom. No sign of Roger. After searching the apartment twice, I was in a full-blown panic. Where could he be?

My friend on the phone said maybe he took himself to the park.

I ran down the stairs and across the complex to the park, carrying my six-month-old and calling Roger's name. I knew I must have looked crazy. I kept calling his name outside, but there was still no answer. A few neighbors came out to help me look. My friend had hung up and started driving over. I ran back up the stairs to look again in every closet and cabinet, and under every bed. The neighbors helped by searching the buildings, but we could not find him anywhere. Where could he be? Kids don't just disappear.

As I was picking up the phone to call the police, I noticed a little movement behind the couch. My first thought was, "Great, not only can I not find my child, but now I have a mouse." I know that was not the sanest thought, but my mind was running a mile a minute.

I dialed the phone.

Operator: "911, what is your emergency?"

Me: "I can't find my five-year-old son. He was just here, and now he's not." I started telling the operator everywhere I had looked.

Operator: "Ma'am, I need you to calm down. When did you last see him?"

Me: "About fifteen minutes ago."

I walked over to the couch to check out the movement I saw for a second time.

Operator: "Okay, now…" This is where I cut her off!

Me: "Never mind. I am so sorry, I just found him! He crawled behind my couch and is taking a nap!"

Yep, Mommy of the Year here.

Operator: "No problem. Glad you found him."

He had squeezed himself behind the couch and fallen asleep. He was completely clueless to everything going on around him. For him, it was a little nap. For me, it was the longest fifteen minutes of my life.

~Pamela Hermanson Camel

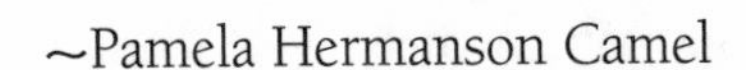

A Bit Too Much Multitasking

A love letter is to be savored; a love e-mail…
is to be forwarded to all your friends, and probably laughed at.
~Erin McKean

I homeschooled my daughter through elementary school. I loved watching her learn and spending time with her. We spent hours every day working on math, science, history, geography, and more.

I was also a full-time writer. I wrote for magazines and anthologies and children's books. I would wake early every morning and write until it was time to teach my daughter. During her lunch, breaks, and when she was doing paperwork or using a computer program for math, I wrote. When we went to story time at the library, her gymnastics class, or doctor appointments, I wrote.

My husband and I were the directors for an all-volunteer ministry to refugees and immigrants through our church. The biggest part of the ministry was an English as a Second Language (ESL) school. Every week, we met with more than twenty volunteers, prepared for 100 students, registered and talked with students, taught or helped in daycare, and more. When there was a lull and I wasn't needed, I sometimes taught our daughter something she needed more help with. Or I worked on an article or story that had a deadline.

In-between the schooling, writing and volunteering, my life as a wife and homemaker still went on. Somehow, I still found time to cook, shop, clean, take care of the dogs, run errands and spend time with family and friends.

"You must be Super Woman," my friends would say.

"Or just plain crazy," I'd respond.

There were definitely times when I was too tired to help out at the ESL school. Or times when I had promised a student I'd come to lunch and forgot. But most of the time, it seemed I was able to juggle things fairly well.

When I heard about an online school that offered writing courses taught by everyday writers, I applied to teach and was accepted. We could use the extra money, and I enjoyed sharing what I'd learned with new and aspiring writers.

One day after a very busy ESL ministry where classes were overflowing and several of our volunteers could not come for various reasons, I woke up tired and thinking of the long day.

My daughter was particularly difficult that day due to upcoming tests and disappointment that the museum we were going to visit was closed after a storm knocked out the electricity. I felt as if I were slogging through the morning and early afternoon, trying to keep us both on task and finally accepting that lessons were going to be shorter and an alternative "field trip" to the neighborhood park was in order.

We came home, both tired and a little cranky. I grabbed at the phone when it rang.

"Hey, hon, did you remember about the plans to run by and spend a little time with the new Bosnian students?" my husband asked. "They've been dying to have us visit. We won't stay long."

I gritted my teeth and grumbled that I'd forgotten. He asked if I could make or get some dessert. I grumbled a lot more, but agreed.

Then I remembered it was the night I always worked on my writing students' e-mails, answering questions and reading assignments. I would be up late that night again.

We had a very nice visit with the family from Bosnia, and I could tell that we were going to be friends. They were thrilled with the dessert I threw together and presented us with a beautiful framed picture from their country.

I was still exhausted, but feeling a little more rejuvenated when we went home. I knew I had been cranky with my husband, and he hadn't said a word about it. I also knew that I'd been so busy with my multitasking life that we'd spent very little alone time together.

That night after I took care of everything for my writing class, I sent out a note for my husband to see in his inbox the next day at school.

"It's time for a romantic evening. Tomorrow there will be candles on the table and a few in our room. You'll dine on your favorite foods, and then we can move our dessert to a more private place. Let me know what you think!"

The next day, I waited to hear back from my husband but never did. Finally, I saw an e-mail from one of my writing students. The subject line was the same one I'd sent to my husband. Her response: "When is this due?"

In horror, I realized I had e-mailed my class instead of my husband.

Immediately, I wrote and apologized for my late-night e-mail.

When the responses came in, I could only laugh.

"We thought it was an extra assignment to write on this topic."

"You shouldn't have told us about the mistake; we never would've known."

I have learned many things about juggling my life. Sometimes I succeed, and sometimes I mess up. But one thing I have learned: Never send a romantic e-mail when you are too tired to check the address before hitting Send!

~Kathryn Lay

The Great Toilet Paper Chase

So many tangles in life are ultimately hopeless that we have no appropriate sword other than laughter.
~Gordon W. Allport

In the morning, I realized we were out of toilet paper. (I won't go into why we were out of toilet paper, but it may have to do with my offspring's habit of dropping whole rolls into the toilet bowl.)

So my two-year-old and I decided to take a walk to the store to buy some more TP.

"Let's use your stroller," I said to Hope, grabbing our smallest stroller.

That was Mistake #1.

After our hike to the store, I folded our little umbrella stroller and loaded Hope into a shopping cart.

After some deliberation, we got our toilet paper. I decided to go with the individually wrapped, lint-free toilet tissue.

That was Mistake #2.

We walked out of the store, and as I was reassembling the stroller, it dawned on me that I had a bulky thirty-roll pack of Scott 1000 tissue to lug home along with two boxes of candy!

My first silly thought was: Oh, no! Now people are going to know that we buy toilet paper in bulk!

"Um… Hope baby. How about we push the toilet paper in the stroller (if I can get it to fit)? Wanna push?"

"Okay!"

I knew it was going to be a looooong walk home—down busy streets, over the railroad tracks, across a crosswalk. As we trudged home, Hope, who was really too short to reach the stroller handles, would happily "dump" our thirty-pack of TP at the most inconvenient times. At one point she got tired of walking and declared that it was time for her to "sit down." I knew that she was going to get tired, but I was hoping we would be closer to home at that point.

So I put her in the stroller and tried to hold the TP pack (and the candy) with one hand against my hip while steering the stroller with the other hand. This was not an easy task on a narrow sidewalk.

As we lumbered along, I realized that the flimsy plastic packaging of my thirty rolls of TP was ripping. A moment later, toilet paper started rolling out into the busy street in several directions.

I started chasing rolls while cars were dodging them. Still in her stroller, Hope thought the whole thing was hilarious. She squealed and giggled every time I picked up a roll and it fell out of my arms.

"Mommy, so funnnnyyy!!!"

I managed to collect a few, but I couldn't carry all the toilet paper and push the stroller. So I finally piled as many rolls as I could on the sidewalk and left them there. When Hope and I made it home, we jumped in the van and drove back to where I had left my toilet paper monument.

Later, when I got home, I noticed the slogan for the toilet tissue:

"Common sense on a roll."

Yes it was.

~Jeneil Palmer Russell

A Reality Check

Reality leaves a lot to the imagination.
~John Lennon

A combined stay-at-home/work-from-home mom to two boys, my days often seem like a three-ring circus. This particular day was no different. With my younger son picked up from preschool and down for a nap, I sank into my chair in front of my computer, determined to complete a project before my fourth-grader arrived home from school. Unlike some afternoons, I actually found myself being very productive. As I pressed the "Save" button and congratulated myself on a job well done, I glanced at the clock: 3:00.

I quickly sprang from my chair and walked to the front door. Where was Skylar? His bus drops him off a few hundred feet from our house at 2:40 every day. I thought he must have been in the yard; maybe he was petting the neighbor's dog that regularly stops by our house to play with the boys. I opened the door and walked down our front steps, scanning the property. No sign of him. I walked down the length of our driveway, past the tree line, to see if perhaps he was merely daydreaming and taking his sweet time coming home, but still no sign of him.

Then I wondered if he went to his friend's house down the road without telling me. Annoyed by the possibility of my older son going somewhere without asking permission first, I called the friend's mother. When she didn't answer and I got her voicemail, I realized that they weren't home so Skylar wasn't there, either. After calling another neighbor who had not seen him, my annoyance began to turn to guilt. Why had I gotten so involved in my work that I neglected to keep track of time and watch my son get off the bus like I normally did every day? If I had only paid attention, I would know what had happened to him.

My guilt suddenly turned to alarm when I thought about his medical condition. A Type 1 diabetic since the age of six, Skylar's life depends on multiple daily doses of insulin and constant monitoring of his blood sugar levels. If his levels are too high, he experiences excessive thirst and becomes nauseous. If his levels are too low, he becomes shaky, cannot concentrate, and must immediately consume a sugary substance such as soda, juice or glucose tablets to prevent his blood sugar from dropping so low as to cause a blackout or seizure. Although he carries his testing supplies with him, his juice is kept at school and on the bus, not in his backpack.

Remembering the phone in my hand, I called the school.

"Hi, I'm calling to learn if Skylar got on the bus this afternoon."

"Let me check for you; please hold a minute," the man said. As I waited, I paced the perimeter of our property and checked the time again: 3:15. Where was he?

"Yes, ma'am," the man responded. "The teacher said he got in line for the bus today."

Trying to swallow the lump of panic rising within me, I explained the situation to him.

"I'll call the school bus driver," he offered. "But it may take five or ten minutes to hear back from him because they're not allowed to talk on the phone while they drive, you know." The safety rule, which I normally applauded, only frustrated me at that point.

"Okay, but please call me as soon as you hear from him," I begged before hanging up. Where was my son? Could the unthinkable really have happened?

I was still pacing in my yard when the phone finally rang. "Yes?" I almost shouted into the receiver.

"Umm, ma'am..." the man hesitated, seemingly unsure of how

to share his news. No, no, no, this can't be happening, I thought. I could barely breathe; my worst fears were about to be confirmed.

Clearing his throat, he continued cautiously: "It appears we were wrong. You signed a permission slip for Skylar to stay after school today to practice for the Battle of the Books competition. He's in the library."

Silence on both ends of the line.

"Oh… yes, the Battle of the Books," I mumbled, red-faced, as my memory immediately recalled the after-school activity. Thank you, God!

Almost in tears from the overwhelming combination of relief and extreme embarrassment, I hung up the phone and made my way inside to wake up his younger brother. Then and there, I determined to do a better job of updating my daily planner and carving out more time with each of my precious boys.

~Dalene Bickel

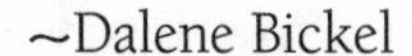

Right Under My Nose

Shared joy is a double joy; shared sorrow is half a sorrow.
~Swedish Proverb

I am the proud and resilient mommy of a little girl who experiences special needs. She is my one and only child, so my introduction to mommyhood was and has been quite different than I had planned for or ever expected it would be.

My days are full of making doctor's appointments, researching treatments, following up on test results, updating family and friends via our Caring Bridge page, coordinating procedures, filling out insurance paperwork, appealing insurance denials, applying for resources, setting up and attending therapy appointments and all the other day-to-day tasks.

They are also full of convincing my daughter to eat (something she hates to do), prying her fingers off the doorframe so we can bathe her (also something she hates), working on her speech, occupational therapy, social and anxiety goals. We have also been teaching her sign language, appropriate manners, how to request things she wants, and how to say "yes, I'd like that" or "no thank you."

Precious minutes are consumed explaining to cashiers in stores why our daughter does not respond when they greet her and why she does not make eye contact when spoken to. We also work to smooth over the hurt feelings of relatives and close friends who feel slighted when our daughter does not return their affection, get excited about their gifts, or desire their hugs.

And yet, the general business of maintaining a life and home are still on the list to be addressed: laundry, dishes, preparing meals, vacuuming, paying bills, and filling the car with gas, grocery shopping, lawn maintenance, trash removal and so many other necessary responsibilities.

The priority list must also include quality time to build, maintain, and nurture my marriage, friendships, a spiritual life, personal health needs, investing in the community and any private goals I might desire to achieve.

My to-do list is endless.

At six months of age, my baby girl stopped sleeping. She would be up every two hours the entire night and it didn't take long for my husband and me to become completely exhausted. We functioned as well as we could, but throw into the mix all of the administrative duties of raising a child who experiences special needs and, let's face it… we were beyond tired.

My husband and I learned quickly that we needed to make some ground rules and agree to be extra forgiving toward one another when we were trying to function in the early morning hours on next to no sleep. We made a pact that any impatience or grouchiness toward one another that occurred between midnight and 7 a.m. was never to be held against the "offending party." Forgiveness and understanding poured forth in our marriage like never before.

On one particular night, when our daughter woke in the wee hours, I went to her room and began rocking her back to sleep. When I did, I noticed that she was missing one of her socks. My husband had stopped in to check on us and I sweetly asked him to look for the sock.

Fumbling in the darkness, my husband looked and returned a few minutes later telling me that he could not find her sock. Note: This is the same husband who will stare directly at an object and insist he cannot see it. During the daylight hours, this was a joke between the two of us and would elicit lighthearted teasing such as "If it were a snake, it would have bitten you." However, on this particular night, his inability to find her sock quite annoyed me and I was in no mood for jokes.

I sarcastically informed him that socks don't just get up and walk away.

So this time, using a flashlight, he picked up her mattress, looked under her blankets and behind her bed.

With every exchange, our voices were getting less sweet and more tense. We were starting to hiss at each other. I was quite irritated and I requested, through gritted teeth, that he look again.

This time, he looked under her bed, by the changing table, and on the floor.

No sock.

My daughter, who preferred to be rocked facing out, was enjoying our nighttime communication dance immensely. (At least someone was having a good time.)

When I had finally had it, I told my husband to come and rock our daughter so that I—finder of lost socks extraordinaire—could locate the sock!

My husband, still using the flashlight in a futile attempt to not disturb the baby, approached the rocking chair. When he was about two feet away, he abruptly stopped. A mischievous grin appeared on his face and an incredibly evil laugh bubbled forth from within him.

By now, I was completely perturbed with my husband and I asked him what was so funny. He was laughing so hard he couldn't even respond, and, instead, pointed to my daughter's left side. I looked down and noticed my precious daughter was waving to her daddy. To my dismay, there, on her left arm, was the missing sock! Somehow, in the night, she had taken off her sock and put it on her arm like a sock puppet! The sock had been under my nose the entire time!

Needless to say, apologies were exchanged, a tiny dose of "crow" was consumed, and we have had many laughs over this very humbling story. My innocent daughter unknowingly played a very funny and timely joke on her tired and overwhelmed mama. Score one for her!

~Amy L. Stout

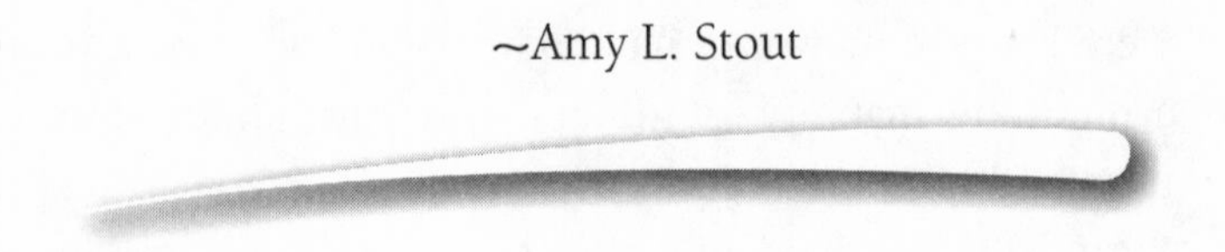

The Longest Day Ever

It would seem that something which means poverty, disorder and violence every single day should be avoided entirely, but the desire to beget children is a natural urge.
~Phyllis Diller

Running a household with a pack full of kids can result in some bad days, even on my day off from work. My day started with a very expensive trip to the grocery store, a broken jar of jelly, three neighbors who dropped in for tea, a missed doctor's appointment and an Avon lady who talked about my sagging chin and crow's feet.

Add on to that the four kids and their eight friends who tracked mud all over the house, the fifteen phone calls (all for the kids), one phone call for me from a guy desperate to sell me a new roof, the bag of un-popped popcorn that split and tumbled out of the cupboard and into the innards of the gas stove, and the roller skate at the front door that I tripped over and thus skinned my shin.

But the event that did me in that day, that tempted me to turn in my motherhood button once and for all, came while I was fixing supper. I told my two-year-old to go down to the family room and turn off the TV. *Sesame Street* was over and Andrew was upstairs insisting that he help fix supper. Believe me, a tired, harried parent doesn't need help from a two-year-old at that time of day.

I knew Andrew could follow simple directions. So I said very clearly and slowly, "Honey, go downstairs and push the button on the

TV and turn off the TV." I repeated it three times, emphasizing the words, push, off, and TV. I knew he'd figure it out. He knew where the off button was. After all, he took delight in pushing it in every night during the climax of every movie we watched.

So downstairs he went, to do a nice deed for Mommy. I went back to the sink to wash the carrots and cut the broccoli. Then it happened. The loudest crash ever heard in our house. I was so startled I couldn't move. I kept waiting for Andrew to scream. But the silence was more frightening than the crash.

I raced down the steps, half expecting to find Andrew lying unconscious midst shattered patio doors. I blurted out a fast prayer. Then I stopped cold.

He was standing there behind the TV stand, smiling a banana-sized grin that said, "Aren't you proud of me, Mom?" That smile just kept radiating across his whole face as he said, "Andrew pushed off the TV!"

There was the TV, face down on the floor. Two of the knobs were broken off. The screen was smashed. The plants I'd watered that morning that used to sit on top of the set were oozing mud and goo into the carpet. Broken plants and smashed ceramic pots were spread all over the room.

And there was Andrew, smiling, because he had done just what Mommy asked. He'd pushed off the TV. Boy, did he.

I pulled him into my arms and sat on the couch rocking him back and forth. I thanked God that he wasn't hurt. I prayed for patience. I prayed that I wouldn't take up child abuse for a hobby. I prayed that this day would end.

That's when my best friend rang the doorbell and walked inside. By the time I got upstairs she was pouring water into the teapot and had crushed a few more popcorn kernels into the new linoleum floor. She asked in her since-you-only-work-part-time-and-today-was-your-day-off envious voice, "Well, what did you do to keep busy today, lady of leisure?"

Somehow, I don't think she'll ever ask that question again.

~Patricia Lorenz

to do list:
- Pay bills
- Get laundry
- call Mom
- Pick up kids from birthday at 6 p.m.
- Buy groceries

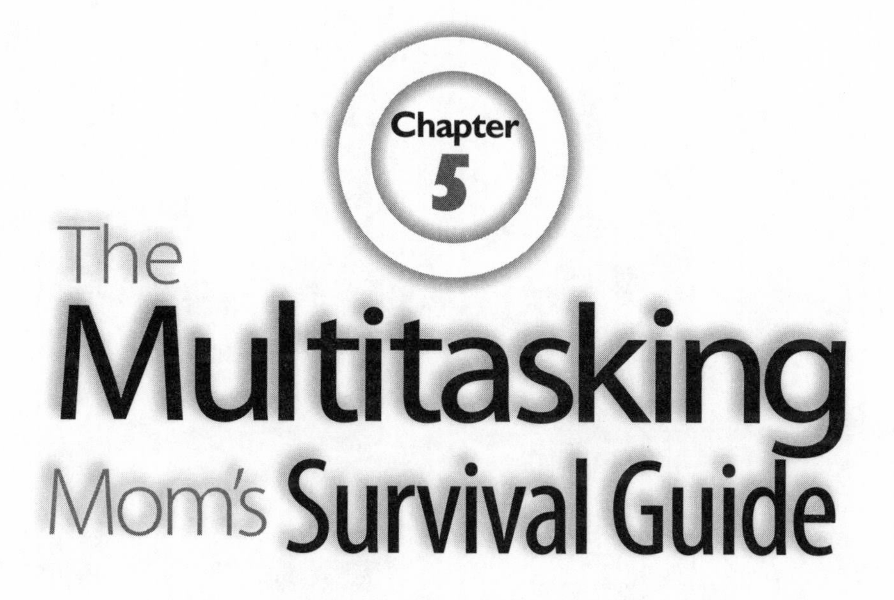

Handling Housework Hassles

Housework can kill you if done right.

~Erma Bombeck

A Busy Mom's Guide to Home Selling

Nothing encourages creativity like the chance to fall flat on one's face.
~James D. Finley

"So your client wants to see our house again before dusk?" I slowly repeated the real estate agent's words back into the phone, perhaps to buy time. My eyes scanned the piles of debris surrounding me. Yesterday's baking spree, last night's dinner, and today's toddler meals occupied every square inch of kitchen counter space. The newborn swing, bouncer, and blanket full of toys crowded the family room furniture. Woven in and out of the baby equipment laid the wreckage of unfinished games, dress-up play, and well-loved stuffed critters.

I mentally reviewed the state of the bedrooms. I recalled the "building-a-mountain" game the kiddos had played earlier and grimaced. They had grinned ear to ear while tugging on my arms to lead me to their magnificent creation—a three-foot-high mound artistically crafted by dumping everything from the toy shelves into the center of the room, including at least a thousand Legos and almost that many puzzle pieces.

"You will arrive in half an hour?" My heart beat louder, and my palm began to sweat against the phone at my ear. I silently willed her to shorten her apologetic explanation. Every second counted.

The client wished to feel the effects of Arizona's hot sun on our west-facing back windows and patio. Understandable. But today? My hands and feet twitched with nervous energy, waiting for her to stop talking—somewhat like an anxious runner waiting for the firing of a starting gun.

At the same time, I was under no illusion that a beautiful, show-ready house could be conjured up in thirty minutes. The task was impossible. But I grew up with the saying, "You just do what you have to do." No excuses, no whining, no holding back.

I had recently given birth to my fourth child—four happy rug rats, four years old and under, who seemed to be laughing in agreement—impossible. Sparkling kitchen: two hours. Tidy family room: minimum of one hour. Sorting of the gigantic toy mountain: a good week.

I had thirty impossible minutes, and unless nature changed its course, a bottle-feeding and one ripe diaper were sure to steal some of those precious moments.

A proper cleaning was not an option. A lousy cleaning was not even doable. I needed a bedroom-sized closet to heave the many mountains into. But even if I had one, homebuyers always opened closet doors to check for storage space.

The agent finally said goodbye, which sounded a lot like "Go!" I rushed to the family room first. The potential buyers should at least get a good view of the carpet. I scooped up armloads of family life while urging the kids who could walk to do the same. As my arms reached maximum capacity, a light bulb went on. My full-sized van was the closet I needed. And its dark tinted windows would never reveal its secondary use.

I struggled to prop open the garage door, and then slid the van door wide open. The floor-to-ceiling cargo space never looked so huge and inviting. I flung my load to the far corners of the auto and tried to suppress the smug snickering of a brilliant plan. The kids shadowed my actions. This would be a fun game.

I quickly found bins for each little pair of hands and instructed them to fill their containers to the brim with anything on the carpet. The treasures they collected were then to be emptied into the van. I used the same tactic in the kitchen. Dishes, silverware, pots, cookie sheets, all nestled into the largest nearby vessel. Stack by stack, they disappeared into the van. As each surface reappeared from under the rubble, a quick rag stood ready to wash down, dust, or polish up.

We maintained a frenzied pace for the full allotted time. No interruptions by bodily functions. Finally, I slid the van door closed and un-propped the garage door. As my eye darted to the grandfather clock for the ninety-ninth time, I lit a candle and began switching on every light in the house for effect. The doorbell rang right on cue.

The children and I stayed out of the way as the real estate agent and her clients studied different areas of the house. They finally let us know they were leaving and made their way back to the front door. They left me with just one comment on their way out. "What an incredible housekeeper you are."

A simple thank you was all I could reply. Then I closed the door so my grin could spread, and I could laugh at the silliness of it all. If only they knew how I kept house.

Phew! We had really done it. Cleaning "by van" had proven fast and efficient—a technique even the most primitive of minds had grasped. The only downside was the inevitable cleaning out of the van. That took quite a bit longer… and a few more organizational skills.

Even so, there was something almost soothing about unloading. With a backdrop of favorite tunes, the slow-paced, methodical excavation of the daily grunge and treasures of life proved immensely more peaceful than the previous panicked sprint to the van.

And the next day we went to contract!

~Ann Kronwald

The Monster in the Closet

Out of clutter, find simplicity.
~Albert Einstein

My three-year-old doesn't read yet, so I feel safe in admitting the truth here. There really is a monster in her closet. It wears last year's snow boots, several mismatched hair bows, and the remains of a July tea party. Silent, but deadly, it hurls missiles from an entire village of Barbie rejects, and is known as The Closet Beast.

The Beast has relatives in the homes of everyone I know—Coat Room Chaos, Mudroom Muddle—even a miniature breed, Junk Drawer Jumble. But the truly mammoth variety hides in the closets of small children. What begins as a reasonable assortment of toys, clothes and books soon grows faster than a pile of dirty diapers after a Toddler Chili Supper. A master of camouflage, the Beast enjoys disguising itself in last season's must-have toys and holey-kneed jeans. It presses against the closet doors, attempting escape, and is held at bay only by the daily struggle to squish, cajole, and jam as many objects as possible back into its den.

The covert union between Child and Beast works against the organized parent. My daughter sings to herself, communing in code with the fiend of confusion. And she cements her loyalty at every attempt to clean out her closet—exclaiming over some "lost" treasure, refusing to depart with dearly loved stuffed animals that haven't seen the light of day in months. Therefore, it is vital that a strategic plan be put into action to vanquish that unwelcome guest. We are at war. I share my tactics here:

The Raid: Not for the faint of heart, this technique is both dangerous and time-sensitive. The prey's accomplice must be out of the house (remember, she can turn giggles into tears before you can say Angelina Ballerina). Remove as many unused items as possible, in the shortest amount of time, before the child returns. This covert operation has a ninety-five percent rate of delayed fallout, culminating in wails of anguish when the pipsqueak with the photographic memory realizes something is missing.

Divide and Conquer: This two-step maneuver has proven invaluable in the case of a child who cannot bear to be parted from even the most neglected objects. Select a chosen few to be reassigned to Grandma's or the babysitter's, then decommissioned after a separation period of two or three weeks to the local resale shop.

Prisoner Exchange: Some mothers swear by this crowd control system. For every new toy brought into the home, the child must release an old one. It effectively cycles items in a kind of automatic closet patrol. It's also an effective exercise for thinking ahead, as the child must decide if a new toy is worth the sacrifice of one.

Invasion: An all-out attack on the Beast, this procedure involves complete restructuring of the area. Empty the room entirely, and then analyze the space for maximum usage. Little clothes can hang above a shelving unit supplied with baskets for similar items and assists in children putting away their own belongings.

I trust your campaign will meet with success, but remember that constant vigilance is required to keep the Beast at bay. Any leave of absence can prompt an invasion. Soldier on.

~Karen B. Nelson

Sometimes You Need to Do the Laundry

Without labor nothing prospers.
~Sophocles

"Mommy, will you play this with me?" My two-year-old peered over a mountain of heaping laundry baskets. She clutched an *UNO Moo!* barn in her hand.

Ugh. I looked at my daughter, then at the laundry, then back to my daughter again. I thought of the advice I've read countless times on blogs and Facebook quips—those popular phrases meant to encourage frazzled moms.

"Days are long but the years fly by."

"Rock and don't sweep, because babies don't keep."

"A messy house is a happy house."

So true! I believed that!

But then I stared down a pile of grubby socks and realized—enough, already. This family is one day short of recycling our dirty underwear. Sometimes the laundry just needs to get done.

I swallowed hard and gazed straight into my daughter's pleading eyes. "I'm sorry, sweetheart, but I cannot play right now. Mom has to do some chores."

Suddenly, a strange sense of empowerment tingled through my veins. It felt a little like rebellion. Yes! I must do the chores! And that does not make me a bad mom!

Quite the opposite, I think.

My house is nowhere near immaculate. I stopped trying years ago, when I discovered babies are messy and moms need naps. But I wonder—have we gone a little too far? Do we encourage each other so much to spend every waking moment relishing fleeting childhood, that any time spent otherwise is deemed a waste or selfish? We don't guilt each other about our dirty floors anymore, and that's great. But now, instead, are we sheepish about cleaning them?

I'm taking a stand for mothers everywhere.

It's okay to clean.

Or to cook. Or to spend a morning running errands, paying bills, making phone calls and folding towels. That's what grown-ups do. And how else will our kids learn unless we demonstrate?

After all, life is not a big game of *UNO*.

Recently, I read an article about a local Amish family. It was a diary of their typical week, written by the father of six grown children. Each day consisted of chores, cooking, and family devotions. The grandkids ran in the barn while the older children milked cows, and everyone helped make pies for the family bakery business. They were all faithfully devoted to one another as they worked side by side from dawn to dusk.

Could it be that the real call on a family is not for the parents to serve the children, but for everyone to serve each other for a greater purpose? It's up to us parents to teach the kids how—by example. So sometimes we work, and sometimes we play. Strong families are built with both.

"Sweetie, I have a great idea." I set my daughter's game on the table and clapped her hands in mine. "You can help me put these clothes in the wash. Doesn't that sound fun?"

"Okay, Momma!" Her face lit up. "Can I push the buttons, too?"

"Absolutely. You are a good button pusher."

"Yay!" She squealed with delight as if I'd just asked her to play, well, *UNO Moo!* or something.

Amazing. It took an Amish diary to show me what a toddler knows at heart. Work is play.

Looks like I'm going to be getting a lot more laundry done around here. We might need bigger underwear drawers.

~Becky Kopitzke

Toilet Talk

Of all the animals, the boy is the most unmanageable.
~Plato

I spend way too much time thinking about toilets. I regularly walk from bathroom to bathroom with the sole purpose of flushing toilets. I've decided this behavior is an outrageous form of multitasking necessary when one has young children. I flush, from time to time, while talking on the phone. My phone-friends do the same thing. We often explain to each other that we are not using the toilet, but merely flushing it. Since we all seem to be in the same absurd predicament, we take each other at our word.

Flushing isn't just a matter of pulling the handle. It's much more. In fact, the innocent act of flushing has gotten me into trouble on occasion, when a proud three-year-old was "saving" the toilet contents "to show Daddy when he got home." I should have known better.

Through the years I've learned to look before I flush. My toilets sprout foreign, unflushable objects on occasion. Toy boats, balls, spoons, and the occasional toothbrush have all found their way into my family's commodes. I've learned to handle such floating objects with the prowess of a professional plumber. In fact, I employ my own patented technique called the Speedy Super Swoop, which involves lightning-fast reflexes and lots of bleach. It's one of those things you have to see to appreciate. Suffice it to say, no undesired items have been flushed down my toilet in at least a month or two.

In the good old days, I never gave toilets a second thought. Oh,

I'd give the white porcelain a good scrub every now and then, but toilet maintenance wasn't a huge priority.

But over the years, we've added little bodies (a.k.a. children) to our household, and with bodies come the need for toilets. I don't like to stereotype, but three of the four bodies are of the male persuasion. It's not that boys are inherently untidy around toilets; they just have farther to aim.

My three-year-old (who refuses any assistance with the commode) routinely announces, "Mom, I sprayed all over."

Believe me, he isn't exaggerating.

The two older boys (three if you count my husband) also experience their fair share of "near misses."

My sister—also blessed with three sons—is a fellow warrior in the tidy toilet quest. Once, despite her unwavering vigilance, she found her bathroom emanating the unmistakable odor of foul urine. She disinfected the toilet and scrubbed the floor, but the smell remained.

She attacked the sink, the walls, the door. It wasn't until she laundered the shower curtain—which was a full six feet away from the toilet—that her bathroom stopped smelling like a diaper pail on garbage day.

I thank God for those handy, pop-up antibacterial bathroom wipes. They are every parent's answer to a prayer for cleaner toilets. You can whip them out, give a quick once-over and be assured it is safe to touch the handle once more.

There may be people who are appalled by such a frank discourse regarding what is one of the most private rooms in the house. A decade ago, I would have agreed with them. But extraordinary times call for extraordinary measures. Toilet tidiness is every parent's business, and I'd bet my last bottle of bleach there are other moms (and dads) out there who are brave warriors in the battle for cleaner commodes.

You may be hesitant to admit it in public, but you know who you are. And the next time we're talking on the phone, don't be afraid to flush. I'll understand. I'll understand completely.

~Jill Pertler

It Doesn't Have to Be Perfect

Always live up to your standards—by lowering them, if necessary.
~*Mignon McLaughlin,* The Second Neurotic's Notebook

It was so sad. I stood in my daughter's bedroom looking at her wood floor. I hadn't seen it in years. But I had driven her to college a few days earlier and now I was starting nostalgically at her partly cleaned up room. I could see the floor, there was nothing on the bed except bedding, and there was even a little room on her countertops.

Even though I am a very neat and organized person, I had never forced my kids to clean up their rooms. The rule was that they couldn't leave one smidgeon of mess in the rest of the house, not even in the family room, but their bedrooms were their domain. As long as we didn't have to work around, step over, or move aside their stuff in the rest of the house, they were in the clear.

This had led to some fancy footwork on my part. When they called from school or from their father's house, asking me to please find a missing something or other in their rooms, I had to tiptoe my way across a floor covered with papers, duffel bags, sports apparel, receipts, and more—all the detritus of teenage life. I allowed this mess for three reasons: 1) because I remembered my own very messy teen years; 2) because they had to live in two houses, mine and their father's, and that made it much harder for them to stay organized;

and 3) because I was too busy to bother with trivia like a messy bedroom that wasn't hurting anyone except its occupant. When I had people over I just closed the kids' bedroom doors.

A wonderful psychologist and expert on stress management named Harriet Braiker wrote the breakthrough book, *The Type E Woman: How to Overcome the Stress of Being Everything to Everybody*. Harriet said: "Striving for excellence motivates you; striving for perfection is demoralizing."

Women in particular, with all their multitasking, really need some help in letting go. Does anyone actually remember if you baked everything yourself the last time you entertained, if your kids' clothes looked perfectly pressed during the five minutes before they got mud on them, or if you have sent out Christmas cards every year without fail? Does your family remember if you used paper plates instead of china at the last big gathering? And does it really matter if your teenagers have messy rooms, when the mess only hurts them and no one else?

The only rule that I did have for those messy rooms involved laundry. The kids were too busy with school and sports and volunteer activities to do their own laundry so that was a "service" that I provided, but only if the clothes were in the hamper. Even if the clothes were in front of the hamper on the floor they did not get picked up and washed. The kids quickly adapted to that rule and used their hampers.

The funny thing was that once the kids went off to college and were in charge of their own rooms, they got a lot neater. And now that they are in their mid-twenties, their own homes are extremely neat, with everything in its place.

There's only one problem. Their rooms, which I now use as guest rooms most of the time, are still pretty messy. The kids claim they are still too busy to go through their things and dispose of them or give them away. At this point, I'm thinking that I might as well leave everything, since they'll have their own kids soon enough, and those rooms will look like a treasure trove to my grandchildren!

~Amy Newmark

No More Overtime

Work expands so as to fill the time available for its completion.
~C. Northcote Parkinson

I sighed at the piles of dishes on the kitchen counter. A quick glance at the clock showed it was almost 8:30. I had just finished putting our daughters, ages two and six, to bed. I desperately wanted to play fairy godmother and wave my magic wand. Poof! Dirty dishes be clean. Poof! Floors be swept. Poof! Laundry be done.

But I'm no fairy godmother, and I certainly don't have a magic wand. No chance of enlisting help from my husband, either. I could hear Derek in the home office, still on the phone scheduling appointments with clients for the next day. There was nothing left to do but tackle the mountain of dishes. But as I fished bits of greasy chicken and mystery food gunk out of the garbage disposal, that familiar and weary discontent returned.

By the time I was wiping the counters, I was shooting furious glances at Derek. He was now relaxing on the couch, watching TV. Couldn't he see how much work remained?

I hinted through gritted teeth, "You know, I sure could use some help in here. Maybe dry these dishes. Or make lunches for school tomorrow."

"Not now, hon. I just sat down. I need a break. I'll help in the morning, okay?"

That was not okay. Couldn't he see I needed a break, too?

"Why don't you join me on the couch, sweetie? We'll finish in the morning."

"I can't. Can't you see how much still needs to get done?"

He gave me a suit-yourself look and went back to flipping through the channels.

I finished in the kitchen and stomped up the stairs. Derek was blissfully (or deliberately) oblivious to my resentment. By the time I was done with the laundry, it was past ten o'clock! So unfair. Yet another late night without a moment of downtime the entire day.

I was about to spit a sarcastic "must be nice" comment Derek's way when I considered maybe, just maybe, he wasn't doing anything wrong. He is a busy real estate agent and works many evenings. To be fair, he deserved a break. He deserved to end his workday.

That's when I had my epiphany: There is no official end to my workday at home. Even if I worked until midnight every night, I still wouldn't get absolutely everything done around the house. So why was I trying? A huge weight lifted as I recognized this futility. What a relief! Since I couldn't get everything done every day, I would just do my best and end my shift at a certain time. Right then I designated 8:30 as a realistic end time to my shift.

The next night looked a little different. After putting the kids to bed, it was already 8:15. Since I only had fifteen minutes until my workday ended, I tackled the kitchen with more enthusiasm than I've ever known. I didn't realize I could load the dishwasher, wash pots and wipe counters with such gusto. All the while I was glancing at the clock: 8:18... 8:24... 8:28 (woo-hoo, only two minutes to go!).

I never got to sweeping the floor or making our daughter's school lunch, but it didn't matter. My relief when I lit a few candles and sat on the couch with a cup of tea was worth it. When Derek came home late from work, he was rewarded with a peaceful, contented wife. No nagging. No stomping. No bitterness. It must have been a relief for him too.

Now I respect my schedule and usually end my shift on time. Nobody seems to care if the floors aren't swept or there's still a pile of laundry in the morning. Somehow it all gets done eventually. I started delegating jobs to my older daughter, who's great at sorting clean laundry and putting away most of her own clothes. I've become more efficient with my chores, and more forgiving of myself (and my husband) when we don't get them all done.

Turns out I didn't need a magic wand. I just needed to set more realistic expectations and give myself permission to stop working overtime every day. Maybe next I'll start scheduling coffee and lunch breaks too!

~Anita Love

When Darth Vader Attacks

If you want children to keep their feet on the ground,
put some responsibility on their shoulders.
~Abigail Van Buren

Getting my eight-year-old son to clean his room should have been a five-minute chore, but in reality it was always the longest hour of my day. Yes, it would have been so much easier for me to just tidy it up myself, but that wouldn't teach him responsibility. It was the same thing every evening. He would whine and complain, and I would try not to lose my mind. So here it was, 8:00 p.m. again. I opened the door to his room and looked around at the oh-so-familiar scene. The towel from his morning shower was on the floor. The sheet and blanket from his bed were halfway off. His books were never on his end table where they were supposed to be; they were usually somewhere on the floor among litters of *Star Wars* toys and dinosaurs. As I looked at the mess, I said to myself, "I'm a creative type. There must be a better way...." Then it hit me.

"Scott!" I sounded alarmed. "Quick, Darth Vader is on his way here, and he's going to aim his death ray on all your men. They're not protected; they're all out on the planet surface." At first, he just looked at me, uncertain if I'd finally lost my mind. "Come on," I said. "You're their commander. Get in there and get them back in the Millennium Falcon."

"What do I do?" he asked with a smile.

"Open the hatch to the Millennium Falcon," I said, pointing to his toy box. "Order your men to pick up all their equipment and weapons, and herd all the dinosaurs inside where they'll be safe."

He rushed as fast as he could to pick up each toy.

"Now you've got to pick up the books with the secret formula in them and put them on the stand with the magic light. It protects them so Darth Vader won't be able to touch them."

"Yeah," he joined me. " Cause if he does try to touch them, this laser light comes on, and it burns a hole right through his hand." He turned on his lamp to show me how it would work.

When he was done with the floor, I adjusted his shower water and called out to him from the bathroom. "Hurry, he's almost here! You've got to get protected with the invisibility shower so he can't find you. Make sure to throw your clothes in the hamper because if he sees them on the floor, he'll know where you are." No child ever ran so fast to take a shower.

"Make sure you use the invisibility soap and get it all over every part of you. If you leave any skin uncovered, he'll be able to find you."

I put his pajamas on his bed. "I left your 'uniform' on your 'escape pod.' Dry off and put it on." I couldn't believe this was working. While he showered, I went into the kitchen to put away the dishes.

When I heard the shower water stop, I returned to his room and noticed that he had dropped his towel next to the one from the day before. "You better pick up both those towels and put them in the hamper so I can wash them tonight." He hesitated. "If you leave them out, Darth Vader will smell your scent on them and find you." Now he rushed to pick up both towels, tossing them in the hamper.

"Make sure you brush your teeth with invisibility toothpaste, too. That way he won't see your teeth when you open your mouth."

Grabbing his toothpaste and toothbrush, he quickly brushed his teeth and, surprisingly, even put away the toothpaste and toothbrush without being told. This was catching on.

"Only one thing left so he won't get you," I warned.

"What's that, Mom?" He was so excited. "Get into your escape pod and pull the invisible sheet and blanket up over you so you won't be seen." He jumped into bed, smoothing out his sheet and blanket.

"Goodnight, Commander." I turned out his light. "You should be safe... this time."

"Wait!" he called out. "He'll see my head. I can't keep my head under the covers or I can't breathe."

"You're right, Commander," I answered. "You need some invisibility dust on your head and even your arms, just in case they come out of the covers."

"We don't have any invisibility dust," he replied.

"The Rebel Force smuggled out some for you just today. I'll go get it," I said as I walked into my bathroom and grabbed the talcum powder. Returning to his room, I held it over his head and arms, sprinkling it down on his arm and a little in his hair.

"I'm good now, Mom," he said, rubbing it all over his head and arms.

"May the force be with you," I said as I left.

"What is the force anyway?" he asked.

"The force is God," I answered. "We almost forgot; you have to say your prayers. Ask that the force of God is with you always."

"For real, right?" he asked. "Not just when the pretend Darth Vader comes?"

"Roger that, Commander. The force is always with you. Good night."

~Diana Perry

The Art of Delegation

Few things help an individual more than to place responsibility upon him, and to let him know that you trust him.
~Booker T. Washington

It was time to put down my foot. For years, I had worked full-time while doing almost all the housework, cooking, laundry and errands, not to mention chauffeur duties. My children grew up, but they were still at home dividing their time between college, part-time jobs and friends. I decided that if I could work all day, come home and do, well, everything, then they could do some things, too. It was time for some changes!

I developed a plan. First, I sat down and listed all the "home work" that needed to be done. Then, I made a delegation list. My husband tried but did not escape. I decided that for my plan to work with the least amount of pain and resistance, I would have to start them out a little at a time.

This was not the first time they had to help at home. My son did yard work with his dad every Saturday. My daughter helped me inside on weekends. Everyone maintained their own rooms, some more efficiently than others. This was a good start, but there were now four adults living in the house, and it was time to balance the load a little more.

I called a family meeting. First on the list, they would begin doing their own laundry. This meant washing, drying, folding and putting away. I was tired of trying to find the dirty laundry, and I was tired of carrying it up and down the stairs to the laundry room. If they didn't do their own laundry, they would be wearing dirty clothes. This was received pretty well. No one seemed to think this was a big deal because they did not know how much work was involved.

I left it there for a while. This went fairly smooth. We had to develop a schedule so that each person had a laundry day. There were a few disasters with bleeding colors and shrinkage in the dryer, but everyone learned the importance of reading the tags in their clothing. There was also an occasional conflict with the schedule if someone failed to do their wash in a timely manner or didn't remove their clothes from the dryer. But soon everything became routine... more or less.

Time to roll out part two, and this was my favorite—dividing kitchen duties. Another family meeting was called. Each person was required to pick a night to cook and clean the kitchen. This time I got a little pushback. "I don't know how to cook." This came from my son who had taken a semester of home economics in junior high.

"All I know how to do is bake," said my daughter. She had made, on occasion, a cake or a batch of cookies.

"Well, now you will learn," was my heartless reply. "We have cookbooks and family recipes. Use them."

In spite of the grumbling, it wasn't as bad as it sounded. After everyone got the hang of it, we began to have some good meals. My husband normally stuck with one thing, baked fish. He was pretty predictable, but this was a good meal every week. He also did some grilling, which was always nice. My children got very creative eventually, even developing their own dishes. In fact, my two children and I have published recipes in two cookbooks together. This was pretty special to all of us.

Little by little, other duties were handed out. The result was a more relaxed household with the burden seeming smaller when divided among the four of us. I still retained the bulk of the work and had more cooking days, but my load was much lighter than before. If someone wanted to do something with friends or was just especially tired on their day, we swapped. Everything became routine.

When my son moved away from home, we had to redistribute the workload. One of our solutions for meals was "on your own" nights when everyone is responsible for their own supper. Laundry day conflicts have diminished with one less person to contend with.

Several good things have occurred as a result of our new lifestyle. The house stays cleaner with less effort on everyone's part. My son's apartment is much cleaner than his old room used to be. He has developed new habits and a stronger sense of responsibility.

My son has also learned that he loves to cook. In fact, he would go to culinary school if he had the chance. His friends always want him to bring appetizers to their get-togethers. His girlfriends have enjoyed dating a guy who can cook a meal for them that matches the restaurants around town. He cooks way over my head now. I am really proud of him.

His former housework responsibilities have fallen primarily to my daughter who now does them automatically. She has also become a very good cook. She likes to experiment with her dishes and has created some tasty treats. She is also chief bakery chef for the holidays. I cannot imagine how I ever did it all myself!

A very special treat for me is on Thanksgiving when we are all in the kitchen together preparing the meal, setting the table, and cleaning up. We chat and joke as each person handles his or her assignment. Cooking, in particular, has created a special bond among us. Family recipes are being handed down to a new generation and often improved upon. New family recipes have been created.

I discovered the best multitasking skills I ever developed were the skills of planning and delegation. Now, I can have some "me time" and read a book or work out.

~Debbie Acklin

The Good Mom

Deep summer is when laziness finds respectability.
~Sam Keen

My alarm clock blasted music way too lively for my early-morning mood. I crawled out of bed with a groan, stumbling over a basket overflowing with dirty laundry. Whatever happened to our lazy days of summer? My mind drifted back to when my girls were younger—back when we slept late during summer vacations. Now, activities like gymnastics, band and volleyball camps, softball games and a number of other commitments had turned our lazy days into crazy days.

I maneuvered my way toward the kitchen through a path of flip-flops. Last night's dinner dishes greeted me at the sink. Oh yes, I thought, remembering our hectic evening the night before. We had scarfed down frozen pizza, grabbed our lawn chairs and rushed out the door for my daughter's six o'clock softball game.

Something is wrong with this picture, I thought, scraping dried pepperoni off a dinner plate. As much as I enjoyed watching and supporting my girls' activities, our busy schedule left little time for housework. Somehow we had plenty of time to make messes, but never enough to clean them up.

Whenever I complained, my husband always gave me the same advice: "Get those girls to help you."

"I know," I said, feeling a twinge of guilt, "but that's easier said than done." They always seemed to have an excuse.

"How about folding some laundry?"

"Okay, Mom, this TV show is almost over."

"Girls, I need you to unload the dishwasher."

"Sure, Mom, but can I do it in a couple of minutes? I'm so close to the next level on this game."

Truth be told, it probably was my fault. I wanted to be a good mom—and good moms didn't follow their kids around nagging them all day. But I didn't feel like a good mom. I was a tired mom. A grumpy mom. I was a mom who needed help, and I knew the perfect way to motivate my girls.

"Okay, guys," I said one morning during breakfast, "today we're starting something new." Three pairs of eyes gazed up at me from their bowls of cereal. "From now on, each of you must complete a chore each day before getting on a screen."

"A screen?" my youngest asked, tilting her head to the side.

"Yes, a screen," I said. "You know, TVs, computers, Wii games, iPhones…"

One by one, each girl's mouth dropped open. They weren't excited, but I was eager to set my plan into action.

I'll admit the first few days were a challenge. Like most kids, they tested me, seeing if I would stand my ground. But within a couple of weeks, doing chores became our daily routine. My plan worked great—and no nagging was needed.

I used to think being a good mom meant self-sacrifice and being able to do it all. Now I have a new definition. A good mom builds a team and teaches responsibility. She is more able to enjoy her kids because she's no longer stressed out, sleep-deprived and exhausted. Once I learned how to share the load, I think I became a pretty good mom.

~Sheri Zeck

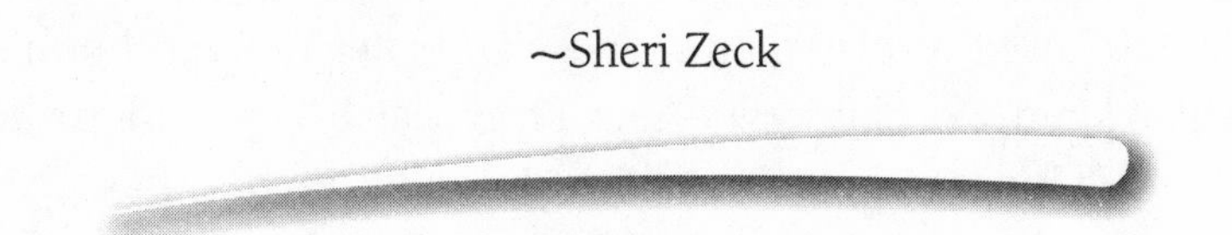

Where Are My Crutches?

Good shot, bad luck, and hell are the five basic words to be used in a game of tennis, though these, of course, can be slightly amplified.
~Virginia Graham

I'm hobbling up a flight of stairs on crutches. Not indoor, carpeted stairs that help grip the crutch legs (and provide a soft landing if I slip), but outside metal steps that are slightly damp from an earlier drizzle.

It's Friday evening. I had knee surgery on Monday.

I'm attending a work function with my husband, who isn't amused by my new infirmity. Not surprisingly, he left for a three-day business trip the day after my surgery. So he hasn't been home to witness my struggles in getting four children off to school while dealing with a heavily bandaged and throbbing knee joint.

This is the first time in my life that I've used crutches, and it's exhausting. Walking with stiff poles poking into my armpits, even though they are padded, takes more muscle strength than I realized. But, by necessity, I'm learning to maneuver them and muddle through life's activities a little better each day.

The reason for the surgery?

My son loved to play tennis, and who better to teach him the basics than Mom? For about two years, I had been his practice partner when none of his friends were available. I welcomed the opportunity for exercise and spending time doing something we both enjoyed.

But then there was the fateful backhand return. I stepped to the right and felt a stinging pop in my left leg. Immediately, I stumbled and then took a few crippled steps. Our game was over, but a little ice and rest would fix it, I thought.

Didn't happen that way. The tennis pro said it was probably torn cartilage. After a couple of weeks, when I continued limping and couldn't bend my leg while doing chores, I had it checked out by an orthopedic surgeon, who confirmed the diagnosis.

The arthroscopic procedure that was supposed to last an hour actually took three as the damage was more extensive than the doctor thought. Pieces of damaged cartilage were cut away, but I'm not allowed to put weight on the leg in order to let the torn ligament heal over time.

My family doesn't comprehend that Mom is somewhat incapacitated. At breakfast time I carry cereal boxes from the pantry to the table, top flaps clutched in my mouth. To do the laundry I lean on the washing machine and dryer to load and unload clothes. For grocery shopping, it requires athletic moves to push the cart and maneuver on crutches at the same time.

At first, my children don't seem to notice these things. In their eyes, Mom is indestructible. And I want to live up to their image of me as strong and capable. In doing so, I find reserves of energy and the will to do the tasks at hand.

Yes, the kids are helpful. The day after surgery, my oldest daughter comes home from school during a class break to refresh my ice packs. They distribute folded laundry to the proper rooms and mostly manage simple meals. They let me rest—after homework is done. They scurry out the door without prodding each morning to catch the school bus. And they cheer me up with stories of their accomplishments. On Thursday, my middle daughter is inducted into the National Junior Honor Society, and I'm in the audience applauding loudly—leg propped up and crutches nearby.

For two months, I carry on this way. Crutches lie on the floorboard of our van when I'm shuttling kids around town. At home I find that hopping is quicker and more efficient for getting from one spot to another than wielding the bulky wooden appendages.

Eventually, physical therapy and a monstrous leg brace improve my mobility.

At a check-up, when the surgeon tells me I'll have a "functionally" normal knee, I reply that I expect a "perfectly" normal knee. After all, "perfect" and "functional" are what Mom is supposed to be.

~Beverly Burmeier

to do list:
- Pay bills
- Get laundry
- call Mom
- Pick up kids
from birthday
at 6 p.m.
- Buy groceries

Learning from the Kids

While we try to teach our children all about life,
our children teach us what life is all about.

~Angela Schwindt

My Little Runaway

If you haven't time to respond to a tug at your pants leg,
your schedule is too crowded.
~Robert Brault

The first child dominates your life. The second child is easier, and the third tips the family balance in favor of a child-majority, yet the workload is similar to before. A little more cooking, a little more laundry, but everyone adapts, and life moves on with a steady hum. And then, sometimes, life throws a curveball in the form of a fourth child, a bonus kid, an honest-to-goodness surprise, at least for us.

We had nine months to prepare, and my fears ebbed as the enthusiasm of the rest of the family buoyed me. No one was more excited than our youngest child, Gavin, as he had long been asking for a younger sibling. His jubilation put me at ease. Surely the whole "riding a bike" adage applied to something as biologically hardwired as motherhood. We'd muddle through.

And then reality hit.

From the first night in the hospital, Baby #4 was nothing like his older sisters or brother. He was curiously opinionated for such a tiny human. He had already developed a particular propensity for his mommy and an aversion to the hospital-issued bassinet. It was like he was morally opposed to sleep, waking from a deep slumber whenever any part of his body touched the bed. And eating? He was intense in his nursing, striking like a rattlesnake, but lacked the functional know-how to achieve the desired results. An apparatus of cylinders and tubes was needed to teach the kid how to eat. Add that to the fact that he was having difficulty regulating his body temperature—a common condition, I was assured, but one I'd never dealt with—and this was one needy kid.

And so instead of an easy transition, Baby #4 disrupted our entire household more than any parenting book could ever predict. Perhaps it was an early sign of his disposition. Perhaps it was an innate understanding that the fourth child needed to make his presence known lest he be lost in the shuffle. Regardless of his reasoning, the transition was particularly hard on Gavin. Reality did not match his expectations, shattered the moment he tried to hold his eagerly anticipated baby brother at the hospital. Instead of an instant bond, the baby wailed until we removed him from Gavin's arms, devastating the tenderhearted little boy.

And the devastation continued when we arrived home from the hospital. Baby #4 became increasingly disruptive in Gavin's little life. TV had to be turned down; the baby was sleeping. Mommy couldn't take him to the park; the July heat was too much for such a little baby. Everyone needed to lie down for a nap; the baby was sleeping and Mommy was tired. The girls were handling the transition better, since changing diapers and picking out clothes for a life-sized baby doll were still a novelty. Gavin just wanted a buddy.

"I'm running away," Gavin told me one day as I worked to nurse the baby.

I vaguely wondered where he had ever heard such a thing. Probably TV. "Where would you go?" I asked.

"I'll go live with Luke," he said, indicating his best friend who lived in the neighboring town twelve miles away.

Now a good mother would recognize her son's plea for attention by dropping everything, issuing a hug and words of love and assurance, and whisking the child away on a special mother-son outing. But I wasn't a good mother. I was a sleep-deprived mess of hormones trying to keep her head above water in the midst of unprecedented chaos.

"You can't run away," I said, too distracted for a longer discourse on the subject. "I'd miss you too much."

It wasn't the answer he sought, but it was all I could give.

Gavin announced his intention several more times, often when the baby was particularly fussy or extremely demanding. Every time I provided the same distracted response. "You can't run away; I'll miss you." He was being dramatic, I reasoned. It would pass. If he was looking for the mother bunny in *The Runaway Bunny*, well, I wasn't capable of that advanced level of creativity.

Several days later, running late for an appointment and flustered, I stopped in my tracks as Gavin descended the kitchen stairs, a look of determination on his face. His pillow and favorite stuffed bear were tucked under his arm, and he carried his child-sized suitcase in the other. It bulged with evidence of his intention.

"What are you doing?" I asked, my heart rising in my throat.

Tears threatened as he answered. "I'm running away."

He finally had my undivided attention. "Where are you going?"

"I'm going to live with Luke." His jaw was set with determination, but his eyes begged me to stop him. "His parents won't care."

The weight of his words slammed into me. Realization dawned that he had been trying to tell me, in his own way, how neglected he had felt since the baby arrived, but I had been too distracted to listen. Even worse, I hadn't taken his feelings seriously. "You can't run away," I told him. "Go put that back in your room, and we'll talk about it when we get back."

Though not satisfied, he obliged, recognizing that I was finally listening to him.

The baby was asleep when we returned home, and I relegated him to the care of his sisters while I went to talk to the little runaway. My heart twisted as I helped Gavin unpack the contents of his suitcase. Plagued with health problems his entire life, he'd packed all his medicines, lotions, and inhalers along with a pair of pajamas and a change of clothes. He didn't have clean underwear or a toothbrush, but these were nonessential in his mind. Love and medicine had sustained him thus far; underwear and toothbrushes wouldn't do much to improve his current situation.

He talked, and I finally listened. The hurt feelings and tears were easily resolved over the next few days with a few more minutes here and some undivided attention there. Gavin's desperate act of rebellion helped me see that I needed to find a way to realign my time to meet the needs of my children—all my children. Time may not increase exponentially with each child, but love does. Dividing it equitably is up to us.

~C. E. Plante

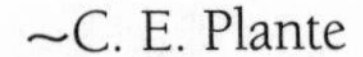

The Green Crayon

Just pray for a tough hide and a tender heart.
~Ruth Graham

It was what I call the witching hour, that hectic interval right before dinnertime. I was exhausted and just trying to survive until the sweet escape of bedtime. I threw a frozen meal concoction into the frying pan for dinner, had the last load of laundry in the dryer and was paying one more bill while trying to keep the children distracted with entertaining videos. Unaware that my four-year-old daughter had left the family room to "help with the laundry," I saw her emerge from the basement holding her brand-new pink Easter outfit streaked with what appeared to be green marker. I jumped to conclusions and yelled, "What have you done? Where did you get that marker? Why would you do such a thing?"

She denied all my accusations profusely and cried, "It wasn't me! Go downstairs and look in the dryer. It's all over everything!"

I ran downstairs to the dryer and found that my daughter was right. As I reached into the dryer and pulled out all the new spring outfits I had purchased on our limited budget, I saw that all the shirts, pants and never-worn clothes were creatively streaked with bright green. I sorted through every item with misty eyes and discovered a pair of my son's OshKosh overalls. They were blotched with a large stain of the same green, and I remembered the green crayon we had placed there two days before while shopping.

I explained to my daughter that the green crayon was destroyed by the dryer and plopped onto the floor sobbing as my four-year-old daughter said, "See, I told you. What are we going to do now?" Feeling totally frustrated, angry and dismayed, I began to aimlessly assess the damaged clothing, only to be interrupted by the sound of the smoke alarm.

I dashed upstairs to find my two-year-old reaching for the pan I had left on the stove, now billowing with smoke and flames. I grabbed him away from the danger and whipped the pan with our dinner into the sink. Totally frustrated with the whole situation, and having no patience with the dinner, the children, the laundry, and myself, I started huffing and puffing, screaming at the children to get out of my way. All of a sudden, I felt a tug on my pants. I looked down at my daughter, peering up at me with tear-stained cheeks. "Mommy," she said, "I think we need to pray about the green crayon!"

I have always heard that many of life's greatest lessons are those we learn through the eyes of a child. That night it was my four-year-old daughter and a melted green crayon that taught me patience, love and appreciation for the gifts that my children are to me each day.

~Peg Arnold

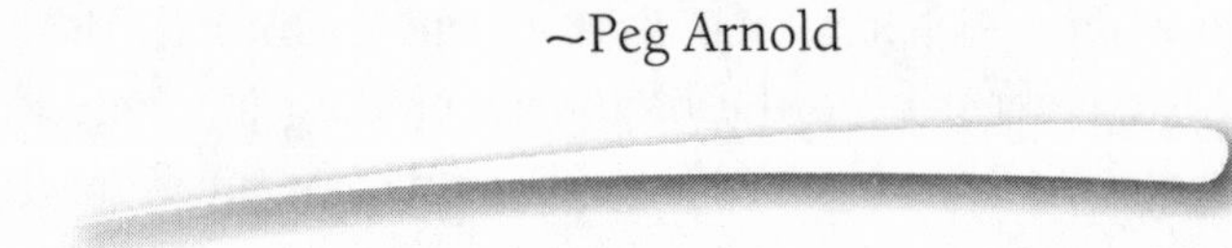

Building Sand Castles that Last

[L]ife is a journey and not a destination...
~Lynn H. Hough

"We gotta fill my bucket all the way up to the top, Mommy," my three-year-old son, Nathan, said. He was standing on the beach, holding a green sand bucket and wearing *Thomas the Tank Engine* swim trunks.

"Okay, buddy, let's fill it up," I said, plopping down in the sand and starting to dig.

He knelt down next to me and grinned. "Let's build a bunch of sand castles and surprise Daddy with them," he said.

My husband was playing in the waves with our older children. I could hear them laughing and shouting as they tried to dunk him. I waved at them and then smiled at Nathan. "Daddy will be so excited to see what you made."

Ten minutes later, the sand bucket was full and ready to be dumped out into a perfect little sand castle. "Where do you want me to put our first castle?" I asked Nathan.

"Right here," he said, pointing to the sand at his feet.

"We can't put it right here," I said. "The water will wash it away as soon as I dump out the bucket."

"I want it right here," he said.

"But it won't work, buddy, because the waves will ruin it."

"That's okay. Then we can just build another one." He shrugged. "It'll be fun."

I sighed, figuring the only way to make him understand was to do as he asked and let him see what would happen. I only hoped he wouldn't be too upset when that first wave destroyed his creation.

But when the water came and washed away his castle, he jumped up and down and clapped his hands. "That was great! Let's do it again!"

We filled up the bucket for a second time, and again Nathan insisted on dumping it out right in the path of every single wave that would crash on the shore.

The third time, I walked up to the dry sand and dumped the bucket there. "Look, Nathan, the waves won't get it up here," I said. "Isn't that better?"

But he scowled and folded his arms across his chest. "No, I don't want to build my castles all the way up there."

"But don't you want to build them where they will last?"

He stuck out his lower lip. "Mommy, I just want to do it down by the water. It's more fun."

"But up here, the water won't..." I began to argue. And that's when I noticed tears in my little boy's eyes. "Is it really more fun when the waves wash away the sand castles?"

"Yes," he said. "Can we please just build them down there?"

"Of course we can, buddy," I said, feeling guilty that I'd nearly made him cry. Building sand castles was supposed to be fun.

We moved back down to the water and built half a dozen more sand castles, none of which lasted more than ten seconds. I still didn't understand, but when Nathan grinned and said, "This is really fun, Mommy," I decided I was finished trying to persuade him to change building locations.

When the rest of our family joined us on the beach, the kids said, "I thought you guys were going to build sand castles."

I smirked and said, "We have been. We've built several, but the waves keep washing them away."

"Does Nathan know that won't happen if he builds them up there?" my oldest son asked, pointing at the dry sand.

I rolled my eyes. "He knows. I even showed him, and all it did was nearly make him cry."

While we were talking, my younger children had sat down in the sand with Nathan and helped him fill up his sand bucket. They dumped it out and watched the waves wash it away. They looked at one another, smiled, and started doing it again.

I looked at my husband, Eric, and said, "I don't know how they can stand to do that. It was driving me crazy, spending all the time building something that was just going to be washed away moments later."

Eric smiled. "It would bug me too, but to them the fun is in the building, no matter how long it lasts."

"It's important to me to spend my time building things that last," I said.

Standing on that beach, Eric smiled and reached for my hand. "You are, babe," he said quietly.

I thought about my life at home. Nothing I did there ever seemed to last. I prepared dinners that were completely consumed ten minutes after I placed them on the table. I washed dishes, and then washed the same dishes the next day. Same deal on the laundry for seven people. I mopped floors only to see someone dirty them on their first trip in from the back yard. My life was just one never-ending to-do list.

It reminded me of the sand castles Nathan built in the wet sand. All of my efforts were washed away by a giant wave called Family Life. Nothing I did lasted beyond the moment.

Because of this, I often struggled with feelings of inadequacy. I wondered if the things I did even mattered in the grand scheme of things. And if nothing I did mattered, that meant that I didn't matter.

I thought of the women I knew who were spending their lives on more important things. They had important jobs. They were making a difference, doing something that would last long past their own lives.

And I was just a mom.

But as I watched my children digging in the sand, laughing and playing together, I realized that my husband was right. I am building something important, something that will last forever.

I'm building a family.

And nothing matters more than that.

~Diane Stark

Fairy Wings

Nothing can be truer than fairy wisdom. It is as true as sunbeams.
~Douglas Jerrold

"Mommy, I need my wand and my fairy wings." I sighed. Up to my elbows in boxes and packing material, my first instinct was to tell my five-year-old that she was out of luck and should find something else to do. But the loving mother in me knew that the poor girl had just moved four hours away from everything and everyone she held familiar, and the least I could do was grant her wish so she could grant the wishes of others.

"I saw your dress-up box in your closet," I said. "Wings and wand should be in there."

Libby cheered and skipped off, her blond ponytails bouncing.

I emptied two more boxes, found enough bedding to get my eighteen-month-old son down for a nap, and started the dishwasher before Libby came in and interrupted me again.

"Mommy, come meet my new friend," she said.

How could I refuse? I walked out onto the porch and met my new neighbors, a delightful couple who had carried over sloppy joes, raw veggies, homemade cookies and lemonade for us and the rest of the neighbors who had become my impromptu movers. Everyone was taking a break and enjoying the feast.

"Down here, Mom," Libby called to me from the yard. I noticed that she was now wearing a pink princess dress under her wings and a plastic "jeweled" tiara over her summer-mussed hair. Her sandals had been long since discarded somewhere in the yard.

My breath caught as I saw my blond-haired, blue-eyed Swedish doll standing next to a tall, dark young man confined to an electric wheelchair.

"This is Nic," she announced.

"Nice to meet you, Nic," I said as I walked down the steps to join the kids. Nic lifted a hand stiffly and vocalized a greeting.

"Yuck! You're drooling again," Libby blurted out as she grabbed a towel from Nic's tray and wiped his mouth.

I blushed at my daughter's bravado. We are, after all, supposed to be discreet about the faults of others.

"Let's go!" Libby shouted, and Nic motored off behind my daughter with a big smile on his face.

Walking down the steps to join me, his mother answered the unasked question about her son. "Nic has cerebral palsy. It was a difficult delivery, and he was oxygen-deprived for a period of time."

"Oh." What else could I say? Nic was a handsome guy—Libby pointed out his resemblance to John Stamos while watching an old episode of *Full House*. It made my heart hurt that what had happened to him was an accident.

Our children came around to the front of the house again. Libby was flitting her wings and waving her wand, while Nic was smiling. Nic's chair was equipped with a computer that allowed him to communicate. It spoke phrases at the touch of a button and could play several nursery rhymes. Libby's laughter rang out when he played "Twinkle, Twinkle, Little Star" and "London Bridge."

Libby twirled to the stairs where I stood and looked up at me. "Can you be the Mama Fairy?" she asked.

"Of course," I responded in my fairy voice. This was a game we had played before.

"Mama Fairy, please let me help this human."

I knew the rules and shook my head. "You know that fairies are not allowed to help humans."

"But, Mama, his legs don't work, and he needs wings to fly with me."

"You're right," I said softly. My voice was a whisper as I gave permission. "You may give him wings."

Libby waved her wand, admired her work and then flew off with her new fairy friend close behind.

With tears in my eyes as I watched, I couldn't help but wonder how my daughter, so young and innocent, was also so very wise and wonderful. How she knew in her heart that we all long for a friend who cares enough to let us know when we've got toilet paper stuck to our shoe, lipstick on our teeth, or drool on our lips. How she was drawn to a young man who was just as worthy of such a friend and far more in need of one. How, as many times as I had used words to tell her that everyone should be treated the same, she knew exactly how to do that with someone who was so very different.

~Becky Tidberg

A Nugget of Wisdom

The ability to simplify means to eliminate the unnecessary so that the necessary may speak.
~Hans Hofmann

I often find myself watching arguments between working moms and stay-at-home moms concerning who is busier. Whenever anyone asks me, I answer simply, "Anyone who takes care of children is busy... all the time."

It really doesn't matter how many things you have going on in your life; you only need one thing to make you instantly busy—children. From the moment you are awake to the moment you sleep, there is something to be done, someone to help, someone to worry about or someone to watch over. And even in your sleep you listen for them, so there really isn't a moment when you are not occupied with something.

I spent several years trying to figure out how to manage a marriage, three kids, a full-time job, a part-time job and all the other things that had to be done in a day. I was exhausted from late-night band practice, middle-of-the-night wet bed changes and project assignments from work. I couldn't remember the last time my husband and I had had a real conversation, and I knew it had been even longer since I had taken a moment to do something for myself.

I was tired, cranky and unhappy, and I knew I was not being a good wife or mother. Something had to change, but I was so overwhelmed that I didn't know where to start. Then my youngest child gave me a glimpse into how to figure out what really matters.

We were getting ready to read a bedtime story after a long day, and he asked me if I was going to be home the next day. I sighed, wearily expecting him to request a trip to the museum or an amusement park. "Yes, Mommy will be home. It is Saturday, and I don't have to go to work."

He got a big smile on his face and asked, "You make me 'hicken nuggets?"

I smiled and said, "Sure, Bub, I can make you chicken nuggets. What else do you want me to do tomorrow?"

"Make me 'hicken nuggets," he said again, and that was it. The next day you would have thought I'd given him the world when those nuggets hit the plate, with ketchup on the side.

The following weekend was the same. He requested his favorite lunch of me, and that was all. I came to understand that to my son the most important thing was that I made his favorite lunch for him. He didn't care about all the elaborate crafts we did or the trips we took or any of the million other things I wore myself out doing for my family. He was simply glad I made him chicken nuggets.

That gave me a lot to think about. Of course, there were things like laundry and food shopping that had to be done, but what about all the other things that took up my time and didn't involve the necessities of life? Who was I doing those things for? And did the people I was doing them for really care if I did them or not?

I looked at all the people I "worked" for in some way, figured out which things I did for them that made the biggest impression, and cut down sharply on the things that nobody seemed to care about, including me. If I wasn't sure how someone would react to me cutting out an activity, I asked. The answers were very surprising, and everyone supported my desire to cut out the busyness in my life in favor of being happier and healthier.

After several weeks, I actually found myself with a few minutes to myself nearly every day. I took up some hobbies I had given up for lack of time. I spent time talking to my husband over coffee, and

I went out to lunch with my friends. I even took a few days away for a mini-vacation to recharge my batteries.

I'd never have figured it out without my son's help. Leave it to a three-year-old to help this forty-something mom turn her life around. I am so glad he did.

~Shawn Marie Mann

The Group I Didn't Sign Up For

A bend in the road is not the end of the road...
unless you fail to make the turn.
~Author Unknown

I didn't sign up for this. These concerns, these remarks and opinions, these lengthy—very lengthy—processes, this autism—I didn't sign up for this.

This was not my plan, not even close. But this plan became reality for me in the year 2005. If I had been told, back when I first found out, that I would have to deal with all that I have dealt with, I would have said, "You're crazy! I can't and won't do it! I can't handle it!" And I would have said these things while burying my face in my arms, curled into a fetal position.

Today I would say different things. Back then I wondered how I was going to cope, how I was going to handle the days and months and years of going through the same motions over and over, addressing the same problems over and over. It might have helped me to know that "handling it" would mean different things on different days. You can't conquer autism in one day, but you can chip away at it bit by bit.

I learned about "handling it" when I became a part of the group I didn't sign up for: the group of mothers of children with special needs. I think the first time I realized that I had become a member of the group was William's first day at the Jane Justin School. It was a special school designed to meet his individual needs, so perhaps I should have been feeling good about taking a tangible, positive step. But I didn't feel like that; I was completely and utterly depressed. I had done it. I had signed up. But I still didn't like what I was signing up for. Sure, it was a highly reputable school based on the science of applied behavior analysis, which I have come to greatly appreciate and respect, but I didn't want William to be different, much less be grouped in the same category as some of those other children. Why? Because it was a reminder for me that he had special needs. Looking back, I realize that I had a lot of learning to do!

Initially, I cringed at the thought of my three-year-old going to an all-day school. It wasn't that I didn't think he would be receiving the best education possible—because I did. I was blessed to find a school so amazingly suited to his needs. No, I cringed at the feeling (rational or not) that a mother feels when she realizes, "I am not enough for my child." William needed more than I could give him, and he needed it right then—hence the term "early intervention." I had to get past my own bitterness and disappointment at the situation and put his needs ahead of my feelings.

I hated feeling like he was "missing out" on his youth. What mother wants her child to be in school—not daycare, but school—at the age of three? Probably all mothers feel something similar when their children go off to kindergarten, but this wasn't kindergarten and William was no five-year-old. But it needed to be done, for his sake. Early intervention is key.

At the end of the first day, a few mothers were waiting in line to pick up their children, and one, whose name I learned was Heidi, began a conversation with me. The first questions were the standard questions exchanged between all mothers, especially on the first day of school: "How old is your child?" "Is this your first year?" It wasn't long, though, before the questions became those that only members of this group, this club, would understand. We began talking about therapies and diagnoses, a conversation common to all parents of children with special needs, and that was when I knew for sure: whether or not I'd signed up for the group, I was in it.

Desperate to convince myself that I could handle this, I remember thinking, "This mother does it. How does she do it with such determination and strength?" I had not yet been exposed to the big shocker. Just as our conversation had reached a lull, the classroom door opened again. Two boys ran up to Heidi, grinning and showing her pictures they'd made at school that day. She had twins! Yes, twin five-year-old boys, both with autism spectrum disorders. Watching the two of them run up to her with open arms of excitement, my eyes began to fill with tears, and it was hard work not to completely lose it. There I was, feeling depressed and anxious about my one boy, and she had two dear, sweet boys in need of her constant attention. Though I had degrees and extensive training, Heidi taught me novels of information in those five minutes of conversation. As I watched her with her boys. I vowed never to let autism overwhelm my family or me to the point where we thought that we had lost the battle or that we were missing out on something better for all of us.

After getting William settled into his car seat and climbing in myself, I closed the car door that day knowing things were different. I couldn't stop thinking about that mother and her two little boys, and I cried in the car as I thought, "Nothing will ever be the same. And actually, I hope that's the case."

~Melanie Fowler

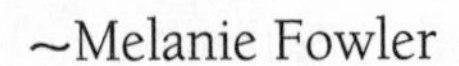

Dandelions

The pyramids will not last a moment compared with the daisy.
~D.H. Lawrence

"Hi, Mom," Kennedie says brightly as she walks up to my car after school. "Here's your flower. I think it might be the last one this year." The cool autumn breeze blows into the car as she opens the door, and I know she's probably right.

"Thank you, sweetie," I say as I tuck the already wilting dandelion behind my ear. Seeing me wear the flower brings her a smile as she launches into the detailed description of her day. Later, someone will point out that I have a wilted weed in my hair. I will smile and say, "Oh, that's just Kennedie's dandelion."

Kennedie picks a dandelion for me every day. I don't know when she started it or what made her think that I would like her to bring me a weed, but from the time they appear in the spring until their last fluffy seeds float away in the fall, she has brought me one every day for years.

I used to set them on the console of my car, and in less than an hour they would become withered stems spreading pollen that was difficult to clean up. Then one day, I decided to tuck the dandelion behind my ear, more fully accepting and displaying the gift. It still wilted in an hour and the pollen littered my hair instead of my car, but wearing it changed it from a messy weed into a bright, cheery flower.

To Kennedie, dandelions are not weeds; they are treasures. And she doesn't seem to notice or care that their beauty is short-lived. To Kennedie, my meager attempts at motherhood are not weeds either. She thinks I'm remarkable. Whenever I cook, or craft, or even type, she says, "You're just amazing with food (or words, or paint, or whatever I happen to be working with)." Soon enough, though, she will become a teenager, and she might see my gifts to her as withered weeds spreading messy pollen in her life.

The daily dandelion reminds me that my time with my children is fleeting. Just as each flower wilts quickly, their childhood will fade. One day, Kennedie will not want to bring me a dandelion or tell me every detail of her day. I can choose to relish this brief season—wear it behind my ear—or I can toss it on the console and watch it become a worthless mess.

For now, I look great in yellow.

~Marilee Herman

A Mom's Talents Run Deep

There will be so many times you feel like you failed. But in the eyes, heart, and mind of your child you are super mom.
~Stephanie Precourt

My talents never cease to amaze me. I may even be superhuman, at least that is how it appears when I compare my capabilities to those of the other beings who live in my house. My elaborate skills seem to be acknowledged and revered, or at least used, on a daily basis.

No one else in my family seems to have these genetic mutations, including my super X-ray vision. I can see practically invisible items that no one else can. My acute sense of eyesight allows me to spot crumpled paper, crayons, Hot Wheels and Legos from five feet away, which is the approximate distance from my eyes to the floor. The non-adults in my family can't see across this vast expanse, even though most of them have eyes positioned much closer to the floor.

My finely tuned eyesight can also make out dog hair on the carpet, food splattered in the microwave and droplets on the toilet seat. My world is a fuller, more colorful place because of my tremendous eyes. I wonder what the world looks like to normal people?

I've also been blessed with supersonic hearing. My ears are nearly bionic. They can detect sounds—like a running toilet, dripping faucet, breaking glass or wrestling in the living room—that are lost to average human ears. The kids living with me (my offspring) were apparently born with normal ears, because they couldn't recognize a running toilet if they were seated atop it.

Sophisticated spatial talents—I've got those, too. They come in quite handy. I feel great sympathy for the people who weren't born with groovy spatial talents like mine. These poor souls aren't able to load and unload the dishwasher, fold clothes or even line up the eighteen pairs of shoes and boots scattered by the back door. These tasks are far beyond the capabilities of people with everyday skills. It takes someone with a fair amount of genius to load the dishwasher.

As incredible as this all may seem, my list goes on. I was born with the empty gene. I possess the amazing and astounding ability to discern whether something is full or empty.

Take a box of cookies. Most of the young people in my house know how to open the box and eat the cookies, but they are unable to determine when the box is empty. They simply take the last cookie and leave the box on the shelf in the pantry. It takes years of practice to be able to lift an empty cookie box and know, without a doubt, all the cookies are gone and it is time to toss said box in the garbage. I am lucky my kids allow me the opportunity for so much practice.

As far as talents go, mine run deeper than the pile of Legos on my living room floor. For instance, I possess instantaneous laundry finesse; this enables me to assess a discarded item of clothing and immediately ascertain whether it belongs in the closet or laundry pile (but never, ever on the floor). I can exchange an empty roll of toilet paper for a full one with just two hands. Pairing mittens—not to mention socks—is practically my forte, and not only am I able to identify when a toilet needs flushing, but I can complete the task with one flick of the wrist.

You might find it hard to believe I possess skills that surpass the dreams of regular people, like my kids. God bless them. They take my talents in stride and treat me like my gifts are completely normal.

Even a superhuman super-mom wants to feel normal a couple of times a week. They are so good to me. What more could I possibly want?

~Jill Pertler

A Change in Plans

Tell me, what is it you plan to do with your one wild and precious life?
~Mary Oliver

Winter had arrived in New York State. Outside, the chill in the air cut clear to the bone, and the fallen, neglected leaves across our lawn were now covered by a thin layer of snow.

Moving slowly after spending a sleepless night with our older son, I was thankful for the warmth of our house and the comfort of our large red sofa. Curled next to me was our younger son, home sick from school. He was not feeling so comfortable. Actually, he was feeling pretty crummy.

To distract him, I started a conversation about severe weather, his favorite thing in the world. I settled into the blankets and prepared for the endless stream of fact-sharing for which this child was known—barely a pause for a breath, just fact after fact after fact.

"So, what sort of work do you think you want to do when you get older?" I asked.

"I'm going to be a storm chaser," he replied with a raspy voice. "Dad says I can start next year when I am ten."

This was news to me. And, suddenly, instead of lying in wait for the merciless stream of weather information, I realized that we were actually starting to converse, albeit, about his upcoming plans... to chase storms... somewhere.

"Dad says we can start by chasing one or two storms in the summertime," he continued. His eyes were round and bright.

"Wait. You mean your dad is going with you?" I said, feeling more than a little rejected.

I didn't make the cut for the imaginary trip to chase imaginary storms? I was hurt.

Fortunately for me, he sneezed me out of my moment of self-indulgence. My sick boy. I pulled a quilt around him in an effort to make him feel better. After all, it's my job to make him feel better. That's what I do. I'm mom. I'm the nurse, the scullery maid, the cook, laundress and caretaker of all things furry, slimy and swimming. I'm the drill sergeant, chauffeur, arbitrator and heavy hand.

In addition to all this, I'm also an autism mom.

Toilet training will perhaps be my lifetime job. And the mess in our bathrooms? Volcanic. I'm an advocate and a home schooler. Special diets, intestinal disorders, comorbid conditions—I've learned enough for a lifetime. Bowel movements. Did I imagine knowing, really, so very much about bowel movements? Really?

A mother of two children with autism, I have stopped amidst the chaos of the day and wondered: how did life bring me to this point?

"Where's my employment contract?" I asked my husband one day. There was a time I had brainpower, you know. How had my life been reduced to this?

He just laughed it off. Only, truly, I wasn't joking. I had plans for my life, after all. Yes, those plans did include children, but did they include special children? All the doctors? All the therapies? Frayed nerves? Diminished patience? Never, ever sleeping again?

That cold winter morning I sat next to my storm chaser on the sofa as he told me of his summer plans, knowing full well that he expected me to be where I always was—where I have always been during his lifetime: at home, keeping those home fires burning. In his mind, while he and his dad were out chasing the great F5 tornado, I was to be in my rightful place, taking care of our older son, the house, the pets and all that comes along with family living.

That's what I do.

I wondered, why didn't he ask me to chase storms with him this summer? I could, you know... if I wanted to...

But, the truth was, I wouldn't want to chase storms. First of all, I think you'd have to be a nut to chase storms. Our son was that kind of a nut. He loved storms. It was his passion.

My children are my passion.

It happened without my realizing, perhaps during one of the sleepless nights as I sat in my familiar spot at the top of the stairs in the hall, forcing our older son to stay in his room during the wee hours. Or, was it while cleaning the tenth, fiftieth or one hundredth toileting accident, knowing that it was a sign of a child just not able to control his body?

Was it the first time our tantruming child hit me, and I realized it was a cry for help and not an act of anger?

I'm hopeless. Somewhere along the very path that will surely drive me to insanity, I had found my life's work and my purpose.

Leaning over my sick child's head, I gave him a kiss. He had just taught me a lesson and didn't know it.

"Yuck, Mama," he said while wiping away any possible remnants of my affection. Too late. I knew I'd already made my mark.

~Amy McMunn

Pink Toilet Paper

You will find more happiness growing down than up.
~Author Unknown

My younger daughter had just turned five when I took her grocery shopping with me one October day. As we rounded the corner to the paper products aisle, her eyes lit up. Behold, there on display was the most beautiful toilet paper she had ever seen, for it was pink.

During breast cancer awareness month, the toilet paper company had turned their product pink, with a portion of each sale's proceeds helping to fund research to find a cure. And my daughter simply had to have it. She begged and pleaded with her very sweetest pretty-pleases. Of course I granted her request, explaining that it was pink to raise awareness and that some of the money we were paying was going towards finding a cure. My mother-in-law had fought and won the battle with breast cancer a few years back, as did her mother when she was even younger, so we always took every opportunity to teach our daughters about the disease, and about the legacy of strong women that preceded them.

The lesson was taught, and we continued through the store with my little girl perched in the cart, clinging to her package of pink toilet paper. I guess simply placing it among the common groceries was out of the question for a product of this magnitude. She could not contain her excitement, and rambled on and on through the aisles about how thrilled the rest of the family would be when she shared her treasure with them. On the way out, she recounted to the cashier everything she could remember about the meaning of the colored toilet paper. Her passion spread among the other customers, and several more packages went through the checkouts that morning. Later that day, amidst all the exciting news of our busy outing, the toilet paper would top her list of things to share with her dad and sister when they arrived home.

She carried the tower of toilet paper into the house herself, a great accomplishment considering the package stood as tall as she did, and dragged it upstairs to unpack while I hauled in the rest of the groceries. After I had everything put away, I went up to check on my little girl's progress with her mission.

I walked into the bathroom to find all the rolls neatly stacked in the cupboard, in the shape of a lovely castle.

"It's sure fun to have a different colored toilet paper, isn't it?" I asked, trying to match her enthusiasm.

"It's not just that, Mom..." she began in all seriousness as she ceremoniously replaced a half-used white roll on the holder with a new pink one, "Every time I use it, I will remember to pray for all those people who are fighting this cancer right now."

~Jaime Schreiner

to do list:
- Pay bills
- Get laundry
- call Mom
- Pick up kids
from birthday
at 6 p.m.
- Buy groceries

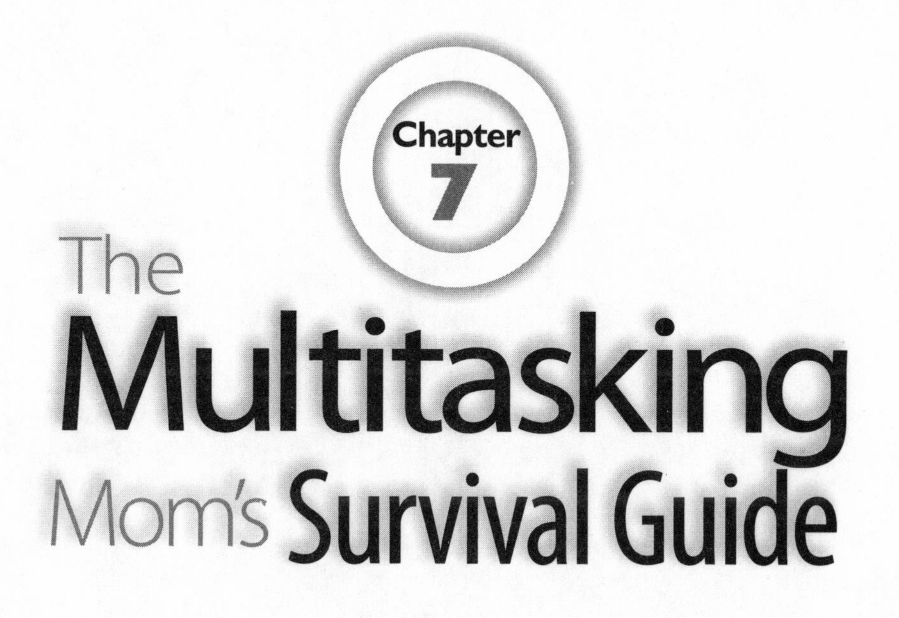

Juggling a Career

When people go to work, they shouldn't have to leave their hearts at home.

~Betty Bender

Witch Wednesday

Where we love is home, home that our feet may leave,
but not our hearts.
~Oliver Wendell Holmes, Sr.

"There's no place like home."

Unless, of course, it's Wednesday.

Wednesday is the only day of the week in which I need to catch the 7:41 a.m. train to Manhattan. If I miss that train, I'm toast. The next one comes at 9:00 a.m., and that would make me late for work.

And that would not be good.

So each week, as I start the Wednesday morning rush, my dear family loses the usual Glinda-like person they know as Mom and are subjected to the harried Wednesday Witch.

"I have to make the train on time! Don't you make me late! Get out of bed! Now!"

My typical, well-paced routine goes completely awry as I make my munchkin boy step into high gear. I've been known to pull a blanket or two off a sleeping body as I spit out the words, "Get Up!"

My threats are thrown around like fireballs through the air: "I'm walking the dogs now, and when I get back, you better be up… and dressed… my pretty!"

I fly out the door, broom-less, walk the dogs in a quick jog, my little Dorothy and Toto looking as forlorn as two oppressed flying monkeys.

When I return from the walk, I set my tornado in motion again. "Wake Up!" I shout up the stairs to the slumbering darlings in their beds, as they rub their eyes and jump out of their beds. My son makes it downstairs in time for his breakfast, his hair uncombed and disheveled like a little scarecrow.

Wednesday, I should mention, is the only day of the week I work. It's a sweet deal, I know. One I'm very thankful for.

Years ago, I worked the regular nine-to-five, five-day-a-week job, but after my son was born, I cut down my hours to be home and raise him. My husband and I decided that would be the best plan (for us) and we're happy we made that decision.

I demoted myself in consecutive steps, from five days a week, to three, to two, and finally just the one day a week. Wednesday.

Wicked Wednesday!

The problem with working one day a week is that if you're late for work, it looks extra bad. Who can't make it to work on time one day a week?

That adds a lot of pressure. The train needs to be on time, and my husband and son must be ready to go with no cause for delay. No excuses.

There is an upside, however, in being the Wednesday Witch.

It's the one day of the week I actually put on make-up, blow-dry my hair and make a conscious effort to look presentable. No fuzzy pullover sweater and pajama pants on Wednesdays! No, sir. It's dresses and tights, and sometimes the pearls even come out.

Once all is set, and the crew has had their breakfast, we're in the car. My husband first drops me off at the train station, my son off at school, and then drives himself to work.

I buy my train ticket and visit my friend, Maria, the crossing guard on the corner, for a few minutes as I listen for the ding-dong of the oncoming 7:41 train.

Once I'm seated on the train, I say a little prayer of thanksgiving, check my phone for e-mails, and take a book out of my bag to read until I arrive at Penn Station. Then it's out into the brisk wind that whips along Fifth Avenue, dodging people left and right—which reminds me that I'm away from home, the place I love the most and away from the family that means everything to me.

I'm not in Kansas anymore, and I don't like it.

I take a deep breath as I enter my building and quickly review the prior night's Mets game with the doorman. Glinda is back... for now.

Once I'm in the elevator, I again realize how much I miss being home.

The elevator doors open, and I whisper a prayer that my boss will be in a good mood. It's 9:00 a.m. Whew! I've made it on time again.

I prepare myself for the world of business. Phones ring, traders are selling, buying, holding, and there are a hundred e-mails that need responses. I'm a mixture now of Glinda and the Wednesday Witch. I need a bit of both right now.

Looking around the office, it dawns on me how differently I live my life on the other days of the week, and I long to be back home. Focusing now, I do my job as well as I can, knowing that soon it'll be 5:00 p.m. when I'll be able to click my heels and go back home. Home!

Juggling family, motherhood, and work—even if only one day a week—is challenging and exhausting. But I do it, as so many other moms do it (five, even six days a week).

I know, as they know, that it's worth it. Because home is there waiting. Home. Like an oasis!

We all just need to breathe and pray and get through the day and focus on what's important—God, our dear families and home.

Juggling it all is hard, but with a little heart, some brains, and a bit of courage, we'll all get to see that rainbow.

~Mary C. M. Phillips

Along for the Ride

You can teach a student a lesson for a day; but if you can teach him to learn by creating curiosity, he will continue the learning process as long as he lives.
~Clay P. Bedford

Volunteer, movie star, spokesperson, relief worker, life coach, dog food model, and published author—an extensive résumé for anyone. Even more impressive when one discovers that these are all jobs previously held by my now fourteen-year-old son, most before the age of six. During the fourteen years I have been a mom, I have been employed in a variety of weird and wonderful positions and pursued equally as many passions in a variety of states, countries and industries. By the time Jackson was seven he had been to Australia, Fiji, the Bahamas, Antigua, Germany, Mexico and a host of other places.

When my husband died, my son was only two and a half—so ever since then we have gone everywhere together, inseparable (in a healthy, non-coddling, creating independence way of course). As we both adjusted to our new lives, I worked hard to create income and opportunities that would provide for us and be rewarding and creative. As I embarked on each new journey, so did he. Here is a brief rundown of my endeavors and my son's role in each as I roped him into one experience after another—like Lucy and Ethel—committed to being a hands-on mom who spent quality time with her kid, while working full-time.

When I was consulting for a talent agency, they couldn't find the right child to play the only speaking kid's part so my son ended up in a television movie with Dean Cain. When I co-founded a relief organization after Hurricane Katrina, Jackson became a relief worker as well as frequent spokesperson on the local news (what is cuter than a seven-year-old asking people to donate and volunteer?). When I was teaching personal development seminars and doing training, Jackson would help greet my clients and could often be heard doling out unsolicited advice he remembered from the countless talks and sessions that he had attended. When I consulted for the Kabbalah Center, my son became our own resident Kabbalist explaining ancient philosophy to random people, including valet parking attendants, barbers and supermarket checkout staff. When I was working as a Master Trainer for Tony Robbins my son firewalked, broke boards and helped deliver food to the homeless for Thanksgiving. Most recently, in my role at Chicken Soup for the Soul, my son has written and published two stories and become the model on our Chicken Soup for the Soul pet food—puppy formula. Sometimes begrudgingly—sometimes happily—he has been a featured member of every team I have ever been a part of. He has learned to interact with adults in a mature and respectful way and has always taken these responsibilities very seriously, even if he didn't understand them and would have rather been home catching lizards or playing Xbox.

Through all of these adventures, one thing has remained constant: the love and connection that my son and I share. I have found ways to incorporate him as much as possible into my work so that we could spend more time together. I have sought out and been fortunate to have found opportunities that would allow for those special moments and ways to create memories. Today, Jackson is proud, resilient and strong. He tells the tales of his adventures with a smile on his face and a sense of accomplishment. My busy life and hectic parenting style have resulted in a child who is flexible and can handle anything life throws at him.

His childhood has certainly not been conventional, but this busy mom wouldn't have it any other way.

~Joelle Jarvis

The Mommy Bed

A good laugh and a long sleep are the best cures in the doctor's book.
~Irish Proverb

"Can we have a sleepover tonight?" my youngest son asks. Others might assume this is a request for a group of rowdy boys to take over the floor of my family room, tucked in sleeping bags with little shut-eye for the night. But in our home a sleepover means something different. It is a family tradition of closeness that my children have grown to adore. It means that all four of my children climb into Mom and Dad's bed in the early evening in lieu of the usual organized bedtime proceedings.

What we do from there varies on any given night. Sometimes we watch *American Idol* or *Wipeout* episodes, with each of us picking a favorite to cheer on. We often take turns reading a few chapters from *Harry Potter* or a favorite novel from Mommy and Daddy's childhood. We study for tomorrow's test on the life stages of the frog *Jeopardy*-style.

Sometimes we take turns around the bed sharing the best and worst parts of our day. In storms, we take flashlights and make shadow puppets on the ceiling. Some evenings my boys bring their Matchbox cars and turn my curled-up snoozing body into a mountain with my legs fashioned as treacherous mountaintop roadways. My daughter brushes my hair and applies glittery make-up to my closing eyelids. We spend the last hours of the day together in this five-by-five cozy tangle of blankets and pillows until we all fall asleep intertwined in each other.

You may think that I am a benevolent and inventive mother who decided to create this family bed tradition in order to foster a safe haven for open communication. Or that I read about it in a new-age parenting book on how to make our children feel safe and secure. The truth is, however, none of the above. It comes from this, pure and simple: I am exhausted and entirely too worn out to put my children to bed properly.

My career choice is a blessing and a curse. I am an obstetric nurse who works night shifts. This means that if I choose, I never have to miss a soccer game or a third-grade recorder concert. It also means that my blood carries as much caffeine as oxygen. It means that quite often I am on hour thirty of being awake with no sleep. At times it feels as though it is the ghost of myself that is cheering on my son from the bleachers. I am lucky to have the flexibility my occupation provides, but I am also so very tired.

I typically work my twelve-hour "graveyard shifts," as they call them, on consecutive nights. After the second night, I typically nap for a few hours if I'm lucky and then power through the rest of the day. By late afternoon, I am queasy and have a mild tremor, but alas there are mouths to feed, sports practices to attend, and arithmetic answers to be secretly Googled on my iPhone beneath the table. The dog doesn't care if I have barely slept in the past twenty-four hours when he needs to be walked. "My mom worked the night shift last night and can barely function" doesn't quite work as an excuse for school librarians, and that pop-up dinosaur book isn't going to find itself.

Years ago, when my children were younger and needed me for everything, the evening hours after a night shift felt like the worst kind of motherhood punishment. I would sit in a haze on the couch with little ones racing around me, dreading the formal bedtime routine that I knew any decent mother should be embarking on. Each child should be bathed and placed in fresh pajamas. Teeth should be flossed and brushed according to hygienist specifications. I should spend fifteen minutes reading or practicing sight words or math facts and then reviewing their prayers before sleep. (I did, after all, check off on their CCD homework that they said the "Our Father" prayer every night this week. The afterlife ramifications of fudging your child's prayer schedule can't be good.)

Then each child would need to be tucked one by one into individual beds while I cleaned up the toy clutter underfoot. I would shut off the lights and melodically call, "Goodnight, my loves." But of course that would not be goodnight. There would be calls for more water and other endless requests. "Mom, Nolan is sniffing, and it's bothering me." "Moooommmmm, do spiders sleep or crawl around your room all night?" "Mom, my left ankle is itchy!" "Mom, can you just lie down with me for five more minutes?"

The thought of the entire production was entirely too overwhelming some days. So, one night in a moment of motherly exhaustion, I announced at six o'clock, "Everyone into the Mommy bed!" They all piled in with great excitement, and we were able to spend quality time together while I was able to remain horizontal. With this, the post-night-shift sleepover in the grown-up bed commenced.

And so it is. If I have just worked the night shift, or let's be honest, am just plain wiped out, a family sleepover is in order. When Daddy comes home from work and we are still awake, he joins in the fun. If we have all drifted into slumber, he carries each sleeping child to his or her own berth. Other nights, Daddy chooses to leave everyone as is and selects the least cluttered of the little one's beds as his own.

I've read all the parenting books. A consistent bedtime routine is essential to instilling proper sleep habits in a child. I should be bathing all the germs of the outside world off my child every evening. My children should be tidying their rooms before bed and reading independently each evening before sleep. Most nights they do. I used to feel guilty on the nights I caved and let everyone pile into our bedroom. Some had brushed their teeth; some hadn't. Some are in pajamas while others remain in gym shorts and T-shirts. But what's the difference really? As the years have gone by, my guilt over these unstructured evenings has lessened.

Maybe it is because my oldest is entering the teen years and more frequently opts out of the family bed. Maybe it is because this is the time when my middle son and budding artist, Jack, seems to share all his creative ideas with me. Maybe it is because my youngest son, Nolan, once asked a friend, "What do you do at your family sleepovers?" When the child seemed confused by the question, Nolan turned to me and proclaimed in hushed horror, "I don't think they have sleepovers! Can you believe that? That's the best night of the week!" Or maybe it is because now that I am a mother of a little girl, I'm actually proud to teach her that some days you do not need to do it all.

There is one thing of which I am sure. When my children are grown, they will probably not remember if I cooked a perfectly nutritious meal every night, or if I followed the bedtime rules created by modern-day parenting experts. But I am sure that they will remember the nights they fell asleep in the crook of my arm whispering their secrets to me and sharing silly stories with each other. Sometimes being too perfect of a parent means missing out on the moments when life's magic mysteriously appears. Our children will most likely forget the routines, but remember the love.

I can't wait for our family sleepover tonight. I'm exhausted from work and can't wait to lie down. But mostly I'm looking forward to the moment when we finish reading the book we've been working on, *The Wizard of Oz*, and we all fall asleep together to the words "There's no place like home."

~Mary Hickey

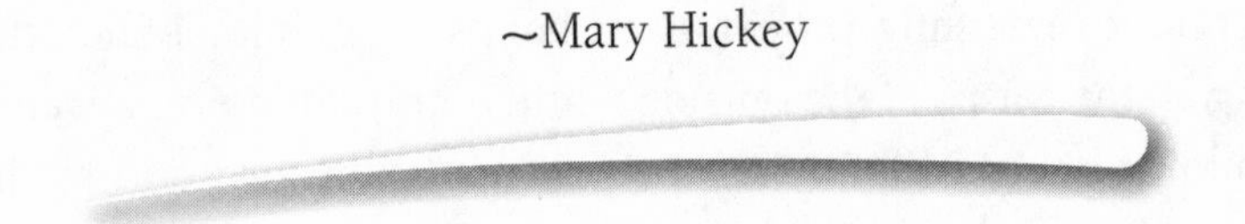

Keeping the Plates Spinning

Help one person at a time, and always start with the person nearest you.
~Mother Teresa

"Do I have everything?" asks my daughter, Betsy, as she hands me the baby she just nursed and adjusts the princess backpack on her first-grader's shoulders. She grabs her car keys, lunch bag, laptop, and breast pump, and trudges to her minivan. After she takes Amy to school, she will work a long day as an aerospace engineer, supervising fifteen scientists working on a project deadline. As I wave to her, I think about the many demands on this multitasking mom.

This morning before dawn, Betsy shared her frustrations as she sat in the kitchen in her nightgown, bleary-eyed and yawning, while I made blueberry pancakes and packed lunches.

"Mom, thank heavens you agreed to fly here to help me! I had another sleepless night and got up several times to nurse Anna. With her fever, she was really fussing. I couldn't get back to sleep so I ended up handling a ton of e-mails from work. With Matt on a business trip to China, the baby too sick for daycare, the plumber coming sometime today, and Amy needing a 'parent' for her field trip this week, how could I handle this on my own? I can answer that… I couldn't!"

As I continue working in the kitchen, I notice Betsy has already put ham and navy beans in the Crock-Pot and programmed the bread machine to begin baking. She'll have dinner ready when she returns home from work after dark. I compliment her on her organization and stamina and ask how she manages everything.

"I feel I have a long line of plates spinning on sticks, and no matter how I rush to keep them from falling, there are always some that begin to wobble."

Later, Betsy grabs a minute to call me from work, where she's working through lunch and pumping her breast milk. She shares what just happened.

"I couldn't believe it! I have this big sign on my office door that says 'Do Not Enter' so I can have privacy while I pump. A guy I work with doesn't bother to read it and walks in on me while I'm sitting there without a bra. We both die of embarrassment."

I empathize with my daughter as she juggles her career and motherhood. She is sleep-deprived, has no time for herself, and can't remember the last time she had a date with her husband.

Betsy needs my support and is grateful I'm her helper, not a guest. I handle the shopping, meals, baths, story time, cleaning, laundry, maintenance calls, school obligations, babysitting and more.

Sometimes, it takes two multitasking moms to keep all those plates spinning.

~Miriam Hill

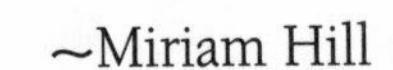

Why I'll Never Be Volunteer of the Month

Enough is as good as a feast.
~English Proverb

I sat in our favorite Florida restaurant on the beach with my husband, Kedron, and our two elementary-school-aged children. The warm January breeze drifted through the door each time it opened, refreshing my tired soul. We had pulled the kids out of school and left the northern cold and our busy schedules behind for one week. I was looking forward to visiting family and friends, and savoring lots of grouper sandwiches.

A week prior, my first book had been released. In a few days, I would run the Disney World full marathon. Needless to say, it had been a busy year. As I savored my fish sandwich, I relished the feeling of being wholly present—my body and mind fully connected to my family. There were no writing deadlines hanging over my head, no training runs that I had to mentally gear up for. Finally, I could just be with my family and not have fear niggling in the back of my mind that I should be doing something else.

A few months before our Florida vacation, my daughter, Ilana, had pointed to a picture of a mom in her school newsletter. "Why can't you win the award for volunteer of the month at my school?" she asked.

I swallowed the foul taste of unnecessary guilt. I volunteer at the school once a week, and I know all the students by name in my children's classrooms. But the women who earn recognition in the newsletter give more than a couple of hours per week. They head up carnivals and give hundreds of hours a month. Our schools are so blessed to have moms who can do that. But I will never be that mom, at least not while I'm writing books and running marathons.

"Honey, those moms give a lot of time to the school, and I am so glad that they do. They help our schools so much," I replied. "But even though I don't go to an office to work, my writing is a job. It's something I believe I am supposed to do and that it helps other people. I do what I can for the school and your classroom, but I can't volunteer like the moms in the newsletter do and still write books."

Ilana shrugged her shoulders and replied, "I understand." She bounced off to go play, as doubt crept into my mind. Did she really understand? Was I giving the kids and my husband enough attention? Was the sacrifice of time worth it to pursue my dreams or was I giving up too much? Even though Kedron assured me that I was keeping a healthy balance, I still wondered if years down the road my kids would gripe to a therapist about how their mom was never there for them and always seemed distracted. Some days, I wished for the defined boundaries of an office and regular working hours.

It was a continual tug of war to keep the balance and not let one area of my life overpower the others. I'd get up early, run a few miles, pack lunches, help at school, write, make dinner, help with homework, write some more, and repeat the cycle the next day.

I found I was always writing—little snippets here and there while the kids munched on PB&Js or between loads of laundry. If I didn't have paper or my computer handy, the words replayed in my mind until I could write them down.

Running got me up early, and I was often home and showered before anyone else was awake. But as the runs got longer on the weekends, I left a sleeping house on Saturday mornings and came home to a day in full motion. Was it okay? Was it worth it? Was I missing too much?

Then she said it. Right there in the midst of our vacation lunch of grouper sandwiches on the beach, between a book release and a marathon, Ilana said, "It's so cool to have a mom who writes books and runs marathons."

Then I knew all that multitasking was okay. So was the forgotten homework, the missed field trips, lunches that weren't creative, or the fact that I will never be volunteer of the month. It was going to be okay.

I was showing my kids the way to work hard and follow their own dreams one day, even in the midst of raising a family. They were learning that sometimes you sacrifice things, like the award for volunteer of the month, in order to reach for different goals. But what matters most—following your passions, being there for your family, celebrating together—those all can be balanced in a way that everyone wins. No matter what, we can support each other and be together, even if Mama is occasionally distracted and writing in her head.

My family cheered me down the finish line at the marathon, and a couple of weeks later we hosted a successful book release party. Each event was a family celebration. My name might have been on the book cover and the finisher's medal hung around my neck, but we had persevered through the past year as a family. I couldn't have done it without their support and understanding.

~Amelia Rhodes

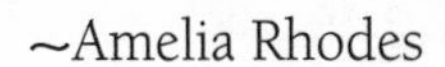

Secret Weapon of a Sleepy Working Mom

People who say they sleep like a baby usually don't have one.
~Leo J. Burke

My husband and I had been sleeping champions. You know how some people love bacon, or traveling, or pets? That's how we loved sleep. In our pre-kid years, we were known to sleep until noon on weekends. Our bed was an oasis of memory foam, the softest cotton sheets, a white noise machine nearby, and a cozy down comforter for cold nights.

Sleep. Was. Everything.

So, of course, when we began to discuss becoming parents, we reassured each other constantly.

It'll just be hard those first few months.

We'll tag team.

Most babies sleep through the night after four to six months.

It'll be fine!

And then Baby Insomniac arrived—beautiful, bright-eyed, and not at all interested in sleep at any point, day or night.

At first, the pediatrician simply advised us that our infant's days and nights were mixed up. He'd adjust soon. But when the mix-up was still going on at twelve months, then twenty-four months—yet there was no sign of a medical problem or bad sleep "habit"—the doctor eventually just shook his head and told us that perhaps our son was one of those rare babies who didn't need as much sleep as "normal" babies. It happens, he said.

Yep, we were proud parents of a Baby Einstein, another person from history who notoriously didn't need sleep. But here's the thing: I really don't think Einstein's mother held down a fifty-plus-hours-a-week job at a fast-paced marketing agency. Because it wasn't working out so well for me.

Our son was about six months old when I fell asleep for the first time in a client meeting. Thankfully, it was a teleconference, so the client didn't actually see me nod off, and I had coworkers with me in the meeting who took over as I descended into sandman-land, virtually in mid-sentence. The only lasting impact was the coworkers' chiding that continued for a week or so.

The next incident occurred on a business flight. It was a fairly short flight, and I was heading straight to a meeting once the plane landed. I had papers out on my lap, reviewing things in preparation for the meeting, when I feel into a deep sleep. The passenger next to me woke me up as everyone else was disembarking. My mouth was hanging open, I had an imprint of the seat in front of me on my forehead, confidential papers were scattered everywhere, and I basically had no idea where I was. Fun times.

In the coming months, I fell asleep in the middle of typing an e-mail. I fell asleep leaning against the office copier. (That hum, that warmth!) I yawned while the president of the company announced I'd gotten a raise.

But the worst incident happened during an in-person client meeting, one of those important meetings when a potential client is deciding whether or not to sign on with the agency—potentially leading to a huge chunk of change for my company. I was slated as the third person to speak during the presentation. But Baby Einstein hadn't slept even an hour the night before, and as was often the case, the baby in question did not want Daddy—only Mama. Even with a triple shot of espresso, I was still in a bit of a daze.

As clients droned on about their needs for attentive account services, I willed my eyes to stay open. As our senior vice president vowed to provide a new energy to the client's communications, I pinched my leg under the table to keep from dozing off. I jotted down incoherent notes, trying to stay focused. I swallowed yawns again and again, trying to hide it all with a mute smile.

But when it was my turn to speak, I'm not going to lie. There was drool.

I wasn't even embarrassed—until I woke up to a strong shoulder nudging and a table full of client representatives looking at me in horror. At that point, it was quite possibly one of the most embarrassing moments of my career.

Colleagues were not amused. And we didn't get the account.

After that, I knew a solution was needed, and stat. And since we could not in any way afford a night nanny, and drugging the kid was frowned upon, I had to think outside the box. Or outside the bed, so to speak.

My solution? During lunch, while other coworkers went to the gym, for a walk, or to the neighborhood restaurants for a quick meal, I headed away from the phone and e-mail and office chatter. And I slept. In my car.

That's right. With an alarm set on my phone, I allowed myself to take a daily power nap in the reclined driver's seat of a Dodge Durango, with no one to hear me snore, for forty-five minutes to an hour.

It was bliss. Short, sweet, close-my-eyes-and-check-out bliss.

It wasn't a pretty solution—people often stared at me in the parking lot and several times someone knocked on my window to make sure I was indeed alive. And once I slept through my alarm.

But it was just enough to save my job and my sanity—until my son finally slept through the night at age three.

~Kathy Lynn Harris

Beat the Clock

When you hurry, you're more apt to make mistakes.
~John Wooden

When my sons were younger, my life as a working mother could be summed up in three words: beat the clock. I had my whole life timed and knew exactly how many minutes it took to complete every task. Mornings were the most crucial, with no room for error. I knew the exact minute my sons needed to get up, finish breakfast, get dressed, brush their teeth and be at the bus stop. I was constantly checking the clock and keeping to our time schedule.

Once the kids were on the bus, a wave of relief washed over me for a few quick moments and then I rushed off to work. I used the five-minute drive to go through the mental list in my head of all the tasks I needed to complete for my job. Some days it seemed like my car was on auto drive because I didn't even notice I was driving.

Summer was always an adjustment. Instead of taking the kids to the bus stop, I had to drive them to summer camp. Books, homework and school planners were replaced with swimming trunks, towels and goggles. I would drop them off, sign them in, tell them to be good, get in my car and try to make it to work on time.

One morning, I pulled into the parking lot at my job with my mind racing. I had done my normal efficient job of mentally preparing for work and had reviewed the list of people I needed to call, paperwork that needed handling and evaluations that had to be completed. I had prioritized what needed to be done in case I didn't have time to complete everything. My system was working. I was in a multitasking mode!

My thoughts were interrupted by a familiar voice in the back of the car.

"Mom, aren't you going to take us to camp?" my oldest son asked.

I turned quickly to the back seat of my car and saw my two sons staring at me, looking confused.

"Oops! I guess I forgot to drop you guys off," I responded with an embarrassed laugh as I took off down the road.

~Denise Seagren-Peterson

Blurred Lines

Any mother could perform the jobs of several air traffic controllers with ease.
~Lisa Alther

I work two jobs: the first is a Sales Executive role with a large North American company. My other job is CEO of Two Young Kids.

To be honest, I look forward to the days that I am going to the office. I know that no matter how busy things at work may be, I will find the time to drink my coffee while it is still hot. I can also be certain that I will be able to take a lunch break without someone asking me to paint their toenails or read them a book.

I do have it pretty good, though. Two years ago, as my maternity leave was coming to an end after the birth of my second child, my husband and I dealt with the difficult decision of whether I should go back to work or quit my job and stay home with the kids full-time. On one hand, I had spent four years in university, earned a business degree, and spent nearly ten years with the same company working my way up the corporate ladder. I didn't want to throw all of that hard work away. At the same time, though, I love my kids, and I didn't want to miss out on a single milestone or on watching my kids grow up in these early formative years.

So being in sales, I made a pitch to my boss asking to go part-time and work only three days per week. I promised I would remain productive and that I would stay connected to the office so that even on my days off, my clients and coworkers would always be able to get a hold of me. Thankfully, I made the sale and thus began the balancing act of being a working mom of two young kids.

During the workweek on my days at home with my kids, there are often important work phone calls and e-mails that I need to respond to urgently. Thankfully, my kids understand when I tell them, "Mommy has to make a phone call for work." When I turn on the Disney Channel or sit them down with a bowl of fish crackers, they know they are not to come and interrupt my conversation. There are times, however, when my little ones are not so understanding.

The other day, for example. My daughter, Priya, was busy working on a craft and my son, Keegan, was in his bedroom intently lining up his Hot Wheels cars. I thought this would be a good time to return a quick phone call to one of my coworkers about a potential new client.

Unfortunately, I was completely wrong about my timing. Three minutes into my phone conversation, down the hallway and through the bathroom door, came a piercing yell from my (extremely) loud three-year-old son.

"Mommy! I'm done going poop. Come wipe my bum!" I tried to ignore Keegan for a minute and quickly wrap up my phone call, but my son did not like to be kept waiting. Again he hollered, "Mommy! I'm ready for you to clean my bum! Come to the bathroom!"

I couldn't help but laugh as I stopped my colleague mid-sentence. "Sorry, John, but can you hold please? I need to wipe my son's bum."

I know I am lucky to be able to enjoy the best of both worlds. I can continue to pursue my career while still sharing in my children's special (and not-so-special) moments. There are times when the line between my two jobs will get blurred. But you know what? I wouldn't have it any other way.

~Ritu Shannon

Creative Thinking

If you don't like something change it; if you can't change it,
change the way you think about it.
~Mary Engelbreit

I was raised to believe that not only could I have it all, but I could do it all too. So when my first son came along while I was working full-time, I saw it as a challenge... until I was losing sleep at an alarming rate, falling asleep at my desk, and had zero energy. After eleven months of barely keeping up, I decided to call it quits—and traded in my full-time job to be a full-time mom. I made a living by watching friends' and neighbors' little ones while they continued to work nine to five. We added two more children to our growing family, and I began moonlighting as a copywriter. I had this multitasking thing down pat—I really could do it all!

Then, suddenly, I found myself going through a divorce and facing life as a single parent. It was the ultimate in multitasking. And this time, I simply had no choice. I began pounding the pavement to find a full-time job that would pay the mounting bills.

I did find a job, but working downtown from 8:30–5:30 five days a week did not make for a happy home. Every day for a year, my one-year-old daughter was the first to be dropped off at daycare in the morning and the last to be picked up, just as the doors were closing at 6:00 p.m. I was exhausted, mentally and physically. I tried to keep up with my freelance writing projects, but I just couldn't swing it, and had to tell my clients I was taking a break to spend more time with my kids. I realized that everything was suffering—my kids didn't eat dinner until 7:00 p.m., we were up late every night fighting over homework, and no one got a good night's sleep. The kids were tired and cranky. And I was never home. At work, my boss—and clients—weren't getting the best of me either because I was forever worrying about my kids.

The turning point came one weeknight after dinner. My two boys (nine and seven, at the time) were arguing over which television show to watch. One of them had grabbed the remote and the other was on top of him trying to take it away. Normally, I'd walk away, or pull one off the other and calmly turn off the TV until they cooled off. But I was tired, my toddler had started to cry, and I couldn't handle it. They ignored my pleas and continued throwing punches at each other, and I lost it. I reached between them, grabbed the remote control and threw it behind me... right into the flat-screen TV. The breaking of glass brought the room to a screeching halt. "This is your fault!" I yelled at both of them. My accusation was met with silence. And tears.

Later that night, I sat on my bathroom floor and cried. My kids were doing poorly in school. I was forgetting to sign papers, pack lunches and thaw food for dinners. I was out of shape, exhausted and had no patience with my three kids. They needed me. What was I going to do? Something had to give. My two-year-old daughter found me in the bathroom and put her chubby, little arms around my neck. "Is okay, Mama," she said, tucking her head into my shoulder.

"Thanks, baby," I whispered. "Mama just doesn't know what to do right now."

Just as I'd done with her many times, she reached up and brushed the hair out of my eyes with her little hand. "You can do it, Mama." She smiled at me.

Hearing her say to me the same words I always said to her made me cry harder. It also got me thinking. Maybe I was going about it wrong. It was true that I couldn't do it. Not the way I had been. But what if I changed the model? What if I could work full-time and be the parent I really wanted to be, the one my kids needed? I knew I was good at my job. I was just not successful now because the stress was consuming me.

It was 2008, and the recession had impacted businesses far and wide. Our small agency was not immune. My boss was considering cutting back hours—having us work four-day weeks, rather than five. Having a full day off during the week might be nice for me, but it wouldn't afford me any more time with my kids. But what if I took those eight hours and spread them over the week instead? If I could leave two hours earlier every day and work late on Wednesdays—when the kids' dad picked them up—I'd have more time to spend with them. I wouldn't have to pay for after-school care, and I'd be able to get dinner on the table and homework started at a decent hour.

My boss agreed to give it a trial run, and it worked. After one year, I was able to begin working from home a few days a week, and return to freelancing to supplement my income. And last year, I was able to quit my job and work full-time from home as a freelance writer and consultant. Most importantly, all three kids are doing well in school, and I'm here when they need me, which is all I wanted in the first place. As it turns out, my little girl was right. I could do it. I just needed to step back, focus on the problem and employ a little creative thinking. Sometimes the answer lies not in changing your actions, but changing the way you see the problem. At one of my lowest points, my little girl reminded me that I still could, in fact, have it all.

~Beth M. Wood

Due Dates

One half of knowing what you want is knowing what you must give up before you get it.
~Sidney Howard

It was unlike my dad to call in the middle of a Thursday afternoon. So, even though I was knee-deep in final revisions of two books and diligently working in the dead quiet of the library, I answered.

"Hi," Dad said. "I was calling to ask if you had seen the news today."

"No…" My voice trailed off. Today happened to be one of my two workdays that week. My two-year-old son was in daycare, and in his absence I was doggedly trying to get some writing done.

Of course I assumed the worst. An earthquake? A bomb exploding in a school? Why else would he be bringing up the news?

"Well," he said carefully, "have you heard the name Hilary Rosen?"

I hadn't. But the next name he tossed out, Ann Romney, I knew. Who didn't? She was the wife of a GOP presidential candidate, and was garnering a lot of attention in the heat of the country's primaries.

Dad told me about how Rosen, a Democratic strategist, had criticized Romney's decision to stay at home to raise five boys. Rosen's comment that Romney had "never worked a day in her life" had set off a nationwide firestorm.

"I thought of you," Dad said quietly. And immediately, I knew why.

Ever since I had been swept into motherhood two years before, the perpetual challenge had rattled me: How to completely throw yourself into the hard work of being a mother without losing the rest of your identity? The paradox grinded at me day in and day out; that motherhood can be so dull yet so lively; that it can feel like no work at all and the hardest work of your life. The struggle intensified now that I was pregnant with our second child and trying to finish not one, but two books.

Every day, I asked myself if I was doing the right thing, being a stay-at-home mom and writer. Not working full-time.

Rosen's comment laid bare the question that so fiercely gripped me.

It had taken me a long time to fully believe in and feel validated by being a mom. The million-and-one decisions that come and go, the moment-by-moment living that being with kids requires, the crucial importance of maintaining confidence day in and day out. Yes, motherhood is hard work. It is legitimate work. Only now, after months of struggle over how motherhood fit into my life, did I really believe that.

My two books progressed along with my pregnancy. The first book, a memoir about growing up as an only child in rural Wyoming, was being pushed along by the publisher and the publication date was looming. I had pitched that book for three years to various publishers and the "yes" had come three days before I got the plus sign on a pregnancy test.

The second book, a project I had begun while my memoir worked its way through the query mill, was a history of my family's small business. It was to be a venture in self-publishing. I wanted to learn the ropes of the trade to be better equipped as a writer during a particularly tumultuous time in the publishing industry. By pure and wild coincidence, both books were wrapping up at the same time, and my baby's due date was fast approaching.

In the chaos and anxiety and self-doubt that ensued, I clung to my mom's persistent wisdom. "How do you eat an elephant?" she'd say. "One bite at a time."

Three weeks before my baby was due, I opened my journal in a desperate grope for comfort. The fear of making life work as both mother and writer was so real I felt I might throw up.

It's all there, I wrote. The haze. The forgetfulness. The failure to finish one simple task before beginning another. The anxiety and million what-ifs.

What if I fail my kids? What if the laundry piles up because I can't find time to do it? What if I fail to write every day? What if, for a while, I do nothing but focus on being a mom?

What if?

My baby came right on time and with him, a flurry of sleep-deprived days and dogged prayers. The laundry piled up. The writing slowed. The publication date loomed.

All because I was doing the hardest and most important work of all, being a mom.

And in those moments of rocking my baby, feeding him while the rest of the world slept, changing his diaper for the hundredth time, I realized: the world wasn't going anywhere. Life comes in seasons, and there is a season for everything.

The writer Hope Edelman, at a 2012 Association of Writers & Writing Programs Conference panel, shared a list of what she can and can't do as both mother and writer. She is really good at budgeting time, she said, and has experienced a whole range of emotions that have enhanced her writing. But, in her own words, she can't "spend three months at a writer's colony… stay at literary events past 9:15 on a weeknight… shower every day… be a foreign correspondent."

My books are out now. I can't promote them with the same zest and vigor I could if writing were my sole focus. I can't tackle my list of marketing ideas fast enough. I can't always write at the very moment the muse strikes.

But I can snatch quiet moments as they come. I can make an important phone call while I'm nursing, jot down an essay idea on the back of a receipt in the daycare parking lot, confirm a book sale via e-mail while my older son catches five more minutes of TV. I can make two solid, blessed hours of work pass in the blink of an eye.

And, I can garner loads of heartfelt material from the range of emotions that come with being a mom. Believe me, I have stories to tell.

In my journal, on a day marked "Nov. 2," is a single line: "I did all the important stuff today."

Days and weeks later, I don't remember what that "important stuff" was. But I know it was good work, the best work, work that mattered.

I can't not be a mom. I can't not be a writer. Only through the dogged pursuits of both have I learned that my work is a daily balancing act, focusing on two fierce loves at once. Give up one for the other, and I am no longer a whole person. I am a better mom because I still make time to write and feed that fire. I am a better writer because I am living the daily challenges and joys of motherhood. I hold two worlds in the palm of my hand.

I trust that, as writer and as mom, I am right where I need to be. My books are out, and people are reading them. My boys are happy and healthy and packed with the pulsating energy of childhood.

Two loves. One life.

Full-time work? You bet.

~Kate Meadows

A Difficult Choice

It's not hard to make decisions when you know what your values are.
~Roy Disney

As a freelance writer and a mom, I often feel like I am the juggler or plate-spinner in an elaborate stage production. Everyone is watching and if I drop something, they will all shake their heads and sigh. I take comfort knowing that other moms and dads feel this way too, but that does little for my confidence when I am faced with a challenge. A few years ago, I had a great opportunity come my way but it presented me with a difficult decision.

My editor at the local newspaper sent me a press release about a well-known author who would be in the area and asked me to cover the story. The author would be giving a lecture and had room for a limited number of press interviews beforehand. I sent an e-mail to the PR person and got one of the interviews, with Judy Blume. Judy Blume! Now that is a writer with confidence.

Needless to say, I was nervous. At the time, I was also taking an adult education class at the local college on writing. The lesson for the week was interviews and having never done one in person before, I felt like this opportunity was also a test. It did not help that my instructor was also my editor at the newspaper. She had given us lots of practical tips and I had thoroughly researched my subject, so as I wrote out my interview questions, I felt a surge of confidence.

The next week was surprisingly chaotic. First, my kindergartener brought home a note from school that announced the school program would be the same night—and time—as my interview. Not good. How could I skip my child's program? But I had already made a commitment. Flaking would be rude, not to mention nix my news story. Then I received an e-mail from the PR person. She had a few too many interviews and could I possibly meet earlier in the day? Somehow I was saved. I could complete the interview in the afternoon with plenty of time to go to my son's program. I tried to conceal my enthusiasm in my reply.

Foolishly, I told my son the story of my near-tragedy. His wide-eyed reaction to the possibility made his anxiety unmistakable. I assured him that I would be in attendance. But the next day I received another e-mail from the PR person. There were too many interviews scheduled and mine had to be cut. I was still welcome to come to the lecture and ask questions then. I was back at square one: lecture or school program?

The stage was set and my curtain call had come. I was going to drop one of those stupid spinning plates, but at least I had a choice. I e-mailed my editor and explained the situation. She said she would do the same in my place.

That night, as the curtains came up on the stage, the kindergarten classes sang "Watch Me Grow." I watched a sleepy little five-year-old yawning on his riser and scanning the audience for familiar faces. I knew I had made the right choice.

~Keri Houchin

Hard Shoes to Fill

If evolution really works, how come mothers only have two hands?
~Milton Berle

"Good morning, Craig," I said to my boss as I entered the small real estate appraisal office where I worked. It was a little after nine o'clock in the morning but my boss was flexible with my start time. He knew I liked to be the one to drop off my kids at school in the mornings.

"Good morning," he said. He grinned, looking suspiciously like the proverbial cat that swallowed the canary.

"So, did you forget something this morning?" Craig asked, the grin never leaving his face.

I looked myself over—all necessary body parts were covered. I had my purse, my keys. Okay, so I wasn't wearing make-up, but that wasn't anything new. Mornings were too hectic for a luxury like make-up!

"No," I said, "I don't think so." He could hardly contain himself.

"Well, your son's school called," he said. That's never a good way to start a conversation but I assumed it wasn't anything serious or he wouldn't be smiling so much.

"Yes?"

"Apparently you sent Josh to school without his shoes!" Craig could no longer hold it in and he started laughing. "How did you not notice he wasn't wearing shoes?"

I had no answer.

"I'll be back," I said, walking back through the door without even stopping at my desk. I headed to my car and began retracing my way back to Josh's school.

In my defense, my son wasn't completely shoeless. He had socks on… and flip- flops. Not exactly barefoot, but not exactly a fashion statement either. He was so embarrassed he refused to go to class and insisted on waiting in the office until I got there with shoes.

"Hey, buddy," I said, handing Josh his sneakers. "What happened?"

"I don't know, Mom. I meant to put on my shoes, but I guess I forgot. I'm sorry." I gave him a hug, sent him on his way, and began the thirty-minute trek back to work. I wondered—how was it that I sent my son to school in socks and flip-flops? What can I say? Life was hectic, shoes were forgotten and this mother didn't notice.

I considered myself a multitasking master; I had to be as this was a very busy season of life. It was a season filled with the many activities of two school-aged children—school projects and sports, social events and scouts, among other things. I was grateful for a job that allowed me the flexibility to take them to school and to be there for after-school activities. It wasn't a challenging job, but I was in college part-time to finish my bachelor's degree and that provided all the challenge I could handle. Therefore, doing two things at once became second nature during this time of my life.

Did you know that Chuck E. Cheese's, the children's pizza and game parlor, is a great place to pay your bills? After the pizza and soda were ordered and the tokens bought, I would find a nice booth to set up shop. Notice I didn't say a quiet booth. If I did, you would think this was a fairy tale. Then I would spread out my equipment—pens, checkbook, bills, calculator and tokens. Locking my fingers together, I would stretch them back till I heard them crack and then off to work. Pay a bill, dole out some tokens. Pay another bill, dole out more tokens. When the last token was gone and the final envelope stamped, we said goodbye to Chuck E. Cheese's and headed home. I felt a certain amount of satisfaction for getting my bills done but I also felt a good deal poorer.

While most college students would find a quiet table at the library to study, I found that the bleachers at Little League baseball games work just as well. Thankfully, baseball is a slow-paced sport—I might never have passed my college courses if my son had played soccer. But with baseball you have a lot of down time, time spent waiting for your little player to get up to bat or make a play. While those base hits, slides home and outs are precious moments, so were the minutes squirreled away during the down time. I never went to a game without my textbooks. It was such a regular sight that the other parents would often ask, "So, what class are you taking now?"

Yes, multitasking served me well, but it was not without its glitches. This state of busyness and juggling was bound to have mishaps—like the time I went to my first college statistics class and forgot my calculator. Another student graciously offered to let me borrow her extra calculator, but considering you needed a PhD to know how to use it, it didn't help me much.

But the agony of defeat was balanced out by the thrill of victory, like the time I received an honorable mention for a personal essay writing contest sponsored by the college. Sure, I was the oldest student at the awards ceremony, and the only one who brought her children. But there was nothing like sharing that special moment with my kids and seeing their pride when I was handed my winnings—a large volume of *Roget's Thesaurus*. The size of the tome impressed my children and they figured I must have done something great to get a book that big.

I wish I could say that the day Joshua forgot his shoes was our last shoe escapade, but sadly it wasn't. After I finished my college degree I took a corporate job. I still wanted to have the ability to be there for my kids' after-school activities, so I chose a job that allowed me to start at six in the morning. The worst thing about six in the morning is not that it is so early, though that was not pleasant, but that it is still very dark. I often dressed in the dark so I wouldn't wake my sleeping husband. One day while at work I noticed that I was walking with a limp. As I looked at my shoes I realized that I had grabbed two different shoes with different sized heels. Unfortunately, I had no one to call to bail me out, and embarrassed or not, I had to limp through the day.

My kids are grown now but I learned a lot during that season of life. I learned to be an accomplished multitasker. I learned to accept less than perfect outcomes. I learned to laugh at the mishaps that were bound to happen. And I learned to always check your shoes, and those of your children, before you leave the house.

~Lynne Leite

to do list:
- Pay bills
- Get laundry
- call Mom
- Pick up kids
from birthday
at 6 p.m.
- Buy groceries

Feeling Guilty

Guilt is universal.

~Tennessee Williams

Multitasking 101 for Germophobic Moms

That which does not kill us makes us stronger.
~Friedrich Nietzsche

In hindsight, I was a real germophobe as a first-time mom. When my first child, Lindsey, was born, I sterilized everything. If she dropped her pacifier for a half-second, I cleaned it. Heaven forbid if the dog so much as sniffed at her pacifier from ten feet away. Forget about sterilizing it. I'd just throw the pacifier away. I was that paranoid.

In fact, I was even more obsessive about dog germs than Lucy from the *Peanuts* comic strip. "Get some hot water! Get some disinfectant!" Unlike Lucy, I sterilized even theoretical dog germs with hot water and disinfectant, not just actual dog germs that came from Fido licking my baby's face.

Lindsey didn't get into situations that involved nasty germs anyway. She was a typical little girl—mostly interested in her stuffed animals, finger painting, and arts and crafts—not dirt, bugs, worms, grime, and slime—the things that boys like.

As you might guess, by the time our second child Cory, a boy, came along three years later, I had trouble keeping up with my own impossible standards of cleanliness.

You know how it goes. Regular math doesn't apply when it comes to counting your children. One plus one actually equals four children—or, at least, it feels like four times the work—when you're as anal-retentive as I was.

It's the same with the picture-taking. You take a million photos of child #1, but when you have #2, you have less time and energy. You just can't give #2 the same amount of attention as you gave #1.

I don't even want to think about what it's like when you have more children than two. It's probably impossible to dote on them all equally. There isn't enough time in the day!

Sorry to digress. Getting back to my multitasking/germ story...

Something big happened that changed me forever when Cory was about ten months old. I still get pale and sweaty when I think about what he did.

Normally, if I had chores to do and had to multitask in the kitchen, I let Cory roam free on the floor while I worked. I figured it was safe since the kitchen floor was squeaky clean and the cabinet doors were safety-latched. Boy, I was wrong about our resourceful little scamp. He found trouble where I thought none existed.

The event in question happened while I was loading the dishwasher. Because I was exhausted, I apparently zoned out for a few minutes as I worked. I don't remember where my mind went, but I was probably daydreaming about what it would be like to actually get some sleep. When I snapped out of it, my heart nearly stopped in fear. I realized my baby was gone. "Oh, no! Where's Cory?" I panicked.

Cory must have sensed my inattention during that zone-out time. It was as if he had radar and knew exactly when to make his move for mischief.

Where was my sneaky little ninja? He was at the doggie door that led to the back yard, and he was doing something indescribably icky—especially from the perspective of an anal-retentive, germophobic mom.

Our doggie door was the clear vinyl kind. Or, at least, it started out clear. By this time, it was a few years old, and it was filthy—literally impossible to see through. It was more like a medium brown color with areas of darker brown and khaki green. There were some yellow splotches on it, too, and some bumpy things of unknown origin. I think one of the bumps might have been a fly that was petrified in dog snot. The point is that it was nasty.

If you're a mom, maybe you can guess what my ten-month-old boy was doing at the doggie door. Yes, I'm embarrassed to admit it because I should have done a better job watching him (not to mention I should have at some point cleaned the doggie door), but... my little Cory was teething on the nasty, repulsive, disgusting doggie door!

More accurately, he was gnawing away at the bottom corner of the doggie door like there was no tomorrow. I imagine he did it to soothe his aching gums. Judging from the way he smacked his lips, it appealed to his taste buds, too. I imagine it tasted tangy. Maybe salty-sweet with a little crunch, too, from the bumpy things.

After seeing the large area he managed to clean, I suppose more time passed than I realized before I caught him. A solid six square inches of doggie door were now squeaky clean. The part he cleaned was the only part of that flap that was see-through. I mean it was crystal clear. It was even cleaner than the day we first installed it.

After the ringing in my ears cleared up and my heart rate and blood pressure started returning to normal, I realized that my baby had just been inoculated with every slimy germ known to mankind—but he was still alive (so far).

The point is there was nothing I could do about it at that point. The germs were in his system. It was a done deal.

That infamous day marked the beginning of my new philosophy about germs. From then on, I realized, "What doesn't kill him can only make him stronger." My new favorite saying became, "Well, I guess that's why God gave Cory stomach acid."

Interestingly, when I showed my now thirteen-year-old son the rough draft of this story, he had a different perspective from my own. Whereas I claim to have multitasked by doing housework while I watched him, he claims that he was actually the one who was multitasking during that episode. "Think about it, Mom. Who was the one who cleaned that filthy doggie door for you? I was the one helping YOU!"

Point well taken.

~Rita Hancock, MD

The Best of Intentions

Everything has positive and negative consequences.
~Farrah Fawcett

I wore many hats as the mother of four young children. At times I was the nutritionist making sure the kids ate a balanced diet, or the fashion expert as they wore color-coordinated, ironed outfits, or the mental health expert helping them have happy and fulfilling lives, or a dance partner for the Mickey Mouse song. But of these, my most prized job was that of an educator. I read to the children daily, took them to the library, and instilled a love of books. I wanted to encourage them to become familiar with words, so I printed "Toys" on a piece of tag board and taped it to the toy box. I followed with other concepts such as "Door," "Wall," "Bed," and "Window." I beamed when my preschool children recognized these words while I read a story or when they pointed out words on signs and billboards.

After the kids became proficient with numerous nouns, I tried other words. A sign with "Up" and an arrow pointing in that direction went near the ceiling, "Down" and its arrow was placed near the floor, "Push" went on one side of the door, and "Pull" decorated the other side. "Around" with a circular arrow went on a toy top. My chest puffed with pride as my children's reading vocabularies grew.

One day they all came down with fevers, coughs, and stuffy noses. I should have had a sign on my forehead that said "Exhausted." Miraculously, all four fell asleep at the same time, so I joined them. I woke from my deep slumber when a little finger poked my arm and my toddler announced, "That's yummy." My eyes flew open, and I stared at the orange stain around his mouth.

I rushed into the kitchen. Just as I feared, the orange-flavored children's aspirin bottle lay on the counter—empty. I dialed the Poison Control Center and gave thanks I'd posted their number by the phone—even though I thought I'd never need it due to my extreme vigilance.

"Yes," I answered when asked if I had syrup of ipecac. "Of course," I replied when queried if I had placed the aspirin bottle out of the reach of children. "Certainly," I said when asked if the bottle had a childproof cap. But even with all the correct answers, I felt like I should pin an "A" for Awful Mother on my clothing.

After the dose of ipecac caused my three-year-old to "fro-up," the waiting voice on the phone asked to speak to the culprit. I eavesdropped on the conversation.

"How did you get the orange pills?"

"I climbed up."

"Did you open the bottle?"

"Yes. It was hard."

"How did you do it?"

"I read the directions."

"Well, Super Mom," I whispered, "looks like your great idea doubled back and kicked you." I gave a sigh of relief that my little son was okay, then readjusted my Mom Hat and trudged on.

~Sharon Landeen

Getting Over the Guilt

Guilt is always hungry, don't let it consume you.
~Terri Guillemets

Your friends warn you about the money-absorbing powers of diapers. Your cousin tells you about the sleepless nights. And your mother reminds you how it will all be worth it. But no one gets you ready for the never-ending trial, the one where you, the mom, are both the defendant and the jury. The one where no matter how you defend your choices, you declare a guilty verdict.

My trial began on Valentine's Day—the day I found out I was pregnant. I second-guessed what I ate, how I worked out, and any whiff of secondhand smoke I inhaled inadvertently. Ms. 4.0-perfectionist-who-was-once-going-to-conquer-the-world-with-her-brilliance couldn't even eat salad without having a minor panic attack. (I mean, what if someone hadn't washed the lettuce?)

The worst part was I had no real reason to be paranoid. No real reason to feel guilty about taking a swim in the lake with my ever-expanding belly or walking past a smoker without holding my breath. I was thirty-three. I was healthy. And my pregnancy was problem-free. Still, I bit my nails, picked my lip, and enjoyed a non-stop eye twitch. By the time I gave birth to Baby M in the fall, I had taken so many guilt trips I had practically acquired silver status.

And then came motherhood. It was time to go for the gold.

Like many new mothers, in order to convince the jury I was innocent, compromise became my middle name. I would work 60 percent, be a mom 70 percent, and go completely out of my mind 110 percent.

My husband, since he was a father, seemed immune to guilt. He took a three-week unpaid paternity leave and went right back to his old life, with the exception of Friday nights, when he stayed home so I could go swimming.

"No," I told him. "You are not babysitting. You are watching your child."

"Right," he'd shrug, guilt-free, as he got out the PlayStation to play *FIFA Soccer*—his version of entertaining a baby.

While I swam, drowning in guilt for leaving Baby M for the insane length of two hours, I couldn't help but wonder why I was the one with all the remorse while my husband spent his limited father-daughter time playing games or redesigning his website. After all, it was guilt that kept me from eating cheese while pregnant. It was guilt that kept me pumping my breasts, even when my daughter would no longer nurse. And it was guilt that kept me from going back to work full-time.

When people asked my plans (and they always ask), I'd tell them, yes, I was going back to work, but only on Mondays and Tuesdays plus one day working from home on Wednesdays so Baby M would really only be in daycare two days a week even though I would be working three days a week. If it sounded like a mouthful, it was because it was one; I always bit off more than I could chew.

My mother-in-law listened to my spiel, but still didn't believe me.

"She'll take one look at that baby and forget about going back to work," she predicted before Baby M was born.

Which probably would have been true, if I had been a child of the 1940s.

But it was the 21st century, and I had been blessed with something women didn't used to have: choices. But give an American woman too many choices and she will take them all. I couldn't help but think my mother's life had been easier. As she tells it, when she went to college, her choices were pretty much teaching or teaching.

When she had a baby, her choices were pretty much stay home or stay home. When I went to college, there were so many options that I double majored and still felt like I was missing out on something. Eleven years and a baby later, nothing had changed except my concentrations, which had now switched to motherhood and advertising copywriting.

"What are you going to do... sing jingles to your baby?" the older generation would ask. Then I would belt out a fake laugh and think about the alternatives: 1) a résumé gap or 2) a child raised exclusively by daycare workers born after 1987. Either way, the horror music played. Either way, the mental institutions beckoned. Either way, I needed industrial-strength Advil. After all, I was an American born in the 1970s. If I didn't chop myself in half, I wasn't whole.

When I dropped Baby M off at daycare for the first time, I waited for the jury. I was outside the daycare. My six-month-old was inside. With other people. My little pumpkin, for the first time in fifteen months, was not kicking me from the inside or the outside. The sky was dark. Raindrops dripped down my black coat like tears. I waited for them to flow from my eyes as well. But instead, a strange thing happened. I smiled.

Stop the press. Hold the camera. Aim it at something you've never seen before—a selfish mother. Clearly, I was a good example of one. I should have been bawling, right? I should have been consumed with separation anxiety, no? But as much as I wanted to be Ms. Model Mom and get an "A" in motherhood, this moment would then involve feeling crushed, broken, and in need of a reality show with which to share my angst with the entire world. So that one morning, I failed. I didn't feel sad. I didn't feel guilty. All I thought, aside from the charming little girl whom I loved, was, "Well, this is kind of nice."

I should have rejoiced in that moment longer. Skipped to my desk in my new, non-nursing bra, a binding device that was somehow, at that moment, the epitome of freedom. But as I boarded the train to go to the office, something terrible took over my mind, body, and soul. Ladies and gentlemen, there I was, Ms. Remorse-Free Me, sitting next to the window on my way back to 60 percent of my good old life as a professional working woman, watching my reflection as my smile turned to a grimace, all because I felt guilty for not feeling guilty.

~Chantal Panozzo

Framed

Photography deals exquisitely with appearances,
but nothing is what it appears to be.
~Duane Michals

I have never (purposely) had professional pictures taken of my family. You know the kind, everyone grouped together in matching sweaters. All of us looking at the camera smiling with the "We are such a happy family" gleam in our eyes. Don't get me wrong, we are a pretty happy bunch. It is just that our kind of happiness doesn't seem to photograph all that well.

I think that part of the problem is that my kids don't know how to have their picture taken. This is not for lack of trying. I have spent much time trying to get just one good shot of them together. I have hundreds of family shots, but none where they are all looking at the camera. Getting all of them to sit still and look in one direction for more than a half-second is nearly impossible. Somebody invariably turns his or her head. Somebody bends down, or sneezes, and then... there is Oscar. My constantly moving, curly-haired boy. For years, I don't think that people believed I had a second son. I would patiently explain, "He's the one on the right. See that blur over by the window? That fuzzy blue thing? Yup, that's Oscar!" Needless to say, I have an awful lot of incomplete family photos.

Candid shots seem to work best for us. Our home is filled with them. My children are quite lovely... until they are asked to pose. I don't know what happens when posing; they seem to take on another persona... a certain gooniness. They don't look like themselves. They look strange. Nothing proves this better than the dreaded school picture.

I don't make a big deal of picture day at school. I don't buy special outfits or dress up the kids. I send them in like I do any other day. I have told them if they choose not to have their picture taken, it is okay with me. I do this especially for Oscar, as he has told me that he doesn't like it. I don't intend to buy them anyway. Regardless, they always choose to have them taken, even Oscar.

About three months later, they come home with the pictures. Large packets of them. Eight by tens, five by sevens, wallet size, bookmarks, keychains, refrigerator magnets. Just how many photos does one family need? Judging by what the photo company sends home, apparently hundreds. Hundreds of the worst imaginable pictures ever. There's Sammy with the enormous head... balding Lily… and Oscar, who after being prompted to smile five million times, looks like the before picture in a laxative ad. Yes, they are that bad. The worst part? Not only do my kids want me to buy them, but they get upset when I say that I don't want to.

"But Mama…" Sammy says as tears pool in his dark green eyes, "don't you want a picture of me?"

"Oh, Sammy, buddy... but it doesn't look like you."

"Yes, it does!"

"No, honey, your head couldn't possibly be that large. If it looked any bigger, NASA would send a space probe."

"But don't you want it, Mama (hiccup)... a picture of me?" A single tear runs down his rosy cheek.

I say the only thing any self-respecting mother would: "Okay, buddy, if it means that much to you…." I smile, but I am seething inside.

I know what those evil companies are doing. Instead of sending home one picture, they send home the entire package. They know the odds are that our children will guilt us into buying them all.

This year I decided to do something different. Instead of buying them, I just wasn't going to return them. If the photo company wanted them back, they could come to my house and get them. They could talk to Sammy. Let them have a taste of their own medicine. So I took the packages of pictures and put them in a box in my attic—the same box where I put last year's and the year before's pictures. My kids haven't missed them. I figure that one day, after I am gone, they will find them and wonder, "Just who are these odd-looking kids... and why does Mama have so many pictures of them?"

In the meantime, I haven't heard a word from the photo company. Cowards.

~Kathleen Leopold

A New Resolution

There's never enough time to do all the nothing you want.
~Bill Watterson

Last night, I tiptoed into your room to turn off the lamp. There you lay in blissful sleep, Nana Mouskouri crooning in your ear, Winnie-the-Pooh snuggled under your arm. I paused for a minute to ruffle your hair and remembered the half-baked promise I had made to come and tuck you in later. Whatever I was doing seemed more important than spending some time with you. My intentions were good, but all too soon you were fast asleep.

I sat in that big, old rocker by your bed and recalled the way you bounded into the kitchen each morning, bright-eyed and bursting with life while I was being jump-started on caffeine.

"Good morning, Mommy!" you sang, forgiving of broken promises, accepting of anything thrown your way. Breakfast was a jumble of "Be careful—don't spill the milk—put your plate in the sink—brush your teeth—get your school bag—hurry up, find your jacket—no, not that T-shirt, where's your other shoe?—will you ever learn to tie them?—of course, I like you!"

A quick peck on the cheek, and you were gone, trudging off to the bus stop, dawdling, kicking stones, looking forward to seeing your classmates. I wish I hadn't hollered so much during those chaotic breakfast hours.

The day would pass quickly, and once again you stood on the doorstep, anxious to tell me stories of your school day. So often, I brushed those stories away with an impatient reminder for you to empty your bag. I half-heard you say you liked your new teacher, but I forgot to tell you I was glad of that. Supper was uppermost in my mind, I guess. I recall the time I stomped outside and humiliated you in front of your little friends, something about getting dirty in the sand pile. How pathetic! A child not being able to get dirty at play? They write books about ballistic moms like me! Still you grinned all the way through supper and shared more stories with me.

Bath time was one jumble of "Don't splash water on the floor—wash your hair—hang up your towels—put your underwear in the hamper," and on and on. I heard you rummaging in your dresser for pajamas, and then a timid knock at my door.

"Aren't you going to tuck me in?" you asked.

I sighed and turned around as you flew into my lap and planted a sloppy, little-boy kiss on my forehead. A whispered goodnight and you padded off to your room, dragging old Pooh. I continued whittling down my paperwork backlog, meaning to come and tuck you in before you fell asleep, but I didn't. Not last night, nor many nights before that.

So here I sit looking at you, feeling terrible, missing the way I used to read you to sleep, vowing that tomorrow will be different. Tomorrow, I will listen with every fiber of my being to your stories. I will giggle with you as you show me how high your frog can jump, and it lands in the toilet. I will sniffle with you as you complain about the inequities of playground friendships. Yessirree, son. Tomorrow, I will be back on track for you.

Tonight, I've realized that your childhood is far too fleeting to elbow aside in the name of Important Work. You are my important work. Please forgive me, little man. I'll do better tomorrow.

~Gloria Jean Hansen

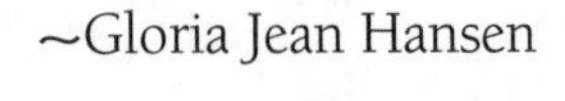

First, Feed the Heart

The seat of knowledge is in the head, of wisdom, in the heart.
~William Hazlitt

I've heard the saying before: It takes a village to raise a child. I understood that in the abstract, but it wasn't until I forgot my son that the reality of the phrase took root in my heart.

I was a young mom. My son was in preschool, and I worked a part-time job at a local college as an academic advisor. My husband and I spent our mornings making sure breakfasts were made and lunches were packed before we dropped our son off for his half-day of school. I went to work, my head full of thoughts for the day, and my husband drove to his office at the church where he was a pastor.

I was fortunate. I had a great career at a local college and was able to work a schedule that allowed me to still be a mom—the other job I loved. During my hours at the office, I stayed busy helping college students with the tasks of choosing a major and selecting classes. I attended meetings and planned projects. It was a career I had invested considerable education in, and I loved the focus and challenges it offered.

This particular day was especially packed with appointments and meetings. I glanced at the clock several times, mindful of my need to pick up my son from preschool. But an impromptu meeting occurred right before I had to leave. Giving my full attention to helping the student, I stopped watching the clock, caught in the flow of the conversation and the student's needs. By the time the appointment was over and I thought to glance at the time, I was almost twenty minutes late. My stomach sank. My little boy! Was he waiting alone outside the school? It was cold! Would the teachers notice he was alone?

Quickly grabbing my coat and purse, I flipped off my office lights, offered a hasty goodbye to my coworkers, and flew out to the parking lot. I closed my eyes. How could I be so stupid? What was more important than my son? Was he frightened? I quietly thanked God that we lived in a small town.

With a sick stomach, I pulled out of the parking lot and headed to his school. Tears stung my eyes as I berated myself. How could I ever let anything take priority over my child? By the time I pulled up to the school, I was in a full-blown panic.

Had I been thinking more clearly, I would have been less upset. I stopped my car and saw my son sitting on a bench in front of the school, his short legs swinging back and forth and his backpack sitting next to him. Beside him, another mother sat waiting with her own daughter, her arm around him, a big smile on her face. I rushed up the sidewalk. "I'm so, so sorry. I got stuck in an appointment…." I started the explanation.

"No problem," she said with a smile and without a suggestion of reproach. "We knew you were just running a bit late, so we thought we'd just wait here together." She stood up, took her daughter's hand and smiled at me. Not another word, a hint of guilt or an implication that I was a bad mother.

"Hi, Mommy!" My son was so completely at ease in the company of his classmate's mom, I doubt it ever occurred to him to worry or notice I was late. Taking my son's hand, I climbed back into the car, my heart finally at ease. I offered him an apology for being late, which he barely had time to acknowledge as he rushed to talk about his exciting day at school.

Still, the day haunted my conscience. It was so difficult to let myself off the hook. Why was it so much easier to extend the gift of grace to others and not myself? I knew being a little late picking up my child wasn't evidence of terrible parenting. But maybe it was a manifestation I had let myself get over-busy.

I had let myself go on overload without taking a little time for exercise or meditation, for nurturing my soul. Was I eating well? Did I explore hobbies or interests? Or had I been so busy meeting all the demands in my life that I'd neglected to feed my heart and soul? The lessons I learned that day didn't go unheeded. I decided to take more hikes with my dog, nurture my friendships, and even took a few classes at the local arts center. As for my little boy, I'm happy to say he grew up, graduated college and has managed to successfully thrive... despite my mistakes.

~Julie Luek

Mother for Life

Things which matter most must never be at the mercy of things which matter least.
~Johann Wolfgang von Goethe

All I wanted to do was go home, eat a sandwich, check in with my two teenage children and my dad, and then spend the afternoon at the university library. And I'd do a load of laundry and put supper in the Crock-Pot while I was home. On the way to the library, I'd stop by the post office to buy stamps and mail a package to return a bathing suit that was too small.

I had to get the research finished at the library for my thesis. And I had to get at least two chapters of my paper written before school started in a couple of weeks. After school began, I'd barely keep my head above water—teaching sixth grade, finishing my thesis for a master's degree, parenting a high school student and a college student, helping Dad, and just day-to-day married and home life. I sat at the kitchen table with my daughter as we ate lunch—ham sandwiches and apples.

"Mom, do you think we should get matching bedspreads? Can we go shopping this afternoon and look for ideas?" My daughter Alicia was excited about decorating her new dorm room and having a college roommate.

Eric, my son, answered the ringing phone. I heard him say, "Sure. She's eating lunch. Come on over." He turned to me and said,

"That was Papa. He wants to talk to you, Mom. He's coming over to eat lunch." After Mom's death four months earlier, Dad had moved from their home forty miles away to an apartment just a half-mile from my family's home. I saw him almost daily, and he often ate meals with us.

"And, Mom, my practice uniform is ripped. Can you fix it before tomorrow? I'm going to the Y," Eric said. His summer schedule was to work out with his basketball team in the mornings and lifeguard at the YMCA during the afternoon. I'd waited to take summer classes until he had his driver's license and could drive himself to all his activities. After spending the past several years taking one graduate class a semester, this was the summer I was taking two classes and working on my research paper. I hoped to finish by December.

"Maybe. Remind me later. Have a good afternoon," I told Eric. I turned to my daughter. "Alicia, I really must go to the library today. Let's shop over the weekend. I promise I'll help you get things together for your dorm room. Just not today." She nodded her head, but her whole body slumped with disappointment.

Alicia opened the refrigerator and said, "I'll make Papa a sandwich. I know you're busy, Mom." Dad walked into the kitchen carrying a manila folder. He'd adjusted well to being a widower, but needed me to share in his daily life and decisions. He kissed Alicia's forehead as she placed his lunch on the table.

"Look what I found," Dad said. He raised his eyebrows and smiled. "A house for sale and not too far from you. Close to town and all the space I need." He opened the folder and laid a picture of a gray brick home on the table. "I saw the inside of it this morning and told the realtor I'd be back this afternoon. You can go with me, can't you, Susan?"

I'm sure Dad didn't know why Alicia laid her sandwich on her plate and stared at me, but I did. Quite often, since Mom's death, I'd put Dad's needs in front of everyone else's. He was seventy-nine and had some health problems. "We'll go whenever it's good for you," Dad said. "I just need to call the realtor."

"I'm not sure," I told Dad. "Let me make a phone call. I'd planned to go to the library."

I hid in my bathroom and stared into the mirror. Tears streamed down my cheeks. I breathed deeply. Controlled, long breaths. How did this happen? My children were almost grown at ages sixteen and eighteen. And yet, they still needed me. Fix something. Look at this. Look at that. And now, Dad wanted me to do those same things.

I hated that I'd just told my daughter that I couldn't spend the afternoon with her and then felt forced to go along with Dad's plans. I'd often heard Mom say, "This, too, shall pass." When? When would being pulled in all directions pass? Or would it ever?

I had a talk with myself—as mother, daughter, and student. At that moment, I knew my priorities needed to fall in that order—mother, daughter, student. After a short, intense prayer, a few hard sobs and a cold-water face wash, I walked back into the kitchen. Dad and Alicia were eating chocolate chip cookies. "Are you okay, Susan? Your eye is red," Dad said. I told him that a hair had gotten in it and I'd made matters worse trying to get it out. Alicia's grin let me know that she didn't believe me and knew why my eye, both eyes, in fact, were red.

"About the afternoon, Dad," I said. "Do you think the realtor could meet us at the house about 4:45? Alicia and I have some shopping to do first. So how about we see the house just before suppertime and then you and I and the whole family can eat out somewhere together? Then I'll go the library tonight."

The next morning, I mended my son's uniform, a five-minute chore. Alicia and her roommate, with very little hands-on help from me, decorated their dorm room a month later. My husband, son, and I helped Dad move into his new home two months after that. I walked across a stage to receive my master's degree the following May. It all got done.

And I had many more face-to-face mirror talks. That day, when all I wanted to do was eat lunch, check on everybody, and get back to the library was a watershed time. A turning point. A time that I revisited often. My children were just that—children. Their needs changed, just as Dad's did. One thing didn't. Being a mother was for life.

~Susan R. Ray

The Best Kind of Mother

Humor is perhaps a sense of intellectual perspective:
an awareness that some things are really important, others not;
and that the two kinds are most oddly jumbled in everyday affairs.
~Christopher Morley

Years ago, before I had kids, I read an article by humorist Erma Bombeck called "What Kind of Mother Would...?" I laughed at her exaggerated descriptions of motherhood. It was only after I became a mother that I saw beyond the humor to the heart-wrenching emotion that often accompanies that question.

I was reminded of this one day when I received a note from the mom of one of my students apologizing for something she felt would cause me to think she was a bad mother. The funny thing was, until she called the incident to my attention, I wasn't even aware of it. She had recently given birth, and the mistake she had obviously agonized over was simply one of those humorous things that tend to happen with a new baby in the house. I couldn't help but wonder at the irony of the situation. No doubt exhausted and sleep-deprived, she had felt compelled to use what precious time and energy she had to write a full-page letter apologizing for something I hadn't even noticed. She was, no doubt, asking herself the question: "What kind of mother would...?"

I knew just how she felt. One cold January day, I awoke to snow on the ground and the announcement that school would be delayed two hours for students, with teachers reporting as usual. This meant that my son, Seth, a high school senior, would be responsible for getting his eight-year-old sister, Ally, to school.

I peeked in at my daughter, sleeping peacefully with rows of tiny pink curlers in her hair. She had asked me to put them in the night before and was no doubt dreaming of the bouncy curls she was sure they would produce.

Seth groggily assured me that he would handle getting Ally to school before rolling back over in bed. I left, feeling guilty about not being home making hot chocolate and warm memories with my kids.

What kind of mother would leave her children to fend for themselves on a day like this?

By afternoon, the sun was out. I drove to my parents' home to pick up Ally. When I got there, I saw a girl about her size on the floor watching cartoons. It took a moment for me to realize I was looking at my daughter. Great globs of matted, mangled hair stuck out from her head in every direction.

"Hey, Mama," she said, looking up at me.

"Ally," I managed. "What happened to your hair?"

"Oh," she said, "we had a hard time getting my curlers out. Seth tried to help me. He finally said to just wear a hat. Guess what!" she continued. "We picked up Seth's girlfriend and went out for breakfast!"

What kind of mother would send her child to school looking like her hair had been combed with an eggbeater?

When I saw Ally's teacher a few days later, I felt I should offer an explanation for my daughter's appearance the morning of the snow. There was no need. Ally had told the class all about her adventure.

"What a wonderful memory she'll have of hanging out with her brother before he leaves for college," said the teacher.

We finished our conversation and went our separate ways, but I couldn't get her comment off my mind. I'd been asking myself that same old question, but now I sensed the true answer.

What kind of mother would leave her children to fend for themselves on a snowy morning and send her daughter to school with her hair a mangled mess? What kind of mother would do a thousand other things she thought she'd never do?

A real mother. A good mother. A mother a lot like me!

~Martha Hynson

The Super Dad Blues

Certain is it that there is no kind of affection so purely angelic as of a father to a daughter.
~Joseph Addison

It started when I was in the hospital with our first child. I was laid up post-C-section, and so my hubby initially was on solo diaper duty. It didn't matter that Jon had never changed a diaper before in his life—and that I had years of babysitting experience on my side—baby Evelyn helpfully provided plenty of practice, and suddenly Jon was a diaper-changing ninja.

It was the beginning of what would become a trend: the birth, not just of our darling little girl, but of Super Dad, the one who could beat me in just about any parenting task that didn't involve lactating breasts.

I would've been content to let Jon reign as the diaper-changing king (it gives me an excuse to recruit his help for a few of the really nasty blowouts). But soon it became apparent that he was also a better baby burper. And then a better baby shampooer. (I credit his superior arm strength, which gives him a better grip while holding a wet, wiggly baby under a running kitchen faucet.) For the first year, while I was nursing Evelyn, I held the baby-soothing card at least part of the time. But then we weaned, and suddenly Evelyn decided that her dad was her number one choice for comfort. An unfortunate run-in with a wall? Her dad is the only remedy for the pain. When she's a river of snot? She turns to her dad's arms. When she wakes up howling in the middle of the night? Ninety-five percent of the time, only her dad's gentle rocking can lull her back to sleep.

I realize that parenting isn't a competitive sport, but c'mon—throw Momma a bone!

I know I should be grateful that they have such a terrific bond; that he's so willing to be an active parent; that he also spoils me by handling much of the cooking and laundry. And I am grateful. He's a dream husband and Super Dad, and sometimes I feel guilty about just how much he does. Part of this is due to circumstance. As a teacher, Jon almost always finishes his workday before I do, and he's a stay-at-home dad during the summers. He likes to cook, and an unkempt house gives him the heebie-jeebies.

But despite my gratitude for his skillful mastery of so many household tasks, it still stings a little when my daughter turns to him over me. Once, when she was crying after a tumble, Jon swooped her up in a big bear hug, and I tried to join in, wrapping my arms around them both. Her chubby little toddler hand flew out and pushed me away. Message received.

It doesn't help that most of the other little kids I know seem to prefer their moms. It's a cultural expectation: Crying babies and toddlers are supposed to prefer their mothers above all else, right? There are just some things moms are supposed to be better at. And I'm a warm, nurturing person—so what does my hubby have that I don't?

Jon tries to rationalize away Evelyn's clear preference. He notes that I'm naturally more spazzy and stressed under pressure, and Evelyn probably senses that and so reaches for her less-rattled dad.

My maternal insecurity was also eased a little when I heard a stay-at-home mom complain about the fact that her son rushes straight into his father's arms every morning. She was always a little hurt until her son explained, "Daddy's soft and warm. You're cold and boney." I doubt her husband appreciated that description of his physique, but as a fellow thin-framed woman with hands that can chill a drink faster than the freezer, I can understand the appeal.

I used to joke that I wanted a second baby "because this one doesn't like me as much as I had hoped." My mom had warned me that Evelyn would end up a daddy's girl—"they all do"—so I was more than a little curious about whether I'd regain the baby-comforting upper hand if we had a boy. So far, our son is an equal-opportunity cuddler, so at least that's a step in the right direction.

In the meantime, I try to cope with my parenting inferiority complex by concentrating on what business executives might call my "core competencies." I make killer homemade mac and cheese, and my cookies and brownies are always a hit. When Evelyn transitioned from kitchen-sink shampoos to hair washing in the "big bath," my gentler touch yielded fewer tears than her father's attempts. I'm always the one to sing to Evelyn when we tuck her in for the night. And sometimes, just sometimes, I go in to comfort her in the middle of the night and successfully soothe her into sleepy silence. And when she lays her head on my shoulder or reaches up to lightly touch my hair, I look down into her little face and know with a certainty: I may not be a perfect mom, but I do okay.

~Nicole Sweeney Etter

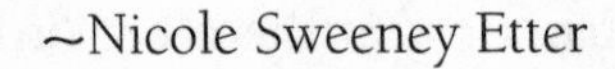

Multitasking Mom of Multiples

Adopt the pace of nature: her secret is patience.
~Ralph Waldo Emerson

Friends told me I had the "best of both worlds," as a stay-at-home, as well as work-at-home, mom. But some days could seem like the worst. I recall a particularly bad one when lunch at "Donald's House," as my two-and-a-half-year-old called her favorite restaurant, seemed a great idea.

Children skittered about the bright playroom in their socks. Moms sat at the tables in the fast food franchise and talked. Usually, we shared these lunch dates with my friend Janet and her two-and-a-half-year-old Jonathan. One day my friend joked that she told her husband she wished for a divorce just so she could count on a break in parenting every other weekend. We laughed about the current difficult stage in our children's development.

But on this day, my daughter Elizabeth and I just sat and ate. Even talking was too much multitasking for mom and daughter. I also felt the sting of a bad parenting moment the night before that sent her scurrying under the dining room table, as I took out my ire on her older brother, a high school senior, for dropping his soccer gear by the stairs, and her junior high school sister for dropping out-of-season Easter grass used for a science project all over the kitchen floor.

Not that a clean house and a little responsibility aren't important. But when the wrath of Mom broke loose, the older siblings looked up from doing their homework, and I remembered they are good kids, and perhaps I had overreacted.

So, maybe that's why one mom in particular got my attention. She seemed unusually attentive to her three young children. Her smile, straight-combed hair and a denim skirt with a crisp white blouse made her look the role of a model mom.

I watched as she scooped up a struggling toddler, set him on her lap and Velcroed his shoes in place as she chatted with him. Then she released him with a hug and a smile. She did the same with a slightly taller little girl in a yellow dress. With a kiss on the top of her head, she released this wriggling tot with a smile and a hug, too.

This woman seemed as if she were on display, as if she knew others were watching. Was this genuine? Or was she just showing off how attentive she was to her children, and I caught her on a good day? I'd like to see her when her children are taking charge of their own lives.

Soon I had the chance. She chased down another little girl, dressed a lot like the first, except for the color of her dress. Little green dress struggled. She kicked and screamed. It required that seat belt maneuver that every parent recognizes, where you hold the child facing the ground, with one arm under the shoulders, and the other between the kicking legs, locking your hands in the middle.

As little green dress loudly protested, her mom gently jiggled her daughter as she walked, repeating softly, "I know, I know, I know, I know...." She must be very tired, repeating that to comfort herself, I smugly thought. But she smiled as she released little green dress, too.

I was curious about how old her children must be. They all seemed to be close in age. I got my chance to find out as her child in the green dress played near my daughter. I commented on "how cute" and asked her children's ages.

"They're two and a half years old," she said proudly.

"Oh, your girls are twins?" I queried.

"Oh, no! They're triplets!" She beamed.

I was floored. I wanted to exclaim, "How do you do it?" But as the mother of two teens and a toddler, I got that question a lot too, and hadn't figured out the best way to respond. Now I understood why she seemed on display. Everywhere they travelled, the entourage must have drawn attention—and my unasked question. I missed my golden moment to be enlightened. Little green dress went one way and Elizabeth another. I didn't even get to see the super mom and her triplets walk out. Did any of them want to be carried? Did they hold hands? What if one—or all—didn't want to leave "Donald's House"?

It left me hoping to meet up again with Multitasking Mom Times Three. In the decade-plus that has passed since then, I never have. I've always wondered about her possible words of wisdom. But her actions already said it all. Be kind. Be gentle—yet use the seat belt maneuver when necessary, and always remember to smile and give hugs.

I think we would both agree to be patient—because nothing lasts.

~Jane Miller

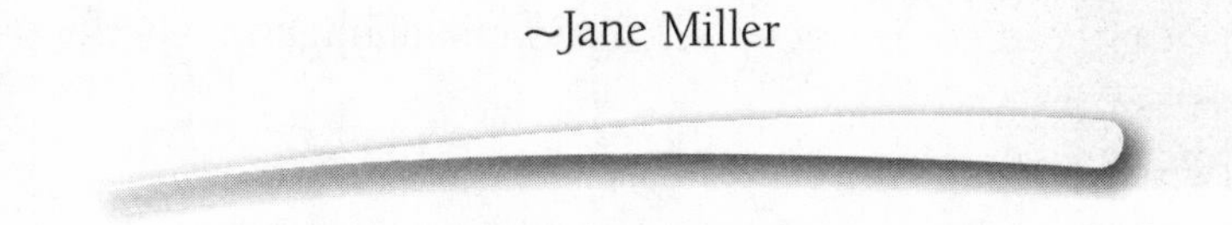

Not So Guilty After All

Forbear to judge, for we are sinners all.
~*William Shakespeare*, Henry VI

"Great game, Maggie," I said to my sixteen-year-old daughter. "Your team did well. And so did you." We had just returned home after her basketball game. I was scurrying about the kitchen trying to get dinner on the table.

"You didn't even pay attention, Mom," she said, with all the scorn a teenage girl can put in her voice. "You were highlighting. Becky saw you."

"I was watching. You scored."

"You weren't looking when I shot the free throw. Becky saw you reading with your yellow highlighter in your hand. You always work during my games."

There's a lot of down time in basketball games. Time outs. Substitutions. Fouls. Of course, I had reading for my job with me at her game. I couldn't just sit there, not with all the deadlines I faced at the office.

But I made it to most of her games. Didn't she appreciate that?

"Go Cougars!" I yelled from the stands, as loudly as any parent. Surely, she could see I was paying attention... most of the time.

"Your mother's always been that way," my husband told Maggie. He'd been at the game too, sitting on the bleachers, elbows on knees, chin in hands. Looking bored, never cheering. Yet Maggie gave him credit for being there, while I got chastised for reading.

"Why, back in February 1980," he continued, "Mom couldn't take a vacation because seven cases were set for trial. You know what? All of them settled, but we didn't go skiing."

In 1980, I was a new attorney. The senior litigator in our department told me there were seven trials scheduled. How could I know they would all settle? But for the next twenty-five years, every time I told my husband I couldn't do something because of work, he'd say, "And there will be seven trials in February."

And every time I said something about my daughter's activities, she told me I shouldn't bother coming if I had to bring my highlighter. I was supposed to focus on her—and only on her—at these events.

My work was a perpetual issue in our family. Somehow my husband's job (also as an attorney) and his civic responsibilities were never a problem. But my career as a corporate lawyer interfered with all the fun we could be having.

I know my husband appreciated me working. He told me many times that my salary took the pressure off him so he could spend his time on activities that were meaningful to him without worrying about increasing his billable hours.

I know my husband thought highly of my intellect. We'd met in law school, for God's sake. He knew I was smart and worked hard and focused on doing things well.

So I thought we were partners in every sense. I thought splitting our home obligations and childcare responsibilities was the deal we had. But the message I got was that my work wasn't supposed to interfere with anything anyone else in the family wanted to do.

We'd both grown up in traditional homes where the mothers didn't work. I think subconsciously my husband expected his adult life would repeat his childhood experience. Even though he knew I wanted to work and he wanted me to work.

When the kids came along, they joined in his refrains about my job.

Our older child, Josh, was a dreamer. He hated being hurried, but what could I do? If he wasn't ready to leave the house by 7:15 a.m., I wouldn't get the kids dropped off so I could get to work by 8:00 a.m. If I wasn't at work by 8:00, my entire day would be off track. So I rushed him. Every day. And he resisted. Every day.

Maggie was more organized than Josh—more like me. But also more vocal than my son when she was unhappy. Hence, the "you're always highlighting" comments that came more and more frequently as she grew older.

Yet somehow we survived. Both kids went off to college. I changed careers, then retired. Life got easier.

Both Josh and Maggie are now focused on their own careers. Josh is not involved with any organizations other than his work. He can be found at his office late into the evening. Maggie is a lawyer like her parents, now working at a large law firm and facing her own pressures to increase billable hours. She is still athletic, but struggles to find time to exercise.

On a recent family vacation, both children had interruptions due to work obligations. Maggie made us stop at a coffee shop on our drive to the ski resort so she could participate in a conference call. Josh stopped skiing early one afternoon so he could send an urgent e-mail.

Now that I'm retired, I had no interruptions. No highlighters in hand.

They don't have children and neither of them is married, though they are both older than I was when Josh was born. I always thought they'd shy away from working as many hours as I did. But at this point in their lives, they are as hardworking as I was thirty years ago.

Maybe they have shied away from assuming family obligations because of watching my struggle. I hope that is not the case, but I wonder what lessons they took away from my years of highlighting.

We all have to find our own work-life balance. As for me, I do not beat myself up for highlighting during basketball games. And I don't point out my children's similar behavior on our vacations. They will figure it out for themselves soon enough.

~Sara Rickover

Coasting

A memory is what is left when something happens
and does not completely unhappen.
~Edward de Bono

I was blessed with a career as a financial analyst while I was raising my kids. I could work from home and I could also ratchet up or down my commitment depending on how much time I had available to work. I was even able to take a whole year off when I moved from New York City to the suburbs and had my second child. Then I gradually ramped up the job again, ultimately doing it full-time from home. With the proliferation of cell phones things got even easier. I remember talking to one of my traders while watching a bunch of kids on the roller coaster at a local amusement park one day and thinking *I can't believe I am trading stocks and chaperoning a class trip at the same time.* I even ran my own hedge fund from home—after all, the market was only open from 9:30-4:00—so I could trade during the day, spend the afternoon and evening with the kids, and then prepare for the next trading day after they went to bed.

My kids were two years apart, so I had twenty years of childrearing until the second one turned eighteen and went off to college. I managed to work from home for seventeen and a half of those twenty years. The problem was the other two and a half years, when my kids were preteens, during which I commuted to New York City and traveled all over the country in a very intense senior executive position with a technology start-up. I also got divorced and moved twice during that same period.

Those years were my undoing as a multitasking mom, or so I thought. I had managed to be class mom every single year, alternating between the two kids, and I did lunch duty, drove on numerous field trips, and did other volunteer work for school and sports. But during those couple of bad years, I felt completely disconnected from school, not really knowing what was going on, not signing up for volunteer work, and not driving on a single field trip.

I wasn't even home for the emergency phone calls. My son was a "frequent flier" at the local emergency room and I would get calls at work, an hour away from home, with scary messages like "there isn't enough skin left to put in the stitches" and "he was only not breathing while he was unconscious." The worst was when I got a call that Mike rode his bike, unauthorized of course, down an icy, rocky trail through the woods and was found lying in the dirt at the end of a dead-end road. He ended up in an ambulance and I almost quit my job that day.

But the New York City job ended and things went back to normal. I was once again class mom, team mom, driver, and volunteer, juggling my work-at-home career and all the mom duties I could handle. I still felt guilty about those two and a half lost years however. That is, until I discussed those years with my kids, and they both told me exactly which field trips I drove on. They vividly remembered me participating in all my motherly duties during those commuting years, and yet I checked my calendar and I really hadn't!

There is a great piece of poetry from T.S. Eliot that includes the following lines:

> Footfalls echo in the memory
> Down the passage which we did not take
> Towards the door we never opened

That poem describes exactly what happened in my family. My kids gave me credit during my commuting years for driving on field trips, being class mom, and all the other wonderful things that I had stopped doing, but which I had done in earlier years. Somehow, I got a pass and was able to "coast" through those two and a half years, living off my good reputation. The kids are absolutely certain, to this day, that I never took a break from being the fabulous multitasking mom that I most certainly was not during that time. It just shows, your kids won't be nearly as critical of you as you will be of yourself. You have a little leeway. I just wish I had known at the time.

~Amy Newmark

to do list:
- Pay bills
- Get laundry
- call Mom
- Pick up kids from birthday at 6 p.m.
- Buy groceries

Slowing Down

We do not remember days; we remember moments.

~Cesare Pavese

Crazy Lady on a Bicycle

Living involves tearing up one rough draft after another.
~Author Unknown

A few months ago, my kids and I went to a movie on opening night with another family. The kids had been scattered at sporting events and play dates. The grown-ups were busy, too, with errands and last-minute attempts to clean cars and fold laundry. We got a late start. There was traffic. There was no parking. The ticket line was long. The popcorn line was even longer.

Everyone kicked it into high gear. Scouts were sent to save seats and take popcorn orders. Orders were texted to the people assigned to the popcorn line. Two of the seat scouts returned to help carry copious quantities of sodas and candy and popcorn. The lights dimmed. The previews played. The treats were passed down the line. When the last soda was inserted into its cup holder, I sighed. It had not been easy, but now we got to sit back, relax, and watch the movie!

Later, when the kids were asleep, I had an epiphany. This long, crazy night of executing a small military exercise to see a movie was a microcosm of my life.

Over the past several years, I have taken on three jobs. The first, and most important, is raising my boys, ages fifteen, thirteen and ten. On the weekends, my kids have both Mom and Dad driving them around, watching their games, and hassling them about homework. But during the week, it's mostly me. My second job is running a small law practice. I work for a larger firm where the partners meet with clients, which on a good day means I can operate from home in my pajamas. On a bad day, I'm stuck in court an hour from my kids' school. My third job is writing. I am nearly finished with my third novel.

Having three jobs has placed me in precarious, and sometimes amusing situations. I have left the house wearing slippers. I have negotiated property divisions and TV time simultaneously. And I have changed my clothes in the back seat of my SUV more times than I care to admit. But it was Thursday of the epiphany week that took the prize.

For over a month, the service light had been on in my car and I had not been able to figure out how to get the car to the shop. Finally, I made arrangements with my sitter to meet me there after I dropped the boys at school and take me home to my old, second car.

With the plan in place, I embarked on my journey. I got up at six and dressed for job two—attorney. I woke up the kids, made breakfast, put their coats in the dryer (because a warm coat gets them out the door faster), packed the backpacks, loaded the car, and drove them to school.

I had just gotten back on the road when my sitter called to say she wasn't feeling well. I felt my heart race and my mind focus. I would not go one more day with the service light on! I believe that there is a solution for every situation. This is completely untrue but my survival depends on this delusion so I hold on to it like a fragile newborn. I checked the clock. I had plenty of time. I came up with a new plan.

I peeled into my driveway and raced inside. I grabbed sweatpants and sneakers. I went to the garage and inspected the assortment of old bicycles. I found the one with the tires that weren't flat and that had the least amount of dust and congealed grease around the chains. I threw it in the trunk and drove off.

At the shop, I waited impatiently at the line behind a woman in yoga clothes. I checked the car in, then removed the bike from the back. This was my thinking. My house is just four miles from town. I could certainly bike the short distance. I would be home in twenty minutes—plenty of time to clean up and get to court. I hopped on the bike and started to pedal.

The bike belonged to my ten-year-old, but he's tall for his age. Plus, it was a mountain bike, so it's very sturdy. I adjusted the seat as high as it went. The first block out of town was a snap! Cruising down the main drag I felt almost young again. I continued on a suburban straightaway. Cars whizzed past me, but I was making great time. I turned the corner on the next road. That's where the trouble started.

Connecticut roads are long. They're winding. And they're hilly. My son's bike only has three gears.

Thirty minutes later, I was staring at a forty-five degree incline. My pace had slowed to a crawl. With my eyes glued to the road, determination surging through my body, I forced my foot to press into the pedal and make another turn. The bike moved an inch. I stood. I sat. I pushed on the pedal with all my might. I would make it up this hill! I would get home and get to court! I did not consider stopping to call for help or to postpone my hearing. I had a plan and it would work!

A red Suburban slowed down beside me. The woman inside looked over. Our eyes met and I saw her expression morph from disbelief to sheer horror. I snapped out of my trance and became acutely aware of my situation.

There I was, a forty-six year old woman wearing sweatpants, sneakers and a business suit jacket, sweating profusely as she rode a child's bicycle so slowly it was a miracle it didn't tip over.

I got home in forty-five minutes. I just made it to my hearing. And my car got serviced. In short order, I forgot just how absurd my plan had been, and how often I push things to the brink of disaster just to squeeze in one more task. And worse, I forgot how many times I say to my kids, "Just a minute...."

What had kept me going through days like the day I serviced my car was the belief that someday this would all stop. Someday, the work would be done and I could sit back, enjoy the fruits of my labor, and watch the movie.

There was just one problem. And this was the epiphany. When it comes to life, you never get to watch the movie. You are the movie.

I gasped, sighed, then said out loud, "Oh! I don't ever get to watch the movie!"

After the epiphany, I have approached my juggling act with greater attention. I think carefully about the tasks I take on. I let things go to have lunch with a friend. And I don't put off spending time with my kids to answer one last e-mail.

Because if I am the movie, I want it to win an Oscar. And I certainly don't want it to be called "Crazy Lady on a Bicycle."

~Wendy Walker

Special Hour

Lost time is never found again.
~Benjamin Franklin

Even though I was a stay-at-home mom, there were never enough hours in a day to accomplish everything I set out to do. My husband helped me around the house, my three-year-old son was unusually well behaved, and yet I constantly felt pressed for time.

It seemed like we had a revolving door in our home. Our social life was active. People dropped in knowing they'd be welcome. There was always a pot of coffee going, along with an abundance of home-baked goodies. I was always available for friends with problems who wanted to talk. If someone visited at mealtimes, there was plenty to fill an extra plate.

I prided myself on being a friend whenever needed, but while I was accessible to everyone else, I began to notice I was becoming less available to my own family.

One afternoon in particular opened my eyes. It was a gorgeous summer day, but I hardly noticed. I was intent on getting my groceries home before the ice cream melted. My son was dawdling like most three-year-olds, inspecting every flower, blade of grass and crack in the sidewalk. I barked for him to hurry, yanking his arm less gently than I normally would. He reluctantly toddled behind me, his little legs pumping to keep up with my impatient pace.

As we approached the park at the corner of our street, he stared longingly at the swings. He resisted my hold on his wrist, and I took a deep breath.

"Not today, honey," I informed him, making an effort to soften my voice. I was expecting three friends for dinner, not counting last-minute drop-ins, and I still had a lot to do. There simply wasn't time to stop at the park, even for a few minutes.

I tried to ignore the pleading look in my son's eyes, feeling even guiltier when his little shoulders slumped in quiet, resigned acceptance. It occurred to me that I'd seen him do that far too often lately. I cringed inwardly, remembering all the times I'd shooed him away when he asked me to play with a new toy or watch a cartoon with him. Lately, we'd even stopped reading bedtime stories, too. Instead I'd rush through our bathtime ritual, get him into pajamas and tap my foot anxiously while he brushed his teeth, ushering him off to bed so I could return phone calls or get back to a card game with company.

When we got home, I sent my son to play in our back yard while I quickly unpacked the groceries and put them away. I hurriedly tidied up and was about to put the roast in the oven when I noticed I didn't hear him babbling to himself the way he always did. I hurried out the back door, my heart in my throat, breathing a sigh of relief when I saw him sitting quietly on the top step hugging himself.

"Are you okay, honey?" I asked, checking his forehead to see if he had a fever. It was unusual for him to be so quiet. Satisfied that his brow was cool, I spun around to get back to my preparations, not even waiting for him to answer my question.

"Mummy, sit with me?" he pleaded.

"Not now, David," I told him. "I'm very—

"Busy," he finished for me. "I know." His sad, wistful tone pierced through me, and I turned to look at him as he stared blankly ahead.

That's when I noticed the changes in him. He was losing that baby look. His little face seemed longer and leaner. The pudginess of his soft arms and knees was almost completely gone. When had that happened? When did I last pick him up to nestle my nose in his clean hair or inhale the sweetness of him?

I raced back into the house. Popping the roast into the refrigerator, I checked quickly to make sure I had what I needed to make my son's beloved hot dogs instead. Then I picked up the phone to cancel dinner plans, not caring if my friends would be upset.

Grabbing juice boxes, a few cookies and some fresh fruit, I called my son.

"Let's go," I told him, smiling widely.

"To the store again?" he asked, and I was overcome with shame. It was about the only place I had taken him lately.

"No, we're going to the park," I announced, squirming guiltily when I saw his expression of pure joy over such a small outing. "Get your bucket and shovels and some trucks, okay?" I added, handing him a bag for his toys.

He scurried back less than three minutes later, his bag bulging with assorted treasures from his room. I spotted his white stuffed frog peeking out and ignored my voice of reason. Dirt washes out, I reminded myself cheerfully, grabbing my house key and taking his hand.

My son talked non-stop all the way to the park, and I listened to his chatter with renewed loving interest. For two hours, we played together, digging in the sandbox, swinging, seesawing and climbing on the park equipment. Then we sat on the grass with our snacks while we looked for animals in the clouds.

When we got home, I put him down for a nap, not even bothering to scrub his face or hands. I watched him doze off with a tired but blissful smile and swore to myself that things would change.

The next day, I implemented Special Hour. At least four times a week, I hung a Do Not Disturb sign that David helped me make on our front door. We ceremoniously took the phone off the hook, turned off the TV and set the oven timer for sixty minutes. Then my son decided what he wanted to do with that time—his time. We would read stories, color, draw, build a lopsided castle with blocks, or just talk. But no matter what he chose, he had my undivided attention.

If the doorbell rang, I would ask the caller to return later. As the answering machine collected messages, I lost myself in my son's little world of fantasy, imagination and fun. Depending on what shift my husband worked, he would join us when he could. Many times, we were so engrossed in what we were doing that we ignored the timer going off to finish whatever project we were immersed in.

Special Hour lasted for many years until my son, an only child, began school and had a social life of his own, becoming too active to "amuse Mom and Dad." I often think back on those days, grateful that I discovered the importance of making time for what was most precious in my life—before being a busy mom made me too busy to be a mom.

~Marya Morin

Sick Break

We should read to give our souls a chance to luxuriate.
~Henry Miller

Moms need social outlets. My favorite is book club. Once a month, my literary friends gather for intelligent conversation and homemade coffee cake while our children play in another room under the watchful eye of a babysitter. I look forward to it for weeks. But one morning, when the club was slated to discuss a popular new biography, my two-year-old woke with a fever. So, of course, we stayed home.

Bummer.

"What are we going to do today, beanie?" I crouched to my toddler's level and smoothed her wispy hair with my fingertips.

"Read books." Her eyes twinkled. Then she coughed in my face.

"Okay, bring me three books." And a box of Airborne.

"Five books!"

"Three books to start." I grabbed a tissue and wiped her nose. "Then when we're done reading, you can help me put some laundry in the wash." Might as well take advantage of our quarantine and catch up on the housework, right?

"Okay, Momma!" She ran to her room and returned with—yep—five books. We snuggled into the sofa cushions and started reading. When we finished one stack of favorite stories, she retrieved another from the book bin. Then another, and another.

Before I knew it, our three-book limit blew to nearly an hour of quality time huddled together under a blanket. Then we set the books aside and turned on a movie. My daughter cradled a sippy cup in the crook of her elbow and pressed her head against my chest.

Stillness. Such a strange feeling. I listened to my daughter breathe and sniffle. Cough and sneeze. Munch crackers and giggle at the television screen.

Laundry? Forget it. I had more important things to do.

Sometimes I trick myself into thinking busy is better. That a fulfilling and productive lifestyle requires being with people—working, volunteering, scheduling playdates and coffee breaks, dissecting the meaning of life with friends while holding steaming lattes in our hands.

But when I'm forced to sit in the quiet, slow moments, I begin to see how loud and rushed my life has become. Social commitments. Deadlines. Chores. Routines. They can pack the calendar and crowd out my peace. Then a sick day punches my pause button, and I have no choice but to rest.

Funny, isn't it? All this time I thought social outlets were my "break." Maybe not.

As I sat on the sofa that day with my arms around my daughter and studied her delicate eyelashes, her red-rimmed nose and plump cheeks, it dawned on me—I was not stuck home alone. I was spending precious downtime with one of the people I love best.

That was not a bummer. It was beautiful.

So from that day on, I started scheduling "sick days." They're blank squares on the calendar, purposely left open to enjoy the company of family with no particular agenda or to-do list. Sometimes we eat popcorn for breakfast and stay in our pajamas until noon. Sometimes the kids watch a video while I speed-read the next book club pick. And when one of my children actually does come down with an illness, I'm less likely to grieve over the sudden change in plans and more likely to say something like this: "Awww, sweetie, you have a fever. Bonus free day! Let's pick five storybooks. Better yet—make that ten. Today we're having our own little book club."

~Becky Kopitzke

An Invitation Not an Interruption

Everywhere is walking distance if you have the time.
~Steven Wright

I had four children in five years... on purpose. Two of my sons were born so close together there was only one inch and one pound difference between them for their first five years. People would often ask if they were twins, and they'd say yes, but they were born a year apart.

We lived on a farm so, besides the four children, I had horses, sheep, goats, cattle and chickens to take care of. When four children are born so close together, they often feel they are part of a herd or a flock. It isn't always easy to spend special time with them individually. So, every evening after dinner, I would take each of my children on a fifteen-minute walk.

One at a time, I would take them through the grove of oak trees, or down to the rocky creek, or up the hill. In bad weather, we'd just walk up and down the long dirt driveway. We'd talk about anything, everything, nothing. We'd tell jokes, sing a song, make up poems and talk about the family. After fifteen minutes, we'd go back to the house, and I'd take the next kid out for his walk. It took an hour of my time, but for me, it was the best hour of the day. There were very few days we skipped our walks.

When my children asked me to do something with them, I would stop whatever I was doing and look at them, really look at them, and listen to them. And, if possible, I would do what they asked.

Could I stop washing dishes to play a game of *Chutes and Ladders*? Of course, I could. Would it be nice if the kitchen was clean and the dishes were washed? Sure. What's more important, though, playing a game with my child or washing a dish?

One time, when I was frying a chicken for dinner, my oldest son rushed into the house and begged me to go outside with him. I turned off the burner, moved the skillet off the heat and went outside to see what was so important.

A heavy frost had covered the entire farm. Every tree looked as if it had been covered with white icing. I'd never seen anything so beautiful. My son and I walked through a tunnel of trees bowed almost to the ground from the weight of the frost on their limbs. The earth was silent; we were silent. It was a magical moment we shared.

I could have stayed in the kitchen and fried a chicken, but I didn't. I followed my son outside into a scene of beauty that never happened again. It was a once-in-a-lifetime memory. I'm so glad I didn't miss it.

When my young daughter asked me to go outside to look at the "melted butter" on the hill I went even though I wanted to finish watching a movie on television; there were only fifteen minutes left. I went outside and looked across the meadow. The hill must have had a thousand jonquils in bloom. When we got back to the house, we put jonquils in every vase, pitcher, glass and cup in the house. Every year after that, there were jonquils on the hill, but there were never as many as there were that spring. I don't remember the name of the movie I was watching that day, I don't know how it ended or what it was about, but I'll never forget collecting those armloads of jonquils with my daughter.

"Come quick, Mom!" one of the kids would yell, and I always stopped whatever I was doing and followed them outside to the woods, to the meadow, to the pond or to wherever they led me.

We saw wild geese flying past the full silver moon, honking to each other and landing on the pond with the reflection of the moon on the water. We watched kittens being born in the hayloft in the barn and witnessed the miracle of five new lives. We waded in snow, swished through piles of autumn leaves, danced in the pouring rain, listened to the thunder that was so loud it shook our hearts. On hot summer nights, we'd lie on a quilt on the grass for hours and watch the sky for shooting stars.

Years later, my son Peter said his favorite thing about his childhood was that no matter what I was doing, I'd always stop and give him one hundred percent of my attention, even if it was just to look at a shiny rock he'd found.

Did I make mistakes? Oh, yes, hundreds. Do I have regrets? Yes, I do, but one regret I don't have is that when my kids asked me to do something or to go outside and look at something or to play a game, I never considered it an interruption. I considered it an invitation. They were inviting me to share their life, their special moment, and it was an honor and always an unforgettable experience and a blessing.

Dirty dishes, laundry, sweeping, cooking can wait. These things will wait patiently for an hour or a day or for several days. But moments with my children were really just moments, gone in the blink of an eye. Sometimes you only get one chance to do something.

My children are grown now. They are fine, decent, funny, warm, loving, compassionate people. I'm proud of all four of them. They have never caused me shame or grief.

I watch my children with their own children now. When their sons and daughter come running up to them and say, "Come with me, Daddy. I want to show you something," they stop what they are doing and let their children lead them to adventures.

If I did anything right as a mother, that would be at the top of the list. When children ask you to spend time with them, it's not an interruption. It's an invitation to share miracles, adventures, blessings… and you only get one chance.

~April Knight

Save the Worms

One of the most responsible things you can do as an adult is become more of a child.
~Dr. Wayne W. Dyer

Heavy rain pelted the grocery store parking lot. Dismayed, I wheeled my cart to a halt inside the foyer exit and waited for the downpour to subside, thinking of the work I had left to do at home. At least the kids would be in bed when I got there.

But thirty minutes later, after the rain had stopped, I pulled into the driveway and saw my son Andrew playing on our sidewalk while my husband fixed a broken storm door handle.

"Why isn't Andrew in bed?" I asked.

"He's looking for earthworms," my husband said, as if that is the natural thing for a four-year-old to be doing past his bedtime.

"And why is he looking for earthworms when he is supposed to be in bed?"

"Ask him. It has something to do with *Wild Kratts*."

"Oh."

Andrew's favorite show, PBS's *Wild Kratts*, features brothers who teach children about insects and animals in nature, and if the Kratts say something, my little nature lover takes it to heart. In a recent episode, they implored "creature rescuers" to help earthworms back to grassy areas when they slither out on pavement during rainstorms.

"Mom, we have to save the worms!" Andrew said, running to greet me. "If we don't rescue them, they will dry out and die."

I'd heard of dog rescues, cat rescues, even exotic wildlife rescues. But worm rescues? I hesitated to join the cause. I wasn't fond of picking up slimy creatures, no matter how much they helped the earth.

"Andrew, it's almost dark."

I didn't point out that the worms had all night to slide off the pavement and burrow back into the ground, long before the sun came up the next day and dehydrated them like crispy Chinese noodles.

"I also have a lot to do," I added. I had to plan his homeschool lessons, put together a casserole for company that was coming the next day, and write an article that had a quickly approaching deadline. I was too busy to be doing something as frivolous as rescuing worms.

But then I saw the pleading look in my son's eyes and the expectancy in his face. This mattered to him, the boy who hated to see living creatures die, excluding spiders and wasps. He still goes out of his way to save ladybugs, beetles, and mayflies. One spring, he kept a caterpillar in a jar next to his bed until it spun a cocoon and emerged as a moth. Then he released the moth outdoors.

"Okay," I relented. "Let's go save the worms."

For the next thirty minutes, we splashed through puddles on the shimmering street. Andrew scooped earthworms off the pavement and gently placed them on the grass. We zigzagged across the road, delighted at each rescued worm. The water squished between my toes in my sandals, but I didn't care. I imagined the neighbors, hidden behind their front-window curtains, shaking their heads and tsk-tsking, "Her sanity has diminished more rapidly than we thought." But again, I didn't care. When it grew dark, the neighbors' porch lights illuminated the street while we saved every worm in the vicinity. No worm would die on our watch.

We came home wet, but exhilarated. I felt refreshed, ready to tackle any task. However, the to-do list didn't seem quite so important anymore. I finished what I absolutely had to, postponed what I could, and crossed some items off all together. My most important task that day had been validating something that was important to my son, no matter how trivial it seemed to me.

That night, Andrew reminded me that childhood should never be as structured and organized as I am. There's no way to predict when worms will need rescuing! When I'm overwhelmed with tasks, I take a break and do something whimsical with Andrew and his younger sister, Gracie. We picnic outside, follow animal tracks in the snow, fly kites, or play tag in the spring grass. The time away from work reinvigorates me and gives my children the chance to see their mom join in the spontaneity of youth.

Twenty years from now, my to-do list won't change the world. But my son might. In his own way, he will leave an indelible mark on all the lives he touches. My hope is that he will be selfless and kind, willing to help others in need. I think he is off to a good start. At four, he taught his mom that making a difference begins with taking time to save the worms.

~Janeen Lewis

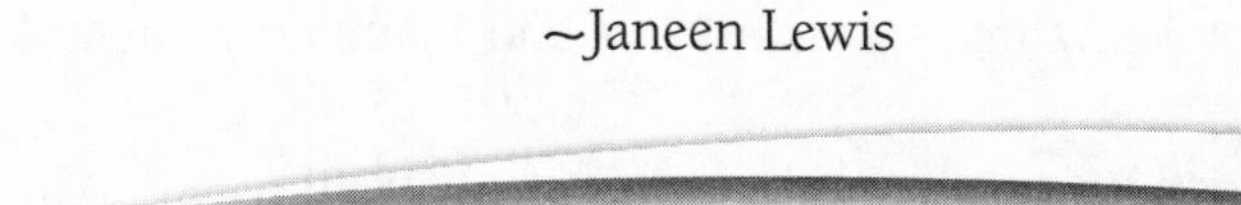

Uncorked

Technology presumes there's just one right way to do things and there never is.
~Robert M. Pirsig

I am not one of those "I Don't Know How She Does It" moms. We have a lot of those in my town. They volunteer at church, blog about keeping life simple, and have three or more kids, all of whom play three sports a week and maintain straight A's in school.

Me, I am a run-of-the-mill mother of two, still trying to adjust from going from a Filofax to an iPhone. When it comes to pulling together my family's much-more-limited plans I am organizationally challenged.

The iPhone might have changed other people's lives for the better, but for me, not so. All the apps look the same. I swipe the wrong way almost every time. I press Delete instead of Save. Sometimes an e-mail I know I received is there; sometimes it's not. And this is just the beginning.

I was a Filofax holdout for a long time because it worked for me. I never lost it; I could erase my pencil marks and make changes; I could see what I needed to do, flip to addresses, and find everything. In fact I realize now that I had most of it memorized.

But gradually, as time marched on, that way of life became too old school. Why carry a phone and a calendar when you can have it all in one place? I was supposed to be a young, hip mother. Everyone had an iPhone, and I needed one too.

I yielded; I gave technology a chance; and my life has never recovered. Plus, it appeared that everyone around me had made this leap with no problem. I was the only one struggling to keep up, to get the kids and myself to where we needed to be at the right time. That is if I didn't forget to show up.

After quietly talking to a few trustworthy friends about my organizational deficiency in the technological realm, I learned that I was not alone. In fact, what I realized was that for me, and others, remembering events, phone numbers, addresses, and things on my to-do list had as much to do with what color they were written in and where they were on the page as what the words actually said.

My brain functioned successfully when there was an image to grasp. Every time I looked at my Filofax my brain took a picture that I could hold onto and recall. In my iPhone all the information was merely data. Even with colors and typeface changes there was no nuance to the lettering or numbers.

I soldiered on for two years, constantly triple-checking my iPhone and still remembering nothing, until a large volunteer responsibility I accepted made me realize that I needed to add a little old school back in.

For about a week I maintained two calendars—the one on my iPhone and a desk calendar. Then I realized I was spending more time calendaring than living. What was I, a visual person, supposed to do?

My answer arrived like manna from heaven in the form of an old oversized cork bulletin board pulled from the attic.

Our Family Calendar now hangs on the mudroom wall for everyone to see and check. It is divided into four sections, one for each person in the family. Each person's section has everything that person needs to know about his or her life and where he or she is supposed to be. Each person has a calendar of school, sports, and activities that I have created for that season. Any reminder that comes in from a teacher gets pinned up in that child's quadrant. Allowance gets pinned up every Friday.

Each child also has a list of what he or she is working on, for example, brushing teeth before school (son) or packing an afternoon snack for dance (daughter). If anyone needs to know something, they can go to our Family Calendar and it's all there.

Today, when I go out into the world I carry my iPhone for texts, e-mails, and phone calls, but if someone asks me about the calendar, I say sweetly, "I'll have to get back to you!" Then I go home and check my bulletin board.

~Jennifer Quasha

All in Good Time

I am not Superwoman. The reality of my daily life is that I'm juggling a lot of balls in the air... and sometimes some of the balls get dropped.
~Cherie Blair

School. Work. A preschooler. It was a juggling act, and every week I had to scramble to make sure everything didn't come cascading down on me. I was recently divorced and I was taking college classes at night, on top of my day job working at a residential facility for children. And in the hours squeezed in-between, I tried to keep up with my daughter.

I had to make creative use of my time. When we went to the park, I took one of my college textbooks along to study while I kept an eye on Virginia as she arced back and forth on the swings and scampered around on the jungle gym. When I was cooking dinner, she would play with the pots and pans and I'd join in. On the drive to work, before I'd drop her off at preschool, I'd talk to her the whole way—about everything. The weather... What I was going to do at work that day... What we were going to have for dinner later that evening. The more we "conversed" (and back then it was more a monologue than a dialogue), the more her speaking skills improved. Every minute of my day had to be used wisely.

After my college instructor would dismiss us for the evening, I'd pick up my daughter from my parents, and we'd go through our nightly routine: a bath, a story and then bedtime... for her. I longed to feel a pillow under my head, but a multitude of things begged for my attention: the spills on the kitchen floor, the dirty dishes, the laundry, the research papers and projects that were due, the quizzes and tests that were looming—there was never a shortage of things to do.

A year of juggling those three things—work, college and my little girl—was taking its toll. At the children's facility where I worked, I was in charge of infants who had been abused. A large part of my day was spent rocking and feeding the babies. I didn't trust myself to spend too much time sitting down in a comfortable rocking chair because there were times I was afraid I would nod off.

During my classes I would occasionally fall asleep mid-lecture. You could look at my class notes and tell the instant I started to snooze because my writing would become illegible and eventually "flatline" across the page. It was like I was on automatic pilot. Even though I was asleep, my hand kept moving across the notebook, as if it had memorized its role.

It was obvious I was beginning to fail as a juggler.

One Sunday afternoon, Virginia was playing with her dolls on the floor. I lay down on the couch with my geography textbook. I had a test coming up the following week and needed to study. From where I was positioned, I could re-read and highlight the chapter on geomorphology while I kept an eye on my daughter. Unfortunately, the diagrams and dull scientific passages failed to keep my attention, and not even my little girl could keep my sleep-deprived brain focused. Apparently, I dozed off because my head jerked upright as I awoke, startled, to a clattering noise.

Rushing to the kitchen where the commotion was coming from, I looked down. Kneeling on the floor was Virginia, safe and sound. However, she was also busy. In front of her was a mountain she had created. Flour. Sugar. Milk. Eggs.

Looking down at the white sloppy mound, tears came to my eyes. That mountainous mess was an obstacle, just like the insurmountable string of responsibilities that made up my life.

I couldn't be angry with her—it was my fault—so I cleaned it up without even a frustrated look cast her way. As I was sopping up the liquid and scooping up the powdery globs, I thought to myself, "Something's gotta give. I cannot keep up this pace anymore."

It could have been so much worse. Virginia could have climbed onto the counter and gotten into the knives. Thinking of all the horrible ways it might have ended, I felt fortunate. It was as if someone had been watching over my little girl, since I hadn't been.

When the semester ended, I quit college. Six years later, I re-enrolled and finished. Keeping up with the pace the college professors set was still difficult, but this time I had a husband who supported and encouraged me. I resigned from work so I could go to school full-time. Eventually, I became a third-grade teacher.

Can women have it all? Can moms juggle a family, career and college, and keep everything from tumbling to the floor?

I don't know about most mothers. I just know that in my case, I realized I could have it all... just not at the same time.

~Sioux Roslawski

The Worst Piano Lesson Ever

Turn your wounds into wisdom.
~Oprah Winfrey

"Mom, remember the time you made me go to a piano lesson with a broken arm?" my elder daughter quipped. As a family, we were enjoying a lighthearted Sunday lunch, laughing over days gone by. Everyone laughed at the broken arm memory, except me. Ouch. That one stung. I don't know what hurt the most: the fact that Megan's arm was broken or the fact that I did, in fact, take her to a piano lesson with a fresh break. However, in my defense, I wasn't quite as bad a mom as that story makes it sound.

I was a working mom, a high school guidance counselor by day and wife and mom of two by night. In the circus I called life, I juggled a caseload of 525 students from 7:00 a.m. to 4:00 p.m. and two precious daughters and a husband from 4:00 p.m. to 9:00 p.m. A typical day was filled with college applications, academic problems, and teenage crises. Five hundred students meant a thousand parents or more, depending on the marital status of the family. My days began early with waking and dressing the girls, dropping them off at two different sites, and then racing to school. I was usually spotted in the parking lot where students talked to me as we walked into the building. Many mornings began with me facilitating a 7:00 a.m. parent/teacher conference where a student was usually academically at risk.

Sandwiched in the middle of the day were more phone calls, e-mails, and students knocking at my door than I could keep track of. My day usually ended with a student following me to the car, talking all the way. I would then race across town to pick up the girls. Then we were off to piano, violin, dance or church activities, snacking as we wove through traffic in the blue minivan. Thinking back, it's all a blur, but I vividly remember the day of the broken arm.

As I picked up the girls, Megan calmly stated, "My arm hurts. I can't lift it."

"What happened? Why does it hurt?"

"I fell playing blind tag on the jungle gym during recess."

"What! You mean you were playing tag on the top of the jungle gym with your eyes closed? Why would you do such a thing?" My very precocious fifth-grader responded with a shrug.

"Did you go to the nurse's office?"

"No. I asked Mr. Smith, but he said I needed to take the spelling test. By the time the test was over, it was time to go."

"Humm," I grunted. Obviously Mr. Smith, Meg's teacher, was focused on the task at hand and not listening to my child. When the bell rang, she was off to the after-school program, never having visited the nurse.

By the time we finished this discussion, we were in front of her piano teacher's house. There was no such thing as a cellphone in those days, so my plan was to call the doctor from the teacher's home phone while Megan attended the lesson. The lesson was already paid for, right? Might as well kill two birds with one stone, or was that two activities with one little broken arm? While on hold with the doctor's office, I peeked around the corner to check how the lesson was going. There sat my brave girl, holding her arm up to the keyboard with her other hand. Stoically, she was doing what she was told to do. As I finished arranging for a doctor's office visit, Meg finished her lesson with tears in her eyes.

We hurried to the doctor's where an X-ray showed that, in fact, she did have a fractured arm. I watched her face, teeth digging into her bottom lip, while the nurses moved the arm into the right position to support it and set it.

By the time we arrived home, supper was long overdue. I hurried to pull together a quick meal while Megan told the whole story to her dad and little sister. I overheard her say, "Mom made me go to my piano lesson." Wow, had I really done that? Perhaps Mr. Smith wasn't the only person focused on the task and not the child. In the hustle and bustle of my life, had I seen this as another problem to hurry and solve? Had I truly been insensitive to the pain my child was in? By the end of dinner, I knew what I had to do.

Later as I helped Megan gingerly into her pajamas, brush her teeth, and climb into bed, she asked, "Mom, do I have to go to school tomorrow?"

"No, sweetheart. How about you and Mom stay home tomorrow?"

"Really? I would love that," she exclaimed with a big smile on her face.

I called in a sick day for both of us the next day. We both had a break that needed to heal. We spent the day in our pajamas, curled up in bed together reading books and talking. By the end of the day, I knew that there was more broken here than Megan's arm. Luckily, the broken arm would heal physically, and thankfully, the bigger broken issue would also heal. The pace I was living could slow down, and I would learn to listen to the verbal and nonverbal messages of the ones I love. It's funny that life presents us with opportunities to reset fractures that we don't even know are broken. I'm just glad to have caught this fracture when it could still easily heal.

~Gwyn Schneck

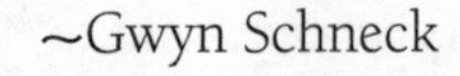

Say It Again, Sam

If I have a monument in this world, it is my son.
~Maya Angelou

"Mom, did you hear me?" my son Samuel asks.

"Hmmm," I say.

"The cookout. For youth group. It starts at four."

"Gotcha," I say. But truth be known, it probably didn't register. I'm admiring my son. He's standing on the deck near our pool. His skin is a warm, cocoa brown. His wet hair stands up in blond tufts, corn-silk salutes to summer and boyhood and swimming and fun.

"I love you, Sam," I say.

"Love you too, Mom." And he's off. His eleven-year-old, gangly preteen body leaps and curls, and now he's a cannonball plunging into the water below. A wild spray of water rains on the deck. On his brothers who are sprawled on a blanket, playing with a green plastic cavalry. And on me.

It's going to be crazy. This cookout that Sam will go to lands right in the middle of a jam-packed day. My husband and I will have to double-team the schedule for sure. We're used to it, though. We have five sons. Sometimes our two family vans run like a hotel shuttle service. Passengers here. Passengers there. Drop off. Pick up. Passing sometimes on our town's main road, the one that parallels the Mississippi River, in red and silver blurs.

I let the sun rest on my shoulders for just a moment before I begin the great withdrawal. Our three youngest sons are playing in or around the pool. There has been an hour of unscheduled goodness. An hour of heaven. An hour of stay-at-home stillness that has become a rare thing. Pulling them from the pool, encouraging them to shower and dress and find all six wayward flip-flop shoes—that will be a chore.

I notice that two of my little guys are in combat with their plastic army men. Their hands are curled around soldiers. Their legs fold like pretzel twists. And their hair, a slight green from pool chemicals, is slicked back like seals. I watch them for a moment. Drink in the sound of their little-boy voices. I want to hold these moments, these sounds, the sights and smells and feel of this day in my heart.

I know they pass too soon.

It's a three-party day. Might sound like a lot, but truly it's not an unusual thing. With so many people under one roof, there is always a friend having a gathering. Today I'll drive two over the river to visit a boy from church. His birthday party will be this afternoon. My husband will have to shuttle Sam and friends to the cookout. And we'll both have to shoot home and get ready for my friend's surprise birthday party. It will all have to work smoothly—synchronized like water ballet. We'll need to be accomplished and gathered and in place when my friend walks, hand-over-mouth, into her birthday celebration at five.

I notice that Sam has taken two or three more leaps into the pool, and I know that I have to get shaking. If we're not on time, the dominos will fall, and the afternoon will crash. Never mind that I also have to make lunch for today and a potluck casserole for a breakfast thing tomorrow.

But I'm drawn to this play of my sons.

They've stacked river rock in a wall. Palm-sized pebbles for the small green men to scale.

My friend says it's my saving grace—this longing to watch, listen, witness the miracles of the small things around me. Our lives move so fast. It's here and there and back to here again. We're always running, doing, committing. If I don't carve a moment to appreciate, to know, to treasure these everyday things, they'll be swept away in yesterdays.

And I want to live these moments. I want to make myself slow down enough to let them run through my senses and settle into my heart.

Samuel trudges over, leaving near man-sized footprints on the boards of the deck. He stands in front of me and gives me a gap-toothed grin.

"Mom, did you hear me?" He smiles. He knows how I am. "The cookout. It starts at four."

Yes, Sam. I know what you're really saying. "Mom, better get moving. There's lots to do, and we have to be on time."

It registers.

The cookout is at four. And being on time is important.

But you may have to say it again, Sam.

Because I want to take a moment.

I'm not willing to miss the fleeting treasure of you.

~Shawnelle Eliasen

Seeking Serenity

Boredom is the feeling that everything is a waste of time;
serenity, that nothing is.
~Thomas Szasz

Watching sleeping babies has never been my thing. While other parents recount that this is one of the absolute joys of parenting, that there is nothing as peaceful in the world, that this simple task makes the trials and tribulations of parenting all worth it—I shake my head slowly, perplexed.

Back in the days when I would have watched my own babies sleep, what I saw was an opportunity to go sleep myself. I was very sleep-deprived, and I've always been very practical.

If, by some miracle, my baby boys actually napped for more than twenty minutes at a time, I saw an opportunity to do something productive. You know—laundry, dishes, cleaning, maybe even take a shower or brush my teeth.

Standing motionless, watching babies sleep, just letting the time pass, did not appeal to me. It was enough to take a quick peek, to make sure their little eyes were closed and their breathing steady, before I was off.

Now, years later, I spend hours each week watching my boys swim.

I often think to myself, perhaps I should do something productive. There is plenty of time to leave swim team practice—to go run errands, to go to the gym next door, to make phone calls to neglected friends and relatives.

There is nothing new or exciting that happens at any given swim practice. It's not like I will miss anything monumental if I leave. Jonah, my nine-year-old, complains that, "Swim practice is the most boring thing in the world."

Ah, my boy. If only you could see it from my point of view. That is exactly what I love about it.

My two boys are most beautiful when they are swimming. Their wiry arms and legs are rhythmic, their lean bodies perfectly controlled, strong and purposeful. Their breathing is patterned and predictable—one, two, three, breathe, one, two, three, breathe. Everything about them is peaceful, planned, and orderly.

It is rare to see them this way—for while they are generally good kids, they are also exploding with the exuberance of young life, full of fresh ideas, fervent eagerness, and, most notably, total chaos. Spending time with them is often like getting swept into a tornado. I love them for their raw zest and enthusiasm—but sometimes, I just need a break.

The other parents don't wait around. They get groceries, they exercise, they chase younger siblings around outside by the little play structure. Some of them even go outside and take naps in their cars. I am one of the only ones sitting—apparently doing nothing—on the very uncomfortable set of metal bleachers. If it is cold, I bundle up in my down parka and drink hot tea.

I cannot tear myself away from this hour of tranquility. Watching my boys in motion—in perfect, rhythmic, orderly motion—is so different from the whirlwind of raw energy, the flailing limbs, and the unpredictable explosions of chaotic motion that mark the other hours of my day. I know that as soon as swim practice ends, there will be an argument about who showers first, about what we're having for dinner, about taking out the garbage, about going to bed.

But here, during swim practice, my boys are breathtaking.

I sit at peace in the eye of the hurricane.

I have found my thing.

~Lisa Pawlak

to do list:
Pay bills
- Get laundry
- Call Mom
- Pick up kids
from birthday
at 6 p.m.
- Buy groceries

The Multitasking Mom's Survival Guide

Meet Our Contributors
Meet Our Authors
Thank You
About Chicken Soup for the Soul

An excerpt from
Chicken Soup for the Soul: Just Us Girls

Meet Our Contributors

Debbie Acklin has stories in numerous Chicken Soup for the Soul books and was featured on the front page of her local paper and dozens of papers nationwide. She has been interviewed by a local TV station and a national radio station. Her first novel is almost complete. Contact her via e-mail at d_acklin@hotmail.com.

Beth Andrews, LCSW, LAC, is a therapist, supervisor, college instructor, and mother. She has authored three self-help books for children: books about parental depression, parents with PTSD, and a military kid's book about deployment, as well as numerous articles on parenting issues. Contact her via e-mail at bethandrewslcsw@aol.com.

Peg Arnold received her master's degree in 1995 from Johns Hopkins University. She freely shares her life experiences as teacher, counselor, wife, mother and grandmother of twins in unique, humorous, entertaining and touching ways through her writings and her Wonder of Women ministry. Visit her blog at pegarnold.wordpress.com.

Dalene Bickel, writer and editor, is passionate about preserving life stories and family histories. She earned her B.A. degree in English and History from Chatham University in 1996. She is a volunteer and board member with JDRF Coastal Carolina Branch, which supports Type 1 diabetics. E-mail her at DBickel@lasting-legacies.net.

Freelance writer **Florence Calderone Blake** has had more than 1,600 articles published in newspapers, magazines, and anthologies in the past decade. She's currently a reporter for various newspapers. Since its publication in 2010, she's appeared on over 950 radio and TV stations discussing her memoir, *The Sicilian Nobleman's Daughter*.

Beverly Burmeier is a former public school teacher turned freelancer. She writes for a variety of national and regional publications on topics including health, travel, lifestyle, family, and gardening. She lives in Central Texas and loves sharing stories about her children and grandchildren.

Pamela Hermanson Camel received her Bachelor of Science in marketing from Bellevue University in 2010. She currently is a stay-at-home mom and autism blogger. E-mail her at noguile04@yahoo.com.

Lucy Lemay Cellucci is the author of the Young Adult novel *True Colours*. She currently resides in Ottawa, Ontario, where she teaches dance. When she's not teaching, writing, or child rearing, she enjoys mountain biking, and administering first aid on herself. Please visit her blog at www.lucylcellucci.net.

This is **Sharon Love Cook's** third story for Chicken Soup for the Soul. She's the author of the Granite Cove Mystery series and lives north of Boston with her husband and assorted rescued cats. Her babysitting ordeal has become a family legend. E-mail her at cookie978@comcast.net.

D'ette Corona is the Assistant Publisher of Chicken Soup for the Soul Publishing, LLC. She received her Bachelor of Science in business management. D'ette has been happily married for twenty-one years and has a seventeen-year-old son whom she adores.

Heather Davis is a momma, a writer and a blogger. She blogs at www.Minivan-Momma.com. She is the author of the TMI Mom books, which include *TMI Mom Bites the Big Apple*, *TMI Mom: Oversharing My Life* and *TMI Mom: Getting Lucky*.

Linda C. Defew divides her time between writing and entertaining family and friends. Living on a farm, the summer involves gardening and food preservation; the fall and winter are spent taking pictures of wildlife out of her fourteen-foot enclosed tree stand. E-mail her at oldwest@tds.net.

Lynn Dove is the author of the award-winning Wounded Trilogy for young adults. She is a frequent contributor to the Chicken Soup for the Soul anthologies and her popular blog "Journey Thoughts" has won a Canadian Christian writing award. Readers may connect with her on Facebook, Twitter and on her blog at lynndove.com.

Shawnelle Eliasen and her husband Lonny raise their bevy of boys near the Illinois banks of the Mississippi River. Shawnelle home teaches the youngest three. She contributes regularly to Chicken Soup for the Soul series and *Guideposts* magazine. Follow her adventures at "Family Grace with My Five Sons" on shawnellewrites.blogspot.com.

Nicole Sweeney Etter is a freelance writer/editor in Milwaukee. She's constantly inspired and challenged by life with her spirited preschooler and toddler, and she dutifully memorized the *Thomas the Tank Engine* theme song so she can sing it on command.

Melanie Fowler, author of *Look At My Eyes*, holds B.A. and M.A. degrees in Speech Language Pathology and Special Education. Her son, William, was diagnosed with autism at the age of two. She and her husband, Seth, continue to help others through speaking engagements and outreach initiatives. Learn more at www.lookatmyeyes.com.

Angela Glenn received her bachelor's degree from Central Missouri State in 2004 and master's degree from Johns Hopkins University in 2010. She lives in Maryland with her husband and their two daughters and writes about the journey of motherhood on her website "Time with A & N" at http://glennbabies.blogspot.com. E-mail her at glennbabies@gmail.com.

Anastacia Grenda is a writer and editor who lives with her family in Southern California. E-mail her at babyonkeyboard@gmail.com.

Gina Guilford received her M.F.A. degree in Screenwriting from University of Miami in 2003. A freelance writer for more than twenty years, Gina's been published in magazines, newspapers and books. She's currently writing restaurant news and reviews for the Examiner and working on a murder mystery set in Miami. Go Canes!

Rita Hancock, MD, ("Dr. Rita") specializes in musculoskeletal medicine and pain management. She appears on national radio and TV and is a blogger (www.AskDoctorRita.blogspot.com) and the author of Christian health and wellness books (*Radical Well-Being* and *The Eden Diet*). For more information about Dr. Rita, visit www.RitaHancock.com.

Gloria Jean Hansen has penned columns and articles for local newspapers and magazines and written books for many years. She is a nurse educator/writer/bluegrass musician and hopes one day to retire to a cabin by the river to write full-time. Contact her at glowin@persona.ca or arielgroup.ca link "Gloria Hansen".

Kathy Lynn Harris is the author of two Amazon bestselling novels: *Blue Straggler* and *A Good Kind of Knowing*, which earned the top NFPW literary award in 2013. She also blogs and has written children's books, magazine articles, short fiction, essays and poetry. Learn more at kathylynnharris.com.

Kimberly Henderson is a writer who lives in the Upstate of South Carolina with her handsome husband, three giggly girls, and one seriously spoiled Schnauzer. You can find this recovering perfectionist pressing through the toughest of days with humor, honesty, and the Word of God at her blog, www.aplantingofthelord.com.

Marilee Herman received her Bachelor of Arts degree from Brigham Young University in 1996. In addition to being a busy mother of four, ages 6-16, she teaches tap dance at San Juan College, helps in the family businesses, and serves in her church. E-mail her at marileeherman@msn.com.

Mary Hickey is the mother of four children, three of whom are on the autism spectrum. She is a registered nurse in Boston, and has previously written for Chicken Soup for the Soul. She enjoys writing about her experiences of motherhood and raising children with special needs. E-mail her at maryhickey_4@yahoo.com.

Miriam Hill is a frequent contributor to the Chicken Soup for the Soul series and has been published in *Writer's Digest*, *The Christian Science Monitor*, *Grit*, *St. Petersburg Times*, *The Sacramento Bee*, HCI books, and Poynter. Miriam's manuscript received Honorable Mention for Inspirational Writing in a Writer's Digest Writing Competition.

Erika Hoffman has authored several stories included in the Chicken Soup for the Soul anthology. She also writes essays, travel pieces, and humorous tales. Before she began penning her life one story at a time, she taught school, raised four kids, and took care of her elderly dad. Occasionally, she cooks a meal for her husband!

Keri Houchin graduated from Howard Payne University in 2006 with a Bachelor of Arts degree in Cross-Cultural Studies. She lives in the Dallas-Fort Worth area with her husband and two children. When not writing, she runs a handmade business with her husband called Houchin's House of Wizarding Wares.

Martha Hynson is a veteran multitasker. She raised three children (with a little help from her husband) while teaching preschool and earning a degree in Early Childhood Education. She then taught first grade and kindergarten. These days she enjoys encouraging a new generation of multitasking moms through her website www.welcomelord.com.

Joelle Jarvis's passion has always been personal development. She has worked with many of the world's most inspirational names, including Tony Robbins, and now has her dream job as Vice President of Marketing for Chicken Soup for the Soul. Her greatest love is her son Jackson. E-mail her at joellejarvis@mac.com.

April Knight is an artist and freelance writer. She enjoys riding horses and beachcombing. She collects antique inkwells. E-mail her at aknightscribe@gmail.com.

Mimi Greenwood Knight is a freelance writer living in South Louisiana with her husband, David, and four spectacular kids. She enjoys gardening, baking, karate, knitting, Bible study, and has recently jumped on the backyard chicken wagon. Mimi is blessed to have essays in two dozen Chicken Soup for the Soul books.

Debbie Koharik teaches ESL and GED courses in Illinois. She served as a Korean linguist in the Army and, after completing an

M.A. degree in English, earned a commission in the Air Force. She is a military spouse of seventeen years and mother of two busy teenagers. E-mail her at debbie81k@gmail.com.

Jacqueline Davidson Kopito received her Bachelor of Arts degree from Syracuse University and a master's degree in Corporate and Public Communication, with honors, from Seton Hall University. She is a member of the Writers Guild of America. She lives with her husband and two sons in Short Hills, NJ.

Becky Kopitzke is a freelance writer, devotional blogger, lunch packer, snowman builder and sidewalk chalk artist. She lives with her devoted husband and their two young daughters in northeast Wisconsin, where a pink indoor trampoline fills half the living room. Visit her blog, www.beckykopitzke.com, for weekly mom-to-mom encouragement.

Kimber Krochmal lives in rural North Carolina. She has a large family consisting of not only her own children but other children she "adopted" over the years. They keep her young and are a constant source of inspiration.

Ann Kronwald holds a master's degree from the University of Hawaii, and has a passion for writing. Her articles often highlight one of God's Old Testament names, or narrate a tale of the wee folk in her life. She received first place in the 2011 Writers-Editors Network International Writing Competition.

Sharon Landeen, a retired elementary teacher, is a volunteer reading mentor and art teacher, blanket maker for Project Linus, 4-H leader, and avid University of Arizona basketball fan. Topping her list of favorite things to do, however, is spending time with her children, grandchildren, and great-grandchildren.

Lori Lara is a writer, blogger, photographer, black belt martial artist, and homeschool mom. She passionately shares the hope and healing of Jesus with people struggling with addiction, PTSD, grief, and depression. She lives in Northern California with her husband Robert and two sons. E-mail her at lori@lorilaraphotography.com.

Kathryn Lay is the author of twenty-five children's books and 2,000 articles, essays, and stories, including eleven in the Chicken Soup for the Soul series. She loves speaking to school children and writers. She and her husband own an antique/vintage business, Days Gone By. Visit her at www.kathrynlay.com or e-mail her at rlay15@aol.com.

Arlene Ledbetter holds a Bachelor of Arts degree from Dalton College. She has written adult Sunday school curriculum, magazine articles, and is an active member of the Chattanooga Writers' Guild. Her story "Chosen Last" appeared in *Chicken Soup for the Soul: Think Positive for Kids*. Sample more of her work at www.arleneledbetter.com.

Lynne Leite has two great loves — faith and family. She is a speaker and author and desires to be a blessing to others by sharing stories of hope and inspiration. You can learn more about Lynne and read her devotional blog by visiting her website at www.CurlyGirl4God.com.

Kathleen Leopold is the mother of four very active kids. In addition to writing about her family adventures at www.autismherd.blogspot.com, she co-runs the Autism blogs directory and is a writer and correspondent for The Autism Channel. E-mail her at kathomar@aol.com.

Janeen Lewis earned degrees in journalism and elementary education from Eastern Kentucky University. She has been published in more than a dozen Chicken Soup for the Soul anthologies. Janeen lives in Smyrna, GA with her husband and two children.

Patricia Lorenz is the author of thirteen books and contributor to nearly sixty Chicken Soup for the Soul books. She's mother of four, grandmother of eight, wife of one and enjoys following her dreams while she's still awake in Largo, FL. If you'd like her to speak to your group, e-mail her at patricialorenz@juno.com.

Anita Love taught high school English until she had her first child. She now redirects her teaching passion into writing anecdotes to help busy families stay happy, intimate and intact. She started swinging trapeze lessons, and lives in Port Moody, B.C. with her husband, children, and chocolate Lab. Learn more at happyfamiliesblog.wordpress.com.

Julie Luek is a nationally published writer and mom living in the mountains of Colorado. She enjoys hiking with her dog, Blue, and is a regular contributor to the websites Joyful Home and Life, and She Writes. She loves connecting with readers on Facebook at Julie Luek or Twitter @julieluek.

Shawn Marie Mann is a geographer and writer living in central Pennsylvania with her family. When not cooking chicken nuggets, she likes to travel within her home state and document the Pennsylvania Dutch Country for her website www.amusementparkmom.com. E-mail Shawn at shawnmariemann@yahoo.com.

BJ Marshall is a freelance writer and mother of three trying to steer her household in a greener direction. Read about her adventures—the good, the bad and the hilarious—at www.confessionsofagreenmom.com. Though she still occasionally loses her keys, she always checks her e-mail. E-mail her at confessionsofagreenmom@comcast.net.

Brandy Lynn Maslowski is a career firefighter turned quilter. She now follows her passion as a quilt teacher, judge and the new host of *Canadian Quilt Talk*. She takes motherhood to the extreme with a balance of the nitty-gritty vs. snuggles and fun! E-mail her at info@explorefibre.com.

Randi Mazzella is a freelance writer who writes for many publications including *New Jersey Family*, *Life with Teens* and *Your Teen*. In addition, she blogs for the website Barista Kids (kids.baristanet.com). Randi has been married for twenty-three years and is the mother of three children. E-mail her at rmazzella5@verizon.net.

Amy McMunn is a native West Virginian living in Rochester, NY with her two sons, the dog and several creepy animals, which her son adores. She has been a parent to special needs for more than a decade and a past contributor to *Chicken Soup for the Soul: Raising Kids on the Spectrum*. Learn more at fromthemomcave.blogspot.com.

Kate Meadows is a freelance editor/writer and published author who helps communicate life stories. Her work appears in *Writer's Digest*, *Kansas City Parent*, *Chicken Soup for the Soul: The Dating Game* and *Chicken Soup for the Soul: Thanks Mom*, and elsewhere. She lives with her husband and two sons in Kansas City. Learn more at www.katemeadows.com.

Laura Garwood Meehan is a writer and editor as well as mother of three. She participated in the 2013 Sacramento Listen to Your Mother show and also enjoys sharing her parenting trials and joys on her blog. She has a master's degree in publishing and runs her wordsmithing business in Sacramento.

Jane Miller is the founder of The Ruff Writers (www.theruffwriters.com) an intergenerational writing project and anti-bullying program. Jane and her husband Rick, a psychologist, live in Pittsburgh, PA with their sixteen-year-old daughter and dog Sadie. E-mail her at janemiller516@gmail.com or ruffwriterbooks@gmail.com.

Marya Morin is a freelance writer. Her stories and poems have appeared in publications such as *Woman's World* and Hallmark. Marya also penned a weekly humorous column for an online newsletter, and writes custom poetry on request. She lives in the country with her husband. E-mail her at akushla514@hotmail.com.

C. Muse is a writer, reviewer, teacher, and seeker of blue skies. She enjoys quality time with a good book in the backyard hammock. A published writer for over twenty years with credits ranging from *Highlights for Children* to *English Journal*, she continues pursuing the craft of writing.

Karen Nelson has a degree in education and is currently at work on her MFA in Creative Writing. She has published nonfiction articles, short stories, poetry, and educational curriculum, and now homeschools her children on a hobby farm in the Ozark Mountains. Visit her online at kbnelson.wordpress.com.

Chantal Panozzo is an American writer living in Switzerland. Her work has appeared in publications on three continents, including *The Christian Science Monitor*, *National Geographic Glimpse*, *Swiss News*, and more. She is the author of the forthcoming *Swiss Life: 29 Things I Wish I'd Known*. Visit her at chantalpanozzo.com.

Lisa Pawlak is a freelance writer and mother of two mischievous boys. Her work has been featured multiple times in the Chicken Soup for the Soul series, as well as in *Coping with Cancer* magazine and *The Christian Science Monitor*. E-mail her at lisapawlak@hotmail.com.

Diana Perry lives in Columbus, OH. She writes for magazines and newspapers, and also writes juvenile books, teen novels, mysteries and action adventures. Currently she is on tour with *The Weather by Heather* and working on her next book, *The Fairyland Pet Show*. E-mail her at info@bibliopublishing.com or dianaperryenterprises@yahoo.com.

Jill Pertler touches hearts and funny bones with her weekly syndicated column, "Slices of Life," printed in over 130 newspapers across the U.S. She is a playwright, author and has stories in three previous books in the Chicken Soup for the Soul series and two books in the Not Your Mother's Book series. Follow Slices of Life on Facebook.

Mary C. M. Phillips is a writer of narrative essays and short stories. Her work has appeared in numerous anthologies including the Chicken Soup for the Soul series, Cup of Comfort series, and *Bad Austen: The Worst Stories Jane Never Wrote*. Visit her blog at CaffeinatedWord.wordpress.com.

C. E. Plante is a teacher, author, freelance writer, and married mother of four. She recently published her first young adult novel entitled *Out the Other Side* and is a regular contributor for *Grown Ups Magazine*. E-mail her at ceplante@outlook.com.

Jennifer Quasha is a freelance writer, mother, foster dog mom, wife, daughter, friend, volunteer, reader, traveler, and believer. She writes to live and lives to write. She loves Chicken Soup for the Soul and has been published in over ten of their books. Stories make the world interesting!

Susan R. Ray, a retired teacher, writes a weekly newspaper column, memoirs for her family, and stories for her grandchildren. She enjoys playing with her six grandchildren, baking bread, and sewing. Read her column "Where We Are" at susanrray.com or e-mail her at srray@charter.net.

Kim Reynolds received her B.A. degree in Journalism from Concordia University in Montreal. Her fiction and essays have appeared in newspapers and the fiction anthology *The Company We Keep*. She lives in Canada with her husband, two children, a quiet dog and a noisy cat. Contact her at kimreynoldscreative.ca.

Amelia Rhodes lives in West Michigan with her husband and two children. Her book, *Isn't it Time for a Coffee Break? Doing Life Together in an All-About-Me Kind of World*, offers a fresh perspective on friendship. She enjoys running and drinking coffee with friends. Connect with Amelia at www.ameliarhodes.com.

Sara Rickover is the pseudonym of an award-winning author of short stories, essays, poetry, and novels. Sara has published the novel *Playing the Game*, a financial thriller. For more information about Sara and her novel, please see her Amazon Author Central page, amazon.com/author/sararickover.

Sioux Roslawski is a third grade teacher in St. Louis, a freelance writer and a dog rescuer. As one of the five founding members of the infamous WWWP writing critique group, she's constantly refining her craft. You can read more at siouxspage.blogspot.com.

Marcia Rudoff is a retired educator, teaching memoir writing to adults on Bainbridge Island, WA, a short ferry ride from Seattle. She is the author of *We Have Stories—A Handbook for Writing Your Memoirs*, and a frequent contributor to the Chicken Soup for the Soul series.

Jeneil Palmer Russell blogs at rhemashope.wordpress.com about life with her Army husband Brandon and their daughters Rhema, who is nine, autistic, epileptic, beautiful, brilliant, funny and gentle-hearted, and Hope, who is six, silly, joyful, imaginative, kind and full of all the best of childhood. Jeneil is author of *Sunburned Faces*.

Mitali Ruths lives in Montreal, Canada with her family and dances with Ballet Coppélia's excellent Adult Beginner class. One day, she dreams of doing a pirouette without falling flat on her face. Her stories have appeared in other Chicken Soup for the Soul anthologies. E-mail her at mitali.ruths@gmail.com.

Julie Sanders believes moms can find peace that passes understanding. From classrooms to churches to crossing cultures, she writes and speaks to inspire women around the world. Julie loves traveling, camping, and drinking tea with her husband and their two grown kids. Find Julie at "Come Have a Peace" at www.juliesanders.org.

Gwyn Schneck is retired from thirty years of teaching and counseling high school students. Currently she multitasks as a writer, speaker, wife, mom and most recently grandmother! She loves to bring life lessons and humor to audiences of parents, students, and women. Learn more at www.mykidscounselor.com.

Jaime Schreiner is a freelance writer from the Canadian prairies where she lives with her husband and two daughters. She has been published in the Chicken Soup for the Soul series, Hallmark, and numerous issues of Focus on the Family's *Thriving Family* magazine. Find her at jaimeschreinerwrites.wordpress.com or e-mail jaimeschreiner@yahoo.ca.

Denise Seagren-Peterson received her bachelor's degree in human relations at the University of Pittsburgh at Bradford and a master's degree in counseling psychology at St. Bonaventure University. Denise enjoys music, genealogy, history and spending time with her family. She has been writing a book about the Civilian Conservation Corps.

Ritu Shannon lives in beautiful British Columbia with her husband Jamie and their amazing kids, Priya and Keegan. This is Ritu's third published story in the Chicken Soup for the Soul series. In addition to writing, Ritu enjoys tropical vacations, going for long walks, and spending time at the ocean.

Sarah Shipley is a full-time homeschooling mom of four girls, part-time employee and runs a backyard farm. When she's not milking goats or preparing school lessons, she enjoys writing.

Diane Stark is a former teacher turned stay-at-home mom and freelance writer. She loves to write about the important things in life: her family and her faith. Visit Diane's blog at DianeStark.blogspot.com or e-mail her at DianeStark19@yahoo.com.

Amy Stout is a wife, mommy, and autism advocate who loves travel, coffee houses, books and Jesus! As a child of the King, her tiara is often missing, dusty, bent out of shape, or crooked, but will always and forever be His "Treasured Princess." Learn more at histreasuredprincess.blogspot.com or e-mail her at Brightencorner@hotmail.com.

Annemarie (Nuzzo) Thimons is a graduate of Franciscan University of Steubenville in Ohio. She grew up reading Chicken Soup for the Soul books and is thrilled to be a part of their community. Her three wonderful but crazy kids and husband Tom give her constant material to write about—including her first book series coming out in 2014! Keep in touch at www.athimons.com.

Eleanor Thomas retired in 2011 and has spent the three years since doing things she had no time for before. One of those things is writing stories. She hasn't had much luck getting published, but she enjoys every minute of putting a tale together. Eleanor lives in Ottawa, Ontario. E-mail her at ethomas123@rogers.com.

Becky Tidberg is an English, creative writing, and theater teacher in northern Illinois. She has had the privilege of being Mom to more than 100 kids through birth, foster care, and group home work. Please check out Becky's alter ego, the Worst Mother Ever, on Facebook or WorstMotherEver@yahoo.com.

Wendy Walker is an author and practicing attorney in Connecticut. She has two published novels, *Four Wives* and *Social Lives*, and has coauthored four Chicken Soup for the Soul books. Wendy divides her time between her two jobs and her three sons. She is at work on her third novel. You can find Wendy's work at wendywalkerbooks.com.

Samantha Ducloux Waltz specializes in multitasking. Her favorite endeavor is offering readers inspiration, courage and a fresh perspective on life as the writer of more than sixty creative nonfiction stories published in the Chicken Soup for the Soul series and other anthologies. She has also published under the name Samellyn Wood.

Ferida Wolff is the author of books for both children and adults. Her essays and poems appear in anthologies, newspapers, magazines, and online She writes a nature blog www.feridasbackyard.blogspot.com and can be reached via e-mail at feridawolff@msn.com.

Beth M. Wood is a mom of three, writer and marketing consultant. She has been published in several books in the Chicken Soup for the Soul series, and both regional and national magazines. She blogs about life at bethmwood.blogspot.com and about business at bethmwoodblog.com. Follow along on Twitter @a1972bmw.

Sheri Zeck enjoys writing creative nonfiction stories that encourage, inspire and entertain others. She lives in Illinois with her husband and three daughters. Sheri's stories have appeared in *Guideposts*, *Angels on Earth*, *Farm & Ranch Living* and numerous Chicken Soup for the Soul books. Visit her website at www.sherizeck.com.

Meet Our Authors

Jack Canfield and **Mark Victor Hansen** are the co-founders of Chicken Soup for the Soul. Jack is the author of many bestselling books and is CEO of the Canfield Training Group. Mark is a prolific writer and has had a profound influence in the field of human potential through his library of audios, videos, and articles. Jack and Mark have received many awards and honors, including a Guinness World Records Certificate for having seven books from the Chicken Soup for the Soul series on the New York Times bestseller list on May 24, 1998. You can reach them at www.jackcanfield.com and www.markvictorhansen.com.

Amy Newmark has been Chicken Soup for the Soul's publisher, coauthor, and editor-in-chief for the last six years, after a 30-year career as a writer, speaker, financial analyst, and business executive in the worlds of finance and telecommunications. Amy is a Chartered Financial Analyst and a *magna cum laude* graduate of Harvard College, where she majored in Portuguese, minored in French, and traveled extensively. She and her husband have four grown children.

After a long career writing books on telecommunications, voluminous financial reports, business plans, and corporate press releases, Chicken Soup for the Soul is a breath of fresh air for Amy. She loves creating these life-changing books for Chicken Soup for the Soul's wonderful readers. She has coauthored and/or edited more than 100 Chicken Soup for the Soul books.

You can reach Amy with any questions or comments through webmaster@chickensoupforthesoul.com and you can follow her on Twitter @amynewmark or @chickensoupsoul.

Thank You

We owe huge thanks to all of our contributors. We know that you poured your hearts and souls into the thousands of stories that you shared with us, and ultimately with other mothers. As we read and edited these stories, we were truly amazed by your experiences and your great advice. We appreciate your willingness to share these inspiring and encouraging stories with our readers, even the ones where you weren't such a great multitasking mom!

We could only publish a small percentage of the stories that were submitted, but we read every single one and even the ones that do not appear in the book had an influence on us and on the final manuscript. We owe special thanks to our editor Susan Heim, who read all the submissions to this volume, and narrowed down the list to a manageable size, editing beautifully as she went along. Our assistant publisher D'ette Corona did her normal masterful job of working with the contributors to approve our edits and answer any questions we had, as well as helping select many of the stories in the final manuscript. Barbara LoMonaco ran our story database to get the stories in, and then did the final proofreading as we went into production. And managing editor and production coordinator Kristiana Pastir proofread and managed the metamorphosis from Word document to printed book, a process that never fails to amaze me.

We also owe a special thanks to our creative director and book producer, Brian Taylor at Pneuma Books, for his brilliant vision for our covers and interiors.

~Amy Newmark

Sharing Happiness, Inspiration, and Wellness

Real people sharing real stories, every day, all over the world. In 2007, *USA Today* named *Chicken Soup for the Soul* one of the five most memorable books in the last quarter-century. With over 100 million books sold to date in the U.S. and Canada alone, more than 200 titles in print, and translations into more than 40 languages, "chicken soup for the soul" is one of the world's best-known phrases.

Today, 20 years after we first began sharing happiness, inspiration and wellness through our books, we continue to delight our readers with new titles, but have also evolved beyond the bookstore, with wholesome and balanced pet food, delicious nutritious comfort food, and a major motion picture in development. Whatever you're doing, wherever you are, Chicken Soup for the Soul is "always there for you™." Thanks for reading!

Share with Us

We all have had Chicken Soup for the Soul moments in our lives. If you would like to share your story or poem with millions of people around the world, go to chickensoup.com and click on "Submit Your Story." You may be able to help another reader, and become a published author at the same time. Some of our past contributors have launched writing and speaking careers from the publication of their stories in our books!

Our submission volume has been increasing steadily—the quality and quantity of your submissions has been fabulous. We only accept story submissions via our website. They are no longer accepted via mail or fax.

To contact us regarding other matters, please send us an e-mail through webmaster@chickensoupforthesoul.com, or fax or write us at:

Chicken Soup for the Soul
P.O. Box 700
Cos Cob, CT 06807-0700
Fax: 203-861-7194

One more note from your friends at Chicken Soup for the Soul: Occasionally, we receive an unsolicited book manuscript from one of our readers, and we would like to respectfully inform you that we do not accept unsolicited manuscripts and we must discard the ones that appear.

Chicken Soup for the Soul®

Just Us Girls

101 Stories about Friendship for Women of All Ages

Jack Canfield,
Mark Victor Hansen
& Amy Newmark

The New Friend Project

Wanted: Mom Friends

Are we not like two volumes of one book?
~Marceline Desbordes-Valmore

For me, the early days of motherhood were isolating. I had quit a rewarding job to become a stay-at-home mom, and while I loved being with my six-month-old son, what I missed most was adult conversation. Every day, I pounced on my husband, Dwayne, the moment he came home from work, anxious to hear news from the outside world. We both knew I needed to make "mom friends." But how?

Although I often took Ethan with me on errands, shopping at the grocery store didn't exactly provide a chance to make a new friend. Ethan was content to smile at the other customers and look at the brightly colored displays, but I wasn't. "We need to find something better to do," I told him.

Surprisingly, the solution was just a few miles away.

"I want to pick up a few things at the library. Let's all go," Dwayne said on one of his days off. He didn't need to ask twice. I loved to read, but hadn't had much time or energy since Ethan was born. Perhaps a good book would lift my spirits.

After choosing a novel, I decided to venture past the adult department. The children's area looked inviting, and with Ethan in the stroller I felt qualified to take a closer look. A decorated wall displayed schedules of activities for children of all ages, even babies. I picked up one and noted an upcoming playgroup for babies and toddlers. I doubted I would know anyone there, but it had to beat sitting at home.

The next week I gathered my courage, and Ethan and I headed to the library. "We're going to go play, and we'll have a great time," I said to him, partly to convince myself. "Da, da, da," he babbled in agreement.

The library's community room was filled with a play kitchen, a small ball pit, lots of toys for babies and toddlers, and half a dozen moms and their children, none of whom looked familiar. Uh oh.

"Welcome to playgroup. I'm Misty, the playgroup coordinator," said a smiling woman about my age. "How old is your baby? What's his name?" she asked, her friendliness instantly putting me at ease. Misty introduced me to the other moms, and we began chatting about our children's milestones, their favorite baby foods, and their sleep schedules while the babies and toddlers played around us. I left the playgroup feeling energized and excited about these potential new friendships.

After that first playgroup, Ethan and I rarely missed a date. As he grew, I added "Tot Time" and preschool "Story Time" activities to our schedule. And when his younger sister and brother were born, our calendar filled up even more. Together we've learned about gardening, met small animals from the local zoo, played math and alphabet games, and most importantly, we've all made new friends.

I'm grateful for the moms I've met at the library. We share similar backgrounds and interests, and with children in the same age group, we can offer each other a sympathetic ear and advice. To help pass the time when our children were younger, we met at a different park each week during the summer so they could play and we could chat. Nowadays, my friends and I get together for dinner or shopping without the kids so we can enjoy each other's uninterrupted company. And we still attend lots of library activities with our children.

I'm still amazed how one small act of bravery made such a huge difference in my level of happiness. Go ahead and strike up a conversation with the mom at the next park bench. Seek out other moms at your church or your child's school and start your own playgroup or book club. And don't forget to check for activities at your local library. You just may meet some lifelong friends.

~Melissa Zifzal

From Gym Friend to Real Friend

Why not go out on a limb? Isn't that where the fruit is?
~Frank Scully

I have been going to the gym for years, hoping to keep my body strong and my bones straight. My mother had severe osteoporosis and I was determined to do all I could to prevent that from happening to me. So I worked out—hard.

On this particular day, I was pressing through my twentieth pushup with a metal weight perched on the middle of my back, feeling every muscle complain, when I heard a woman's voice say, "I don't like this." At least I wasn't the only one who found working out at the gym trying. When I finished, I looked up and saw a familiar face, a woman who had been going to the gym regularly like me. She was doing sumo squats. We complained to each other about how hard the exercises were today. Our trainer ignored us, as usual.

She finished her workout and left while I was just at the beginning of mine. Our trainings frequently overlapped so we had the chance to talk while we sweated. We were always glad to see each other as gym friends but had never made an attempt to get together outside of the gym.

Later that week, as she was leaving and I was coming in, I said on a whim, "Would you like to meet for lunch some day?"

She seemed pleasantly surprised.

"Sure," she said.

We made a date for the following Friday after our workouts. She would do some errands and come back for me after I was done.

"Great!" I said, and we went our separate ways.

As the date drew closer, though, I wondered what we would talk about.

On the day we were supposed to get together, our trainer handed me a note. It was an apology. My gym friend was called in to work and wouldn't be able to meet me. I thanked him for the message, stuffed it in my purse, and went on with my training. But it made me a little edgy. Had I been too pushy? We had never really chatted about anything substantial. Would it be embarrassing for both of us? Had she thought about our meeting and decided it was a bad idea after all?

When we met again she was the one to bring up our getting together. So we made another date. This time she stayed on the treadmill while I exercised and waited for me. We left together and went to a local restaurant in the same shopping center. It was an unusually warm winter day so we ordered and brought our plates outside.

As we settled down we looked at each other across the table and before we knew it we were halfway through our meals and deep into conversation. We learned more about each other as we ate our salads than we had discovered in all the years during our workouts. We found that we had similar philosophies and interests. We talked about family and travels and whatever else popped into our minds. Almost two hours passed before we decided we had better move on.

We had parked our cars side by side without even knowing it.

"I decided," she said, "that I only want to be friends with someone who speaks to my heart."

Then she smiled warmly and I knew she meant me. And I knew that I now had a girlfriend who would be part of my life in and outside of the gym.

~Ferida Wolff

Wild Bouquet of Friends

A friend is one of the nicest things you can have,
and one of the best things you can be.
~Douglas Pagels

Michelle dropped into my life just when I needed her. Like manna from heaven. Five of my seven closest friends had moved in the past year. I just knew if I stood on the end of my drive, waving goodbye to a sweetheart sister one more time, my heart would break.

Enter Michelle. I met her at church, and she was a master at making friends. Her husband had been in the Navy. And his civilian job brought many transfers, too. Moving was a way of life for her, and she rose to the challenge.

"Want to come over for lunch today?" Michelle asked.

We were scraping glue from eight-foot tables. Day one of Vacation Bible School and the craft room had gone wild.

"Today?" I asked.

I barely knew Michelle. She'd been around church for a while, but our paths hadn't crossed. Until VBS.

"Sure," she said. "I'll make pizza. The kids can play."

Michelle had three young sons and a daughter. I had three young sons, too. Sounded like a good fit. But I was tired and the morning had been full.

"C'mon" she said, as if tapping my thoughts. "I'll make you an iced tea. I have a nice porch and we can sit."

Sold.

My sons and I went to Michelle's that day, and it took about ten minutes for us to feel like we'd all been friends for a hundred years. Michelle had that way about her. And by the time the boys and I loaded into our van and headed home, I felt as though I'd been given a sweet gift. Michelle eased some of the hurt of those relocated friendships.

And I didn't even have to try to find her.

The next day at Bible school, Michelle was waiting by the door. "I need to get groceries tonight," she said. "Want to come?"

I thought of my cupboards at home. Mother Hubbard for sure. But I'd never gone for groceries with a friend. Seemed like a solo task to me. "Together?" I asked.

"Of course," she said. "Another friend is going to go, too. But there's plenty of room in the Land Rover."

I agreed. And when Michelle picked me up that evening, I was surprised. Her other friend was much younger. Single. I wondered where Michelle had met her and what we'd have in common. I expected a thirty-something mama, like me.

But the evening was a delight.

It was fun to meet someone new and to hear about a life that was so different from mine.

And such was life with Michelle. As I got to know her better, I got to know many others, too. Michelle was different from anyone I'd ever met. And she had a lot of friends. Older friends. Friends in their twenties. Single. Married. Friends with no children. Friends with a half-dozen kids. I'd always played things safe, choosing friends who were just like me, but Michelle reached far. She had friends who were working through divorces and addictions. She was a friend even to some who were hard to befriend.

And I was in awe of her. She'd more than filled a void in my life. And I learned from watching her love.

Then came a sad day. The day she told me she was going to move.

"It's a transfer," she said. "But it will be good for my family. I know we'll meet others who could use a new friend."

But what about me? I wondered. Another friend. Moving away. Maybe it wasn't worth it, getting so deep into someone's life. Who would take her place? Who would be my friend?

The weeks rolled by and Michelle's home became a maze of cardboard boxes. I helped her pack her life, and it felt as though I were packing my own heart. Then came moving day. Once again I stood on the end of the drive. Michelle's children waved like wild and mine waved back hard. I kicked a few pebbles with the tip of my shoe as her white truck became smaller and disappeared.

Gone. Another friend.

The next few days were hard and quiet. Michelle was a pursuer. An inviter. An initiator. With her gone, the phone seemed quiet. I missed her smile. Her warmth. The way her kitchen was a haven for women of all walks of life.

Then one afternoon my boys and I were playing outside. Their laughter rose above the high squeal of the swings. But I didn't feel like laughing. I was lonely for a friend.

And that's when I saw the young mother.

She was walking down the sidewalk, newborn babe strapped to her chest. Her bright red ponytail bobbed high on her head. Two young boys ran in front of her, darting off the sidewalk and back on. She was young. Very young.

I pushed gently on my little son's back. His swing flew high. The mother was just about in front of our house. I pushed again. My little guy cheered. The little parade moved closer, this mother so much younger than me.

And I thought of Michelle.

"C'mon, guys," I said. I pulled on the chains and gently stopped their swings. "There's a mama and some boys coming down the block. Let's go over and say hello."

My sons raced forward, filled with the anticipation of a new friend. I moved forward, too, recognizing that desire in my own heart.

"Hi," I said when we reached the sidewalk. "Nice day for a walk."

That young mother and I chatted in the afternoon sun, and in time, she became one of my very close friends. But my friendships didn't stop there. I began to stretch out. Look beyond my own age, life stage, and circumstance. Before too long I had older friends. Friends without children. Single friends. Friends whose lives were very different from mine.

And the blessing was sweet.

I still miss Michelle. But I know she's reaching others, spreading joy, providing a shoulder, loving and teaching others how to love. And I sometimes wish she hadn't moved.

But this special lady left me with the very best parting gift—the ability to see the beauty in a wild bouquet of friends.

~Shawnelle Eliasen

Friends of Susan Society

Remember, you don't need a certain number of friends,
just a number of friends you can be certain of.
~Author Unknown

When Susan—my best friend of thirty years—died, three of her friends and I got together with her daughter to organize a memorial service in her honor. For a week, we turned our grief into lists—lists of things to do, food and whatnot to buy, people to call and e-mail.

The memorial turned out even better than we had hoped, complete with Susan's favorite foods and a slide show that reflected all aspects of her life, from childhood to adulthood, from family to work. After the crowd departed, and her daughter went home, the four organizers sat down for a recap and chat.

Although we all knew Susan, and had met each other on several social occasions, none of us were close. Still reeling from the void in my life that Susan's death had caused, I came up with a suggestion. "Let's keep in touch. Maybe we can go for dinner in a couple of weeks. Sort of a Friends of Susan Society." The three women nodded.

Work kept me busy during the week, keeping my mind off my grief. Evenings and weekends were much harder. Sunday mornings in particular, when Susan and I used to go out for breakfast and a walk, now stretched long and bleak. One of the women and I e-mailed a couple of times, but the other two were busy with family and travel. Several months passed before one of the busier women suggested meeting for dinner.

I arrived at the restaurant first and waited for the others, a little nervous. Slightly younger, and the only one still working, I was also much lower down on the educational pecking order than they had been, a substitute teacher rather than a principal or high-level school board position.

I felt as if I were back in grade school, trying to make friends with kids in my class I knew by sight but had never really talked to. I wiped my palms on my pants, took a deep breath, and pasted a smile on my face.

I needn't have worried. We had a delightful evening and they never made me feel anything other than included. Many of our conversations began, "Remember when Susan did...?" Or, "Let me tell you a funny story about Susan." Or, "I was thinking about Susan the other day and..." We traded stories about Susan's inability to organize anything, her love of travel and hiking, her culinary experiments, the way you knew she was really angry when her voice got very soft. It was almost as if she were there with us, laughing in the background.

At the end of the evening, we promised to get together again, but one woman was off to Europe for two months, a second took care of her grandkids three days a week, a third had a retired husband and daughter with serious health issues.

By the time I got home the glow of the evening had dulled. Something felt off. For the next two days I thought about it—nice women, nice evening, nice conversation—what could be wrong? But I still couldn't shake the feeling that all the "nice" in the world didn't quite add up.

I needed to talk to someone, so I called a friend who knew about the evening.

"How did it go?" Mavis asked.

"Okay."

"Just okay? You were looking forward to having dinner with

these women. I know you were hoping to make some new friends. What happened?"

I tried to untangle my thoughts. "It was a really nice dinner. We traded Susan stories and talked a bit about what we were doing, but..." Still not sure, I hesitated.

"But what?"

"But it was still all about Susan," I blurted out. "I wanted to make new friends, but these were... they were old friends, but they were Susan's old friends, not mine. Apart from all having known Susan, we don't really have any interests in common. I guess I was looking for an instant Susan clone to take over being my best friend. Dumb, I know."

"Not dumb. It's tough to lose a best friend. Wanting to turn people who knew her into your friends is simply a way of keeping her alive, if only by proxy."

I sighed. "Too bad it doesn't work."

"What are you going to do?"

I took a moment to think. "I do need to make more friends, but it should be about me, not Susan. There's a teacher I know slightly at work who seems very nice. Maybe it's time to try yoga again. I'm sure I could meet a couple of people there." I paused as more ideas came to my head. "And the women in my book club. There's no reason we couldn't do things outside book club nights. Like go to a movie or out for coffee."

Mavis laughed. "Sounds like the Friends of Susan Society will need a new name—the Friends of Harriet Society. Just move slowly. Friendships take time and effort to build but..."

"...the right ones are worth the effort," I completed. "Mavis?"

"Yes?"

"Thanks for being my friend."

~Harriet Cooper

Time to Say Goodbye

No person is your friend who demands your silence, or denies your right to grow.
~Alice Walker

I'd just returned from our regular monthly lunch date. As usual, my friend and I had exchanged the latest news, relished the gossip about other friends' breakups, and laughed until our makeup ran. But driving home, I began to feel as I had the last several times.

It started like a wisp, a feather across my mind, and quickly heightened. What irked me so much?

I went to my journal. It always gave me answers.

Warming up, I started writing about the basics to help get me started—the phone call for a day that fit both our schedules, the big discussion the night before. "What do you feel like? Chinese? Italian? Decadent Deli?" Giggling, we chose Decadent—two kids skipping healthy diet school.

Then I described the restaurant. Arriving first, I had time to look around. The booth was roomy, upholstery past its prime. On the table sat the perennial bowl of sour pickles, with little pieces of garlic bobbing in the brine. The plastic-covered menu, three feet tall, promised anything your heart desired. Smiling hello, the gravel-voiced waitress asked if I were alone. From her collar hung a giant wilting cloth gardenia.

Continuing to write, I felt a small nervousness, an excitement that always told me I was getting closer to the truth.

As I studied the menu, my friend rushed in, breathless and flushed. We screamed and hugged. She slid into the booth opposite me and immediately started talking.

"The traffic! This idiot in front of me for six miles! Couldn't make up his mind. Where did he learn to drive, Jupiter? Kept weaving in and out, the jerk!"

I wondered why she didn't pass him or take another route.

She kept talking, interrupted only by the waitress taking our orders for overstuffed pastrami sandwiches and diet sodas.

I kept writing, trusting the moving pen. Reliving our visit, I found, as always, the answers coming.

She lived, I saw, in a state of chronic indignation. Everything—from the curl of the napkins to the highway driver to how others raised children—was cause for her righteous anger.

As she talked, the frown between her eyebrows deepened, and her lips moved like a sped-up cartoon. Her outrage was punctuated by hand motions that alternately clutched the air and flattened in open-palmed incredulity at humankind's folly.

She jumped from one thing to another with quirky logic: shopping on the Internet revealed the stupidity of retailers. Restaurant pasta less than al dente was a sin punishable by leaving the waiter two quarters. The supermarket checkers' sluggishness proved the regression of human evolution and threatened our entire civilization.

After almost an hour, she wound down, sandwich untouched. Now, I thought, I could talk, finally sharing meaningful bits of my life and the news about mutual friends. That was when I knew she would listen and nod in understanding. And we'd laugh with full abandon like we used to.

But instead our conversation reminded her to deplore something else. And she was off again, eyes popping, voice strident in irate virtue.

In the past, sometimes I'd sympathized with her constant diatribes and even joined in. But then I'd come home with a headache, and, despite my lunch indulgence, not at all nourished. Today, I now saw, was no different.

When it was time to leave, we kissed and promised to call.

As I kept writing, the picture grew clearer. I'd really known for a long time but didn't want to admit it. She'd been a friend so many years, and we used to have such fun. But the truths scribbled out in my journal couldn't be denied.

It was time to say goodbye.

~Noelle Sterne

Riding the Road to Friendship

When I see an adult on a bicycle,
I do not despair for the future of the human race.
~H.G. Wells

I was a Northern newcomer to a Southern adult community. I knew no one and was feeling very out of place and lonesome. I wanted desperately to make new friends.

Day after day, I saw groups of cyclers riding throughout the community and beyond the gates. Dressed in black Spandex riding shorts, brightly colored biking shirts, gloves and helmets, they appeared to be having a great time together. I looked longingly at them as they rode in pace lines of eight to twelve riders.

I knew how to ride a bike, but couldn't imagine myself ever accomplishing the level of riding I saw. I read an article in the community newspaper inviting those interested in biking to join a beginner's cycling group. It is not like me to join something where I know no one, but I pushed myself to attend an organizational meeting. I immediately began chatting with two women and we committed to our first group ride taking place later in the week.

Twelve men and women ventured out on our first eight-mile ride. We slowly pedaled in a long line through the quiet streets of our community. We began to meet three times a week, and steadily increased our distance and speed. Stopping for refreshments became the norm and we soon adopted our mantra, "We bike for food." As we sat chatting over coffee, strong friendships began to form. Many of us found we had other interests in common and began exploring them together.

Now, comfortable with several members of the cycling club, I decided to attend a few of their social events, a luncheon, a fifties party, and a holiday gathering. There, I met more folks. Men from the cycling group brought their wives to the social events and wives brought their non-cycling partners. Out of these gatherings grew a small dinner group and again my circle expanded. More opportunities for new friendships opened up when our club members planned a few overnight cycling trips in conjunction with other clubs from various parts of the state.

All of these new friendships were made possible by taking that first step outside my comfort zone. I now ride fifty to 100 miles a week, have improved my health, and have more friends than I ever imagined. Taking that first step and trying something new opened up a whole new world of fun and friendships for me.

~Mary Grant Dempsey

Chicken Soup for the Soul®

www.chickensoup.com